# The Well-Tempered Object

edited by Stephen Travis Pope

# The Well-Tempered Object

## Musical Applications of Object-Oriented Software Technology

The MIT Press
Cambridge, Massachusetts
London, England

Set in Franklin Gothic and VIP Trump.
Printed and bound in the United States of America.

Library of Congress Cataloging-in-Publication Data

The Well-tempered object : musical applications of object-oriented
 software technology / edited by Stephen Travis Pope.
    p.   cm.
Based on articles previously published in Computer music journal.
Includes bibliographical references
ISBN 0-262-16126-5
 1. Music—Computer programs. 2. Music—Data processing.
3. Object-oriented programming (Computer science) I. Pope. Stephen T.
ML74.3.W44   1991
780'.285'51—dc20                              90-20839
                                                 CIP
                                                 MN

# Contents

# The Well-Tempered Object

Stephen Travis Pope

# Introduction

This book is based on articles, published in *Computer Music Journal* over a span of 10 years, in which various musical applications of object-oriented software technology are discussed. Object-oriented programming (OOP) was perhaps the most important new software engineering technology of the 1980s. The technology itself, however, is over 20 years old. It has its roots in work undertaken in Oslo in the mid-1960s by Ole-Johan Dahl, Kristen Nygaard, and their collaborators—work which led to an ALGOL-based simulation language called Simula (Dahl and Nygaard 1966). Work along this path was continued in the 1970s at the Xerox Palo Alto Research Center, where members of the Learning Research Group (later called the Systems Concepts Laboratory) developed a series of integrated programming environments collectively called Smalltalk. The fourth-generation system Smalltalk-80 Version 2, released in 1983 and described in three widely cited books by SCL members: Goldberg and Robson 1983 (updated and revised as Goldberg and Robson 1989), Goldberg 1984, and Krasner 1983. In parallel with this development, Carl Hewitt and his colleagues and students at MIT developed a series of OOP systems based on their "actor" model of programming (Hewitt 1977).

Although the marketing divisions of numerous corporations active in the field often represent OOP technology as something revolutionary, many see it as a logical evolutionary step after the structured procedural programming technology of the 1960s and the 1970s. Many of the basic ideas of structured procedural programming—the virtues of Dijkstra and Wirth, if you will—are stressed even more radically in OOP language and systems. The basic goals have remained more or less unchanged; language developers are still seeking to make large software systems more manageable and easier to design, implement, and maintain. The language techniques used to achieve these benefits include modularization and strict encapsulation of components, the separation of specification and implementation, the hierarchical specification of components, and

the separation of state and behavior within modules (Dahl and Hoare 1972). In the process of casting OOP languages in the lineage of Pascal and Modula, it is also important to say what they are not. OOP is not an artificial intelligence, although object descriptions do bear some resemblance to frame-oriented knowledge-representation systems. OOP is not the same as neural nets or connectionist programming, although such systems are often easier to implement in a well-constructed OOP system. OOP is not logic programming, although numerous systems merge these technologies (e.g., "Prolog-in-Smalltalk" systems) to blend their strengths.

## Object-Oriented Software Technology

The preface of Goldberg and Robson 1989 includes wonderful sections on "the task of book-writing" and "the task of book-reading." The first of these makes four central points that can be widened here to apply to OOP technology rather than only to the Smalltalk-80 programming language and system. The points they cite can be rephrased as follows:

> OOP is a vision.
> OOP is based on a small number of concepts, defined in unusual terminology.
> OOP uses graphical, interactive programming environments.
> OOP leads to big systems.

OOP evangelists tend to see OOP technology as visionary because it mixes the modeling and categorization techniques of psychological classification theory with those of traditional software analysis and design. The idea is to build software systems as collections of interacting objects, each of which models the behavior of some real-world entity. Another part of the visionary nature of early OOP systems is the strong link between their development (at Xerox PARC in the 1970s) and the advent of integrated, interactive programming environments such as Smalltalk and INTERLISP-D.

Several OOP languages (most notably Smalltalk-80 and Actor languages) have been designed with the goal of making the simplest and most consistent language possible by the radical application of a small number of concepts to all facets of the language, the software libraries, and the programming environment. This does not mean that OOP is trivial, however; many of the difficulties that programmers have learning the technology stem from the fact that its concepts are defined using unusual terminology. The notions of "object," "class," "instance," "message," and "inheritance" are all present in the common English usage, but are new in their use as software systems concepts.

To say that OOP uses graphical, interactive programming environments is more a sign of the times than anything else. During the mid-1970s the avant-garde had access to either West Coast (Xerox Alto) or East Coast (MIT Lisp Machine) computers with bit-mapped screens, mouse input devices, and interactive OOP environments such as INTERLISP-D, Smalltalk, and Lisp Machine Lisp. The market's gradual acceptance of bit-mapped graphics and graphical user interfaces followed the commercial introduction of the Xerox STAR, its clone the Apple Macintosh, and the Sun Microsystems UNIX workstations in the first half of the 1980s.

When OOP is viewed as an evolutionary extension of the structured procedural programming developments of the 1960s and the 1970s, it is clear why it can be said that OOP leads to big systems. The technology was developed to better facilitate the design, implementation, and maintenance of large and intricate systems—to push the "software complexity barrier" a bit further away. The primary technique for achieving this is increased reuse of components within software systems. The secondary techniques that support increased reuse (and reusability) of components include those mentioned above: encapsulating components and hiding the implementation of behaviors via well-defined (and narrow) behavioral interfaces, minimizing the sharing of state, and separating specification from implementation.

## The Well-Tempered Object

The articles presented in this book describe the application of OOP technology to a wide range of areas under the general heading of computer music and digital audio signal processing, including music description and composition, real-time performance, and digital signal processing. A number of popular OOP languages are represented, including Lisp, Smalltalk-80, and Objective-C. The book is divided into four topical parts, although the borders between them are somewhat blurred.

Part I presents three progressive tutorials on various aspects of OOP technology. Glenn Krasner's 1980 article from *Computer Music Journal*'s "Machine Tongues" series introduces the concepts of OOP in terms of several example systems that were developed (in Smalltalk-76) at Xerox PARC during the late 1970s. It introduces the notions of object modeling and object-oriented design by describing the design of a set of Smalltalk classes that are based on the components of a real orchestra. It also introduces message-passing and the basics of Smalltalk-80 language syntax. This article ends with several examples of graphical user interfaces for music developed for Xerox Alto computers which had special microcode for real-time FM synthesis. Henry Lieberman's 1982 "Machine Tongues" article describes the actor model of OOP languages using Lieberman's ACT 1 programming language as its basis. Both the actor model of this approach and the relationship Lieberman draws between actor-based OOP and artificial intelligence make this article very valuable. The examples in Lieberman's article introduce the notion of delegation and some important concepts for the management of parallelism in programs. The third tutorial, also from the "Machine Tongues" series, describes the four central object-oriented software design techniques, presenting musical examples of their application. A number of the relevant issues related to analysis, modeling, and software design are mentioned here, though this article can only serve as an introduction to the large and very active area of new object-oriented analysis and design techniques.

Part II presents four very different software sys-

*Pope*

tems that use object-oriented software technology to build tools for music representation and score description. Each of these systems aims to be a general-purpose library that addresses a range of musical and compositional styles. The first article in this part, which also appeared in Roads 1989, discusses C. Fry's Flavors Band package, a Lisp-Machine-based software system for describing musical styles as combinations of *phrase processors,* which are stream-oriented Lisp functions for modifying musical sequences. The system Fry implemented in 1983 and 1984 included real-time output via commands sent to various (pre-MIDI) synthesizers connected to the Lisp Machine, and a sophisticated menu-based user interface for specifying and connecting phrase processors. The FORMES system developed at IRCAM in Paris and descibed here by Xavier Rodet and Pierre Cointe (in an article that also appeared in Roads 1989) is an attempt to provide generality, universality, compatibility, simplicity of program text, ease of use, modularity, and hierarchical construction in a system for music composition and synthesis. Among the areas that the FORMES system addressed in a novel way was the description and generation of families of hierarchically related envelopes for digital synthesis. Flavors Band and FORMES can be considered the first-generation OOP systems for music in that they are widely known and have been widely cited and emulated in the past 5 years. The MODE (Musical Object Development Environment), described in the next article, is a reimplementation of my Hyper-Score ToolKit, a Smalltalk-80-based class library for music representation, score processing, and performance. The goals of the MODE are similar to those set out for FORMES, but the approach and the programming environment are very different. The MODE is programmed in a uniform object-oriented style, and also provides a framework and a collection of components for the construction of diverse graphical music notations. The sound and music kits for the NeXT computer are Objective-C libraries that are part of this novel machine's basic programming environment. The article in which David Jaffe and Lee Boynton introduce these kits presents their design and several examples of their

use. Jaffe and Boynton also discuss several of the underlying issues in sound and music representation, and they address the real-time performance issues that are important within any time-sharing operating system.

Part III introduces three software systems that address higher-level score processing and interaction from unique vantage points. The Kyma/Platypus workstation described by Carla Scaletti is the result of a multi-year project in hardware and software design undertaken by a group at the CERL laboratory of the University of Illinois. Kyma is a graphical programming language designed for sound description and processing, rather than a particular score notation or front end. This article introduces the notion of describing processed sound by means of directed acyclic graphs and presents numerous examples from Kyma's fascinating user interface. In the next article, Henry Flurry describes his group's development of a NeXT-based prototype system called the Creation Station—a multimedia creative artist's tool kit. The intention of those who developed the Creation Station was to use the advanced input/output facilities of the NeXT machine to provide a powerful working environment for several media and art forms. Flurry also presents a short introduction to the terms of OOP and can be used as another tutorial. TTrees are binary trees within which temporal information is represented explicitly. The article by Glendon Diener introduces the TTree system he implemented in Smalltalk-80 at the CCRMA center at Stanford University; it describes the basic notions of why this data structure is useful for temporal data, and it presents several examples of Diener's flexible TTree interactive user interfaces.

Part IV consists of two articles relating the application of OOP techniques to digital audio signal processing. The two central themes discussed in Kurt Hebel's article on Javelina are graphical front ends (where Javelina uses such representations as the complex $z$ plane for defining digital filters) and retargetable back ends (where Javelina separates the definition and optimization of a filter design from the actual code generation). The examples of the use of Javelina presented in the article and the addendum demonstrate the power of Hebel's approach to software development for digital signal processors. The virtual digital signal processing system presented in the article by David Mellinger, Guy Garnett, and Bernard Mont-Reynaud also separates specification from implementation, but along much different lines than those seen in Javelina. These authors have developed a system whereby signal processing operations can be described in a manner independent of the machine and the signal processor and in which the actual representation of data and delegation of operations are determined at run time on the basis of the available general-purpose or special-purpose hardware.

I would like to take this opportunity to thank Curtis Roads, consulting editor of *Computer Music Journal,* who provided much editorial assistance both on this introduction and on a number of the articles. Carla Scaletti also read and commented on an early copy of this text. The computer facilities for the text processing for this book, as well as the ongoing work for the *Journal,* were generously supported by Ariel Corporation, by ParcPlace Systems, Inc., and by the Center for Computer Research in Music and Acoustics at Stanford University. Tom Wadlow suggested the title.

## References

Dahl, O.-J., and C. Hoare. 1972. "Hierarchical Program Structures." In O.-J. Dahl, E. Dijkstra, and C. Hoare (eds.), *Structured Programming.* Orlando: Academic Press.

Dahl, O.-J., and K. Nygaard. 1966. SIMULA—An ALGOL-Based Simulation Language. *Communications of the ACM* 9(9): 671–678.

Goldberg, A., and D. Robson. 1983. *Smalltalk 80: The Language and Its Implementation.* Menlo Park: Addison-Wesley.

Goldberg, A., and D. Robson. 1989. *Smalltalk 80: The Language.* Menlo Park: Addison-Wesley.

Goldberg, A. 1984. *Smalltalk 80: The Interactive Programming Environment.* Menlo Park: Addison-Wesley.

Hewitt, C. 1977. "Viewing Control Structures as Patterns of Passing Messages." *Artificial Intelligence* 8(3): 323–363.

Krasner, G. 1983. *Smalltalk-80: Bits of History, Words of Advice.* Menlo Park: Addison-Wesley.

Roads, C., ed. 1989. *The Music Machine.* Cambridge: MIT Press.

*Pope*

# I

# Tutorials and Technology

**Glenn Krasner**

Systems Science Laboratory
Xerox Palo Alto Research Centers (PARC)
Palo Alto, California 94304

# Machine Tongues VIII: The Design of a Smalltalk Music System

## Introduction

One way we would like to use computers is for the production of music. We can think of an orchestra as a system that produces music—various people, instruments, and sheets of music interact in well-defined ways. It would be nice if we could describe a music system to the computer directly, defining the objects and the interfaces so that they appeared similar to those of the real-world system. *Smalltalk* is a computer programming system whose purpose is to achieve just this sort of object and interface specification.

Let us first consider an orchestra. We will describe it in terms of conductors, players, and printed sheets of music, and in terms of their interactions, such as the conductor telling the players to start to play. We can use this description of a real orchestra to identify the basic components of a Smalltalk system designed to produce music in a way very much like the real-world example.

## A Real Orchestra

The central figure of an orchestra is the conductor. The conductor leads the orchestra and has a repertoire of music that the orchestra can play. The conductor asks the orchestra to start playing a piece and to stop playing. When the conductor wants the orchestra to play a piece, he or she selects (gets) the score for that piece from the repertoire, hands out a part to each player in the orchestra, instructs the orchestra to play and, eventually, to stop playing.

Computer Music Journal, Vol. 4, No. 4, Winter 1980

An orchestra is a collection of players, each of whom has an instrument (such as a violin), and a printed part for the assigned piece. Some players may be assigned a new instrument or a new printed part. An individual player may be asked (typically by a movement of the conductor's baton) to start or stop playing.

The conductor's repertoire is a collection of scores, each of which contains printed parts for all the instruments in a piece. One of the conductor's activities is to retrieve the score of a piece of music from the repertoire and then to distribute the parts to the appropriate players.

In this description of an orchestra, we have mentioned seven kinds of things:

> **Conductor** — one who leads the orchestra
> **Orchestra** — a collection of players
> **Player** — a person who makes music
> **Instrument** — the music generator for each player
> **Printed part** — the pages representing one part in a score
> **Repertoire** — a collection of scores
> **Score** — a collection of printed parts for an individual piece

Interactions between the people in the orchestra occur when the conductor gets a score from the repertoire and hands out the printed parts to the players, when the conductor tells the players to play, and when the conductor tells the players to stop playing.

## A Smalltalk Orchestra

We will now begin to convert our description of a real music system (an orchestra) into a Smalltalk simulation. First we specify the kinds of things we need, then we select particular *instances* of each kind of thing in order to compose our final system. Our description of the real orchestra mentioned seven kinds of things; we will likewise need seven Smalltalk descriptions of kinds of things. In Smalltalk we use the word *object* for *thing*, and the phrase *class description* for *the description of a kind of thing*. The Smalltalk *classes* we need to describe are conductor, orchestra, player, instrument, sheet music, repertoire, and score. We will define each of these classes in terms of its functions (or expected behavior) and internal representation.

## Conductor

We begin with the conductor. Earlier we said that a conductor leads an orchestra and has a repertoire of music. These two pieces of information (orchestra and repertoire) are the identifying properties of all conductors; that is, every working conductor is connected to some orchestra and some repertoire, though the orchestra and repertoire may differ for different conductors. In Smalltalk we will say that each conductor, as specified in the class description of *Conductor*, will have two variables: one named *orchestra*, whose value is the conductor's orchestra, and one named *repertoire*, whose value is the conductor's repertoire. These variables are called *instance variables*, because every instance of that class has its own values associated with it.

In our Smalltalk music system, we interact with the conductor by asking him or her to have the orchestra play a piece or to stop playing. The conductor interacts with the orchestra by asking it to play or to stop playing, and interacts with the repertoire by retrieving scores from it. In Smalltalk all such interactions are defined in terms of *messages* that are sent from one object in the system to another. Along with the instance variables, a class description specifies all the messages its instances can receive. Corresponding to each message is a description of the *method*, or sequence of actions, that should be taken to respond to that message. These methods are described in terms of the messages that the object sends to other objects (including, in some cases, to itself), in terms of

changes to the values of its variables, and in terms of the *value* that is returned as a result of performing that method.

Our conductors can receive two messages: "play a piece" and "stop playing." The method that a conductor will use when asked to play a piece includes sending a message to the repertoire to get a score, sending a message to the score to get individual printed parts, and sending messages to the players in the orchestra to take the parts and to start playing. The method to be used when a conductor is asked to stop playing consists of sending messages to the players to stop playing.

This is the information needed for a complete Smalltalk description of conductors. Here we will summarize the properties (instance variables) and behavior (messages and methods) of the class of conductors in order to have all the information in one place. This will also allow us to state (still in English) the messages that other objects in the system will receive from our conductor.

**Class:** *Conductor*

**Instance Variable:** *myOrchestra* — the conductor's orchestra

**Instance Variable:** *myRepertoire* — the conductor's repertoire of scores

**Message:** *playAPiece: pieceName*

  **Method:** When sent the message *playAPiece* with the argument *pieceName* indicating which piece to play, the conductor will send the repertoire (*myRepertoire*) the message *getAScore. PieceName*, and *myRepertoire* will return the associated score. Then the conductor will hand the score to the orchestra by sending *myOrchestra* the message *hereIsANewScore: score*. Finally the conductor will send the orchestra the message *playOn*, and all players will play.

**Message:** *stopPlaying*

  **Method:** When sent the message *stopPlaying*, the conductor will send *myOrchestra* the message *stopPlaying*; in turn *myOrchestra* will send all the players messages to have them stop playing.

Similarly, we can translate the English description of the other six classes into plans for Smalltalk class descriptions.

## Orchestra

An orchestra has one property, its collection of players, and three messages; one to hand out parts from a new score, one to play a piece, and one to stop playing.

**Class:** *Orchestra*
**Instance Variable:** *players* — the list of players
**Message:** *hereIsANewScore: score*
    **Method:** Send each player the message *getYourPartFrom: score* in order to have it get its printed part from the score.

**Message:** *playOn*
    **Method:** Send each player the message *playOn*, to have it make the sounds for its current piece.

**Message:** *stopPlaying*
    **Method:** Send each player the message *stopPlaying*, to have it stop making sound.

## Player

A player has an instrument, a name for its current part, and the printed part for the piece the orchestra is currently playing. A player will be asked to get the new part from a score, to pick up a new instrument, to play, and to stop playing. The description of a player might be:

**Class:** *Player*
**Instance Variable:** *partName* — my part name in the orchestra, such as "first trumpet"

**Instance Variable:** *instrument* — a simulated instrument or sound
**Instance Variable:** *printedPart* — the printed sheet of music to be played currently
**Message:** *getYourPartFrom: score*
    **Method:** Send the object to which the variable *score* refers the message *getPartFor: partName* to get a copy of the printed part for *partName*. This object will return a value that is to be the printed sheet for this part. Store this value as the value of the variable *printedPart*.

**Message:** *playOn*
    **Method:** Play the current melody with the current instrument. Send *printedPart* the message *restart*. Then, until told otherwise, send *printedPart* the message *nextNote*, to get the next note to play, and send *instrument* the message *playNote:* with that note as argument. (Of course this method must run concurrently with the *playOn* method for the other players in the orchestra.)

**Message:** *stopPlaying*
    **Method:** Do not send *instrument* the message *playNote* anymore.

**Message:** *setInstrument: newInstrument*
    **Method:** Pick up a new instrument. Assign the value of *newInstrument* as the value of the variable *instrument*.

## Instrument

An instrument is the actual sound synthesizer in the system. It is asked by its player to play (toot) a note. Its state includes a description of the envelope of sounds it can play.

**Class:** *Instrument*
**Instance Variable:** *envelope* — the waveform (described as a table of parameters)

**Message:** *playNote: note*
   **Method:** Synthesize the note specified by *note* using *envelope*. This requires access to a machine code primitive which sends a command to a hardware synthesizer, or (after a software digital synthesis process) sends the waveform to a digital-to-analog converter (DAC) and then to an amplifier.

### PrintedPart

This is the sheet music for a part in a piece, such as the second clarinet part in Handel's *Messiah*. It is represented by a stream of notes and rests.

**Class:**  *PrintedPart*
**Instance Variable:**  *partName* — the name of the part for which this music is intended
**Instance Variable:**  *notes* — a stream of notes and rests to be played
**Instance Variable:**  *position* — the current position in the stream
**Message:**  *restart*
   **Method:** Reset position to the beginning of the music. When *restart* is received, the orchestra will be starting the piece over. Therefore reset *position* to the beginning of the stream of *notes*.

**Message:**  *nextNote*
   **Method:** Return the next note in the stream.

**Message:**  *whatIsYourName*
   **Method:** Answer with *partName*.

### Repertoire

A repertoire is the collection of scores, each representing one piece. The scores are collections of the printed parts for all the parts of the piece.

**Class:**  *Repertoire*
**Instance Variable:**  *scores* — the collection of scores
**Message:**  *getAScore: pieceName*
   **Method:** Get the score for the piece named *pieceName*. Send each score in the collection *scores* the message *whatIsYourName*. Return the first score whose name is the same as the value of *pieceName*.

### Score

Similar to repertoire, score is a collection of things, in this case, printed sheet music. A score can be asked for the name of its piece, and can be asked for the printed sheet for a particular part.

**Class:**  *Score*
**Instance Variable:**  *pieceName* — the name of the piece represented by this score
**Instance Variable:**  *pages* — the collection of printed parts of music for the parts of the piece
**Message:**  *whatIsYourName*
   **Method:** Return *pieceName* to the message sender.

**Message:**  *getPartFor: partName*
   **Method:** To each element in the collection *pages* send the message *whatIsYourName* to get the name of its part. Return the first printed part whose name is the same as the value of *partName*.

### Smalltalk Code

We have completed the design of the Smalltalk simulation of our music system. We have taken the kinds of objects in the real music system and defined their corresponding Smalltalk classes by specifying the properties that instances of each class will have and the behavior that instances of

Code Listing 1. The Smalltalk code for the method
associated with the mes-
sage playAPiece: piece-
Name in class
Conductor.

```
playAPiece: pieceName    |   score part sheet each
[   score ← myRepertoire getAScore: pieceName.
             "ask the repertoire for the correct score, and assign that to the temporary variable score"
    myOrchestra do:                                                          "for each player do the following"
    [:each.                                                           "assign the argument to the variable each"
    part ← each whatIsYourPartName.                                          "get the part name for that player"
    sheet ← score getPartFor: part.                                    "get the sheet music for that part name"
    each hereIsYourMusic: sheet.                                                       "and give it to the player"
    ].
    myOrchestra playOn.                                                           "tell the orchestra to play"
    ↑pieceName                                                     "return pieceName as the value of this method
                                                                            the symbol '↑' means 'return' or
]                                                                                      'send a value back'"
```

each class will exhibit. Properties are defined in terms of instance variables and behavior in terms of messages and methods. Smalltalk's class structure has allowed us to define our system so that it closely resembles its real-world counterpart, the orchestra.

The next thing to specify is the actual Smalltalk code for each method. At this point of implementation, Smalltalk is very similar to conventional programming languages. There are variables, control structures, and sequences of statements to be evaluated. The "procedures" are the methods that are invoked by sending messages.

Code Listing 1 shows Smalltalk code for the method associated with the message *playAPiece: pieceName* in *class Conductor*. Comments are surrounded by double quotes. The name of the argument and those names after the vertical bar are the names of temporary variables. (In Code Listing 1 we assume that *class Orchestra*, of which *myOrchestra* is an instance, is implemented such that it also responds to the *do: [...code...]* message by running the code with each of its elements in turn as an argument.)

A word here about Smalltalk's syntax, which is fairly simple. All statements in the language are of one of three forms (Table 1). Statements are terminated by periods. Messages may take one of three forms (Table 2). Keyword selectors must end with a colon, and there must be a keyword for each argu-

ment. The value returned by a method is an object that may be used (1) as a receiver to be sent another message, (2) as the value to be assigned to a variable, or (3) as the value to be returned by the calling method.

Variables allowed in methods are either instance variables, defined in the class description; *temporary variables*, listed in the message patterns at the beginning of the method; or *global variables*. The pseudovariable *self* is used to refer to the object receiving the message, providing an object with the ability to send itself a message.

Blocks of statements surrounded by square brackets are instances of *class Method*, and may be asked to evaluate themselves (by sending them the message *value*) or to evaluate themselves with an argument (by sending them the message *value: argument*). In Code Listing 1 the argument to *myOrchestra do:* is the Method represented by the code within the brackets. *myOrchestra* is expected to be a collection that will send each of its elements to the Method as arguments to a *value: argument* message, thereby mapping that code onto its elements.

Another example, Code Listing 2, shows the Smalltalk code for the method associated with the message *hereIsANewScore: score* in *class Orchestra*. The instance of *class Orchestra* that receives this message will map its elements, in this case *Players*, onto the code that asks each to re-

**Table 1. Statements in Smalltalk**

| Form | Intention | Example |
|------|-----------|---------|
| Receiver message | Send a message | *each whatIsYourPartName* |
| Variable ← value | Associate a value with an identifier | *part ← each whatIsYourPartName* |
| ↑ Value | Evaluate the expression and return the value | ↑ *pieceName* |

**Table 2. Messages in Smalltalk**

| Form | Example |
|------|---------|
| UnarySelector | *whatIsYourPartName* |
| InfixSelector argument | *+4 (as in 3 + 4)* |
| KeywordSelector: argument | *hereIsYourMusic: sheet* (for multiple arguments this is keywordSelector1: arg1 . . . keywordSelectorN: argN). |

trieve its sheet music from the score. It does this by sending itself the mapping message *do:* [...], in the same way that a *Conductor* sends an instance of *Orchestra* the same message in Code Listing 1.

## Initialization

Now that the description of our music system is complete, we need to create actual instances of the classes. In Smalltalk, rather than go to the store to buy music or hold auditions to get players, we send messages to the classes we have just defined to get new players or music. For example, we send the message *new* to the *class Conductor* (*Conductor new*) to obtain a particular conductor. Similarly, we will request *Player new* once for each player that we want in our orchestra.

To each of these newly created objects, we send messages asking them to initialize themselves. A couple of these messages were described previously (e.g., *hereIsYourMusic: newSheet* for players), but we have left many out for the sake of brevity. The Smalltalk code for instance creation and initialization looks like Code Listing 3.

Once we have initialized our system, we execute the statement *ourConductor playAPiece: 'Bach Third Brandenberg Concerto'* and, assuming the

hardware DAC is on, we should hear music.

This is how design of a system simulation is done in Smalltalk. Whether it is players in an orchestra, instruments, conductors, numbers, files, or graphic objects, the programmer defines the classes of objects that will exist in his or her system. These definitions involve the properties (data structures) that each object will have, the operations on the properties and functions for using them, and the interactions these objects will have with the rest of the system. These interactions are defined in terms of messages sent and received, and are organized by the methods carried out when a message is recognized. Although at the method level Smalltalk resembles other programming languages, it is in the area of system design that Smalltalk offers its unique support. Just as Smalltalk allowed a natural translation from a description of a real-world music system to a computer simulation of a music system, it allows a natural translation between other or imaginary systems to their computer representations.

## Inheritance

Two aspects of Smalltalk that have not been discussed yet are central to the system: one is a

Code Listing 2. The Smalltalk code for the method
associated with the mes-
sage hereIsANewScore:
score *in* class Orchestra.

```
hereIsANewScore: score   |   eachPlayer
[   self do: [:eachPlayer. eachPlayer getYourPartFrom: score]
].
```

linguistic feature, while the other has to do with presentation of information. The feature of the Smalltalk system that is very important to the process of designing a system is *inheritance*, the ability of a class to inherit properties and behavior from other classes. There are many kinds of people or things that have similar properties or behaviors. For example, a chamber orchestra has players with instruments and plays music as does a general orchestra, but the instruments allowed in a chamber orchestra are only a subset of those used by the general orchestra. The chamber orchestra may be thought of as a *constrained* version of a general orchestra. A percussionist behaves like most other players in an orchestra, but often has to play more than one instrument. The percussionist is a version of the general player with *additional* properties.

In our Smalltalk simulations of music and other systems, we would like to capture similarities such as these between classes of objects. That is, we would like to be able to define a class as like another class but with certain constraints and additions. This would allow us to include the shared properties and behaviors in one definition (the description of the general orchestra), and specify the differences only when defining the specific class (e.g., describing the instrument constraint when defining *class ChamberOrchestra*).

Smalltalk allows a class to be defined as inheriting properties (instance variables) and behavior (messages and methods) from another class. The inheriting class is called the *subclass* and the parent class is called the *superclass*. The definition of a subclass may include the specification of instance variables in addition to those defined in the superclass. That is, each instance of the subclass will have values for all the instance variables defined in the superclass plus those defined in the subclass. The definition of a subclass may include messages

and methods in addition to those defined in the superclass. Also, subclasses may *override* messages defined in the superclass, that is, the subclass may define a different method for a message already defined in a superclass. In such a case, the subclass's method will be used when that message is received.

The description of *class Percussionist* in the following example specifies it as a subclass of *class Player*, extending its properties to include two instruments rather than one. In addition to those instance variables defined for *Player*, a *Percussionist* has a *secondPartName*, *secondInstrument*, and *secondPrintedPart*. The message *setInstrument: newInstrument* will be inherited from the superclass. The messages *setSecondInstrument: newInstrument* and *stopPlaying* must be added. The methods for the messages *getYourPartFrom: score* and *playOn* will be overridden to use both parts. The resulting class description looks like this:

**Class:**    *Percussionist* — a player with two instruments

**SubclassOf:**    *Player*

**Instance Variable:**    *secondPartName* — the part name for the second instrument

**Instance Variable:**    *secondInstrument* — the second instrument

**Instance Variable:**    *secondPrintedPart* — the second piece of music

**Message:**    *setSecondInstrument: newInstrument*

*Code Listing 3. The Small-talk code for instance creation and initializa-* *tion of the* Conductor, Repertoire, *and* Orchestra.

```
ourConductor ← Conductor new.                          "Create a new conductor for us to use"
ourConductor hereIsYourOrchestra: (Orchestra new).   "Create and give our conductor an orchestra"
aRepertoire ← Repertoire new.
aRepertoire includeScore: scoreForBachThirdBrandenbergConcerto.
                    "ScoreForBachThirdBrandenbergConcerto was presumably defined
                     elsewhere, within the context of evaluating this message."
aRepertoire includeScore: scoreForMyOpus1.
                    "The instance scoreForMyOpus1 of class Score was defined elsewhere."
ourConductor hereIsYourRepertoire: aRepertoire.     "Hand conductor the initialized repertoire."
ourConductor addToOrchestra: (Player new withInstrument: (Instrument new withEnvelope:
trumpet))
                    "Where trumpet, an instance of class Envelope, is defined elsewhere"
ourConductor addToOrchestra: (Player new withInstrument: (Instrument new withEnvelope:
flute))
ourConductor addToOrchestra: (Player new withInstrument: (Instrument new withEnvelope:
violin))
```

**Method:** Pick up a new instrument for the second part. Assign the value of the argument *newInstrument* as the value of the variable *secondInstrument*.

**Message:**   *getYourPartFrom: score*
**Method:** Send *score* the message *getPartFor: partName*, assign the returned sheet music to *sheetMusic*, then send *score* the message *getPartFor: secondPartName*, and assign the returned sheet music to the field *secondPrintedPart*.

**Message:**   *playOn*
**Method:** Play the current music with your instruments. Send *restart* to both sheets of music. Then, until told otherwise, get the *nextNote* from both *printedPart* and *secondPrintedPart*, and send *instrument* and *secondInstrument* the message *playNote* with the correct notes as arguments.

The Smalltalk system designer might define *class ChamberOrchestra* to be a subclass of *class Orchestra, class StringQuartet* to be a subclass of *class ChamberOrchestra, class MutedInstrument* to be a subclass of *class Instrument*, and so on. In general, the inheritance mechanism is used when we define a class of objects that shares properties and behaviors with another class, but constrains or augments these properties or behaviors. This allows system description to be similar to real-world description, allows the common properties and methods to be defined in one place, and allows the designer to define only the differences for the subclass.

## User Interfaces

Central to the development of the Smalltalk programming environment is the idea that the presentation of information is a very important aspect of any system. Physically this involves good visual graphics, good audio output (especially for a music system), and good input devices. Of course Smalltalk as a language cannot dictate what hardware will be used, but the framework of Smalltalk allows the designer to interact with available hardware in a way that is a natural extension of the message-oriented processing, that is, by sending messages to hardware-device objects. In addition, the subclassing ability in Smalltalk allows the designer to implement graphic objects specific to his or her system by describing extensions to classes

Fig. 1. A Smalltalk music
envelope editor.

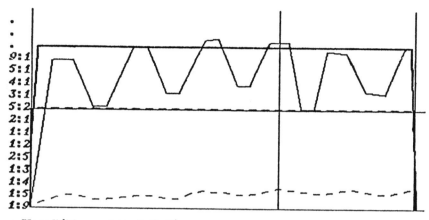

existing in the basic Smalltalk programming system.

A designer of a music system, for example, could use the already-defined *class Window* as a superclass for *class MusicWindow*, a window on the screen in which notes appear. The methods in *class Window* that define window behavior, such as moving around a display, would be used, and in addition to these the designer would need to define only the methods for displaying notes within a window.

Figure 1 is a Smalltalk display of an editor of an envelope of sound (an instance of *class Timbre* in this system) in a frequency-modulated (FM) music synthesis system. The various dotted lines are a graphic representation of the parameters to the FM synthesis as they vary over time. The vertical bars delimit the attack, steady-state, and decay regions of time. The designer may edit each of the dotted lines by drawing new versions with the pointing device. In addition, the words at the bottom form a menu of editing commands.

Although the information is stored in a numeric form, the user's ability to display and manipulate this information graphically makes it easy for him or her to build the desired result. The user could, of course, edit the properties of the timbre object by typing messages to be sent to it. In some cases this is an appropriate way to edit information. In this case, however, and in very many others, the user will find that it is easier and more understandable to edit the information graphically; to point at the picture with a pointing device, indicating the way he or she would like to modify the picture and, therefore, the information.

Multiple views of an object can add to the viewer's ability to understand the nature of that object. In Fig. 1, manipulation of the picture and the sound produced during editing of the envelope provide the user with two views of the information. The Smalltalk message metaphor is one thing that makes it easy to design such multiple *presentations* of an object with a single *representation*. Using the messages *restart* and *nextNote*, an instance of *class Player* in the preceding class description views its *printedPart* as a stream of notes. Instances of another class in our system, for example, *NoteEditor*, might want to view an instance of *class PrintedPart* as a collection of notes and durations. *Class PrintedPart* would contain appropriate messages for this kind of view. The important thing is that a designer should be able to

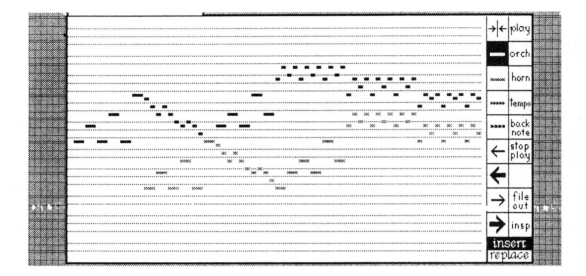

produce multiple views of the system easily so that various users, or users with different purposes, will be able to deal with the information in appropriate ways.

Figures 2 and 3 are Smalltalk screen images of multiple views of pieces of music, one a player-piano type of scroll and the other a more conventional line of musical notation. At different times and for different users each view of the music is important.

## Conclusion

Smalltalk is a programming system in which all components are objects. Objects are packages of properties and behavior. The properties are represented by instance variables and the behavior by messages and methods. The methods are sequences of statements whose syntax involves either message-sending, variable assignment, or returning of a value. Every object is an instance of a class. The class description contains the specification of the instance variables, messages, and methods used by its instances. A class may be a subclass of another class, inheriting the superclass's instance variables, messages, and methods, and perhaps overriding some of the methods.

Smalltalk implicitly provides program modularity, with classes used as program modules. External specifications of modules are provided by the message patterns a class understands, while internal implementation is provided by the instance variables and methods defined in a class. The internals of a class may be redefined without affecting the users of the class as long as the messages, which make up the external interface, remain the same.

A Smalltalk programming system provides a kernel of classes and instances already defined for numbers, objects, classes, methods, text, and graphics. These classes may be used as superclasses so the programmer may have his or her classes inherit their behavior, perhaps to build a system that provides the user with multiple views of information.

The mechanisms that the Smalltalk programming language provides assist in the design of systems; in particular, the class and message mechanisms allow a direct translation between a real-world description of a system, such as an orchestra,

*Fig. 3. Smalltalk view of a line of standard musical notation.*

and its computer-simulated counterpart. Programming in Smalltalk is done by defining the classes of objects we want. These descriptions are in terms of properties that each instance of the class will have, messages each instance will receive, and the methods of behavior that should be invoked when a message is received. Subclassing allows classes to inherit properties and behavior from already-defined classes, providing a powerful tool for system design.

## Acknowledgments

The Smalltalk language was conceived by Alan Kay in the early 1970s and has since evolved through various designs and implementations by members of the Learning Research Group at the Xerox Palo Alto Research Center. The figures in this article are from actual Smalltalk music systems implemented by Ted Kaehler, Bob Shur, Steve Saunders, Kim McCall, and Chris Jeffers. Adele Goldberg and Bruce Horn provided many ideas for this paper. Available

papers about the language and some systems developed using it are listed as References. A book releasing the implementation specifications of Xerox Smalltalk will be available in 1981.

## References

Goldberg, Adele, and Robson, David. 1979. "A Metaphor for User Inferface Design." In *University of Hawaii Systems Science Symposium*. Pp. 148–157.

Goldberg, Adele, et al. 1981. *Smalltalk: Dreams and Schemes*, (two volumes).

Ingalls, Dan. 1978. "The Smalltalk-76 Programming System: Design and Implementation." In *Fifth Annual ACM Symposium on Principles of Programming Languages*. Pp. 9–16.

Kay, Alan. 1977. "Microelectronics and the Personal Computer." *Scientific American*, 237(3): 230–244.

Kay, Alan, and Goldberg, Adele. 1977. "Personal Dynamic Media." *IEEE Computer Magazine* March: 31–41.

Saunders, Steve. 1977. "Improved FM Audio Synthesis Methods for Real-Time Digital Music Generation." *Computer Music Journal* 1(1): 53–55.

**Henry Lieberman**
Artificial Intelligence Laboratory and
Laboratory for Computer Science
Massachusetts Institute of Technology
Cambridge, Massachusetts 02139

# Machine Tongues IX: Object-Oriented Programming

## Introduction

In a previous issue of *Computer Music Journal*, 4(4), Glenn Krasner outlined the basic tenets of object-oriented programming in Smalltalk (Krasner 1980). In this article, I will review some aspects of the object-oriented paradigm using another object-oriented language, Act 1, applied to some simple musical applications. The discussion will focus on areas where the needs of musical applications intersect with those of artificial intelligence (AI), in which object-oriented programming is becoming increasingly popular. Some of the issues we will explore are extensibility of programs, sharing knowledge between parts of programs, and parallel programming. In order to keep the discussion of the technical issues uncluttered, I have kept the musical examples extremely simple. The ramifications of the object-oriented approach for more complex musical applications should be clear.

## Why Object-Oriented Programming?

Musical programming has at least one thing in common with AI programming: the requirements of both domains stretch the state of the software art. In much business and scientific programming, the problems can usually be well specified in advance of coding, and many problems share the same techniques, so new control and data structures are needed relatively rarely. The concern in business and science is often with how to make programs more reliable and efficient. In fields like

Research described in this article has been supported in part by ONR contract N00014-75-C-0522 and in part by ARPA contract N00014-80-C-0505.

Computer Music Journal, Vol. 6, No. 3, Fall 1982

AI and music, efficiency is often less important than flexibility. The nature of the problem often changes as work on the problem proceeds, and new control structures and data structures appear frequently. The AI or music programmer needs a programming environment in which new ideas can be tested quickly and easily. The programming environment should allow extensibility of control and data structures so that programs can evolve smoothly as understanding develops.

Innovative applications in music constantly run up against the *complexity barrier*. Since programs used to compose or analyze music become complex very quickly, it is necessary to have a system that encourages modularity in order to help manage interactions between parts of the program. The same requirements hold for programs in understanding natural language, vision, robotics, games, and systems for expert problem solving. (Two previous issues of the *Journal*, 4[2] and 4[3], 1980, explore the commonality of interest between AI and music in more depth.)

Those interested in musical applications should take notice of a new kind of programming methodology that is becoming increasingly popular in AI circles: object-oriented programming. Object-oriented programming is a philosophy for designing and writing programs by organizing a program as a collection of *active objects*, called *actors*. Each actor can take action independently of other actors, and actors communicate with each other solely by sending messages. An object-oriented style can be adopted in conventional languages like Lisp and, to a lesser extent, even in more primitive languages such as C, Pascal, or assembly language. But the most effective object-oriented programming can be done when the programming language explicitly supports the object paradigm.

Act 1 is an experimental interpretive programming language that replaces all the traditional programming constructs with active objects (the actors) and message passing. Act 1 also allows many actors to interpret messages in parallel. We have implemented a prototype interpreter, written in Lisp, but the language is not really designed for efficient implementation on today's sequential computers. Microprocessors are continually getting smaller and cheaper, so tomorrow's computers will achieve high power by incorporating many processors in a single personal machine. Act 1 is designed to harness the power of parallel machines in an effective and convenient way.

## Advantages of the Object-Oriented Approach

The object-oriented approach allows knowledge to be distributed among parts of the program, rather than centralized in global data bases. Each actor has only the knowledge and expertise required for it to respond to messages from other actors. There is no notion of global state in an actor system. This means that knowledge is always placed where it is used. Knowledge needed to perform operations on an object is part of the object's definition, not of external procedures. Object-oriented languages blur the conventional distinction between data and procedures. If an object is passed from one part of a program to another, the knowledge about how to use the object travels with it.

In actor languages such as Act 1, all communication and interaction between actors consists of message passing. No actor can be operated upon, looked at, taken apart, or modified except by sending a request to the actor to perform the operation itself. This is essential to allow multiple representations of a single conceptual object, which is important, since no one representation may be best for all purposes. A representation that is efficient in one situation may be inefficient in another. Programs that assume a fixed representation become resistant to change, since incremental evolution of programs may lead to the introduction of new representations. In an interview published in this journal (Roads 1980), Marvin Minsky stressed the importance of multiple representations, both for AI and for music.

In Act 1, the object-oriented, message-passing philosophy results in exceptionally clean mechanisms for exploiting parallelism while avoiding the pitfalls of timing errors. In Act 1, an attempt is made to model the kind of parallelism that would result from running many processors concurrently rather than to simulate parallelism with coroutines as is done in Smalltalk and object-oriented extensions of Lisp. In Act 1, only minimal constraints on the ordering of events are assumed so that many actors may send messages simultaneously without interfering with one another.

Eventually, object-oriented languages should prove to be most suitable for taking advantage of a large network of parallel processors, which will become increasingly common in the near future. Parallel systems will be the best vehicles for implementing musical applications, whether for high-speed digital audio processing or for intelligent composers' assistants.

With the object-oriented approach, common knowledge is easily shared by parts of a program, which avoids the necessity of duplicating common resources in every actor that needs them. Act 1 delegates messages, which allows for concentration of shared knowledge in actors with very general behavior and creation of extensions of these actors with idiosyncratic behavior more suited to specific situations.

## The Actor Model

The basic actor model is very simple. It has only one kind of object—an actor. Everything, both procedures and data, is uniformly represented by actors.

Only one kind of thing happens in an actor system—an *event*. An event happens when a target actor receives a message. Messages themselves are actors, too. We can think of each actor as a person who communicates with other people in the society by sending messengers.

Each actor in the system is represented by a data structure with a *script* and *acquaintances* (Fig. 1). The script is a program that determines what the actor will do when it receives a message. When a message is received, the script of the target actor is

*Fig. 1. "Little person" model of the components of an actor.*

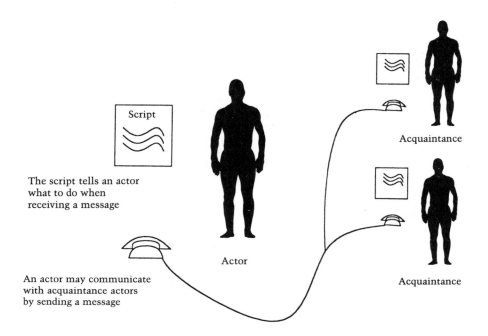

Script

The script tells an actor what to do when receiving a message

Actor

An actor may communicate with acquaintance actors by sending a message

Acquaintance

Acquaintance

given control. If the script recognizes the message, the script can decide to accept the message; otherwise, the message is rejected.

Each actor has to know the names of other actors so that it can communicate with them. The acquaintances of an actor are the local data, or variables associated with each actor. We can think of the acquaintances as the telephone numbers of people. Each actor can call (send a message to) other actors, provided it knows their telephone numbers. Each actor starts out with a set of known telephone numbers and can acquire new ones during its lifetime.

If the script decides not to accept the message, it can *delegate* the message, asking another actor to try to respond to the message for it. An actor that delegates a message is called a *client actor*, and the actor to which the message is delegated is called its *proxy*. Typically, the proxy is one of the acquaintances of the client actor. The proxy of an actor might be capable of responding to a message on the basis of more general knowledge than the original recipient had.

This simple framework is general enough to encompass almost any kind of computation imaginable. Examples will show how the more traditional concepts used in programming can be expressed within the actor model and will illustrate the advantages of doing so.

## What's in a Note?

Let us examine the object-oriented approach by considering one of the first decisions any computer music system must make: How is a note represented? Every music system must have some data structure that is used to represent a note. But existing music systems do not have the same representation for even a concept so simple and fundamental as a musical note.

The simplest music system (say a system for children, implemented on a microcomputer) might implement a note as two numbers: an equal-tempered pitch and a duration. Pitch might be represented by an integer, with middle C represented

Fig. 2. Three different numerical representations of
pitch. Message passing allows different representations of a note to be used
interchangeably.

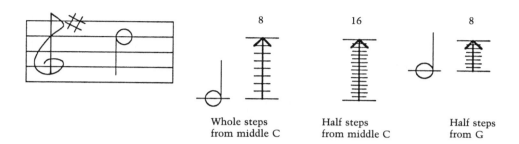

| Whole steps from middle C | Half steps from middle C | Half steps from G |

by 0 and whole steps counted so that C an octave above is 7 and C an octave below is −7. This is far from the only way of representing a pitch. For example, we can agree to count half steps instead of whole steps, providing for sharps and flats so that C an octave above middle C is 12 instead of 7. Or, perhaps it would be better to separate aspects of a single pitch, using two numbers to represent a pitch—one to count octaves above middle C and another for the number of half steps relative to the beginning of the octave.

Perhaps, for this system, it is wrong to think of a note independently of a piece of music. In a simple piece of tonal music, a more useful note representation would contain both the key of the piece and a number saying what octave and what pitch in half steps are relative to the key. Or, for harmonic improvisation, the representation might include a chord for the measure and information concerning whether the note was dissonant with respect to some key (Fig. 2). The problem of choosing an implementation does not end here. For more sophisticated music systems, notes should record their timbre as well. How do we represent timbres, which may be very dependent on details of the particular music synthesis system being used? Choices need to be made for representing duration, for representing such articulation factors as whether the note is staccato or legato, for dynamics, and so on.

Since notes are compound data objects (they contain at least pitch and duration) we must also decide which kind of "glue" to use to hold their parts together. In Fortran or Algol, arrays might be used; in Pascal, records could be preferable; and in standard Lisp, linked lists might be used.

Another implementation dilemma is that often the same concept can be either represented as a static piece of data or computed dynamically by a procedure. If the music synthesis hardware accepts a certain format for pitches, say half steps from middle C, the software designer is faced with two choices. The note may be stored directly in its hardware format, or another format such as octave and half steps relative to the key can be chosen. A procedure must then make the conversion from the alternative format to the hardware format whenever necessary. But a procedure that "just wants to play the note" should not have to "care" whether the hardware format is stored or computed by a procedure.

The proliferation of choices of representation leads to many problems. No one choice can be singled out as best for all purposes. Since different programs may have different representations (especially if they were written by different people), it is often difficult for one program to make use of another if their representations differ. Having multiple representations in a conventional programming language may make it more difficult to change the program to add new features. A program may evolve over time, so that making a change, such as adding another component to the data structure for a note, may involve rewriting every piece of code that uses that note.

The problem is that even such a simple concept as a note can be represented by many different primitive data structures. The raw material for building objects such as notes in conventional languages is primitive data structures (integers, floating-point numbers, and strings) and ways of combining them (arrays, records, and lists). Since programs that use the note must act on it using primitive procedures, *any program that uses the note must know the representation of the note* and is sensitive to any changes in the representation. If programs access the pitch of a note by fetching a certain component from an array, and the component that stores the pitch is changed, all programs that access the pitch must be altered.

## Actor Response to Messages

In object-oriented languages, the raw material for building a concept such as a note is behavior. An actor is defined completely with regard to its behavior, which is the action that the actor takes when it receives messages. Object-oriented languages provide a means of specifying the behavior of an actor when it receives a message, through procedures called *methods* or *handlers*. If two actors respond identically to the same messages, they can be used interchangeably, even though they may have completely different implementations.

For example, we can define two different kinds of PITCHes to go along with the NOTE. We begin by saying, for each kind of actor, what other actors it knows about. An actor can receive messages asking for other actors it knows about. Then, for each message the actor handles, we say how the actor responds to that message. (Descriptions of programs will be given in English, to avoid introducing the details of Act 1's syntax at this point. Important identifiers will be capitalized, and the text indented to correspond to the structure of the program.)

Create a kind of actor called NOTE.
  Each NOTE has a PITCH,
  a DURATION,
    Represented as a fraction of a whole note, and
  a TIMBRE.
Create an actor called PITCH.

Create a kind of PITCH called SIMPLE-PITCH.
  Each SIMPLE-PITCH has:
    an OFFSET-FROM-MIDDLE-C

Represented as number of half steps above middle C.

Create a kind of PITCH called KEY-RELATIVE-PITCH.
  Each KEY-RELATIVE-PITCH has:
    a KEY
      Represented as a number, half steps from middle C,
    an OCTAVE,
      Represented as number of octaves above the middle of the keyboard, and
    an OFFSET-FROM-KEY,
      Represented as number of half steps above the KEY.

This definition enables us to create new NOTE actors by giving a PITCH and DURATION. Each NOTE actor can respond to messages asking, What is your PITCH? or What is your DURATION?

We can define any of these actors so that they respond to additional messages. For instance, another convenient method of creating PITCHes might be by specifying the letter (A to G), of the note, an accidental (if any), and the octave.

If I'm a SIMPLE-PITCH,
  and I receive a message to CREATE a pitch,
  with a LETTER [A–G]
  an OCTAVE [Assuming middle if not specified]
  and an ACCIDENTAL [SHARP, FLAT, or NATURAL, assuming NATURAL]:
I create a SIMPLE-PITCH
  whose OFFSET-FROM-MIDDLE-C is
    The OCTAVE times 12, plus
    The distance in half steps from C to the LETTER,
    Plus one if SHARP, minus one if FLAT.

If I'm a KEY-RELATIVE-PITCH,
  and I receive a message to CREATE a pitch,
  with a LETTER [A–G]
  an OCTAVE [Assuming middle if not specified]
  and an ACCIDENTAL [SHARP, FLAT, or NATURAL, assuming NATURAL]
  in a KEY:
I create a KEY-RELATIVE-PITCH
  whose OCTAVE is the OCTAVE specified
    Minus one if the LETTER is above the KEY note in the C scale.

whose OFFSET-FROM-KEY is the sum of
   The distance in half steps from C to the
   LETTER,
   Plus one if SHARP, minus one if FLAT.

If the sound synthesizer hardware accepts only the number of half steps above middle C as a pitch, we can define both kinds of notes to accept the message ABSOLUTE-PITCH as follows;

If I'm a SIMPLE-PITCH,
And I receive a message asking for my ABSOLUTE-PITCH,
   I return my OFFSET-FROM-MIDDLE-C.

If I'm a KEY-RELATIVE-PITCH,
and I receive a message asking for my ABSOLUTE-PITCH,
   I return the sum of
   my KEY, and
   my OCTAVE times 12, and
   my OFFSET-FROM-KEY.

We have defined two different representations for notes, but since both representations respond to the same messages compatibly, they can be used interchangeably. We can ask a note to play itself:

If I'm a NOTE, and I'm asked to PLAY myself:
   I send my PITCH an ABSOLUTE-PITCH message,
   then I send the result to the MUSIC-SYNTHESIS-HARDWARE object.

This will work with either kind of PITCH object, since both can respond to the message asking for ABSOLUTE-PITCH. One advantage of using object-oriented languages is that they allow many different implementations of an object to coexist in the same system. The program that plays notes does not have to know what kind of pitch it is dealing with. In a conventional language, we would be forced to choose one representation for the note, and programs that use the note would have to convert between representations. Further, if we decide later to implement yet another variety of pitch, such as one that counts whole steps instead of half steps, the old program will still work correctly if we implement a response for the ABSOLUTE-PITCH message.

## Why Must Everything Be an Actor?

As mentioned, several previous and subsequent systems have embodied active objects and message passing. What makes Act 1 different? In Act 1, *all* computation occurs in the message-passing paradigm. This results in an exceptionally uniform and elegant framework for computation. Act 1 is intended to be a vehicle for an uncompromising test of the actor philosophy.

Less radical systems such as Simula-67 (Birtwhistle et al. 1973), Clu (Liskov et al. 1977), Lisp Machine Lisp (also called *Zetalisp*) (Weinreb and Moon 1981) and others generally provide a special data type (or means of constructing data types) to represent active objects defined by a user, along with a special message-passing procedure that operates on the special data type. The predefined components of the system, such as numbers, arrays, and procedures, are not considered as active objects, however. In a nonuniform system, a program must know whether it has been given an actor data type in order to use the message-sending operation. A program expecting a system data type cannot be given a newly defined actor. This limits the extensibility of such systems. (Smalltalk [Krasner 1980; Xerox Learning Research Group 1981] is another language that exemplifies the philosophy of uniform representation of objects.)

The actor theory requires that everything in the system: functions, coroutines, processes, numbers, lists, data bases, and devices, should be represented as actors and be capable of receiving messages. This may seem at first a little dogmatic, but important practical benefits arise from having a totally actor-oriented system. There is a strong kind of modularity that results from having a system made up completely of actors. This kind of modularity cannot be realized without sticking to the principle of organizing systems as actors.

*Modularity* is the ability to treat a part of a complex system as a *black box*. A system is modular if it can be broken up into a large number of small parts or modules, each of which is easily understood in isolation, independent of all the others. Users of a particular module should be able to rely on the behavior of that module without having to know irrelevant details of the implementation. Since in an actor system all communication happens by message passing, the only thing that is important about an actor is how the actor behaves when it receives a message. To make use of an actor, the user just has to know what messages the actor responds to and how the actor responds to each message.

Relying on actors and message passing makes systems very extensible. *Extensibility* is the ability to add new behavior to a system without modifying the old system, provided the new behavior is compatible. In an actor system, the user may always add a new actor with the same message-passing behavior, but perhaps with a different internal implementation, and the new actor will appear identical to the old one as far as all the users are concerned. We can also extend a system by introducing a new actor whose behavior is a *superset* of the behavior of the old actor. It might respond to several new messages that the old one did not respond to, but as long as the new actor's behavior is compatible with that of the old, no previous user will be aware of the difference.

With conventional languages such as C, introducing new data types is not easy. A conceptually new object must be introduced using predefined data objects. The user must be aware of the format of the new data type to make use of it and must rewrite the program if the format changes.

## List Representation Using Objects

Let us consider the problem of representing a melody. The simplest way of representing a melody is as a list or sequence of notes. In Act 1, a CONS (named after the similar structure in Lisp) is an object that receives messages asking for its FIRST element, a list containing the REST of its elements, or a message asking whether it is EMPTY. Linear LISTs of objects are created by putting successive elements in the FIRST part and chaining their REST parts, ending in the EMPTY-LIST.

Create an actor EMPTY-LIST.

If I'm an EMPTY-LIST and I'm asked whether I'm EMPTY,
answer YES.

Create an actor CONS
with a FIRST part and a REST part,
which can return its FIRST or its REST.

If I'm a CONS and I'm asked whether I'm EMPTY,
answer NO.

Create an actor LIST,
which when asked to form a list of several ELEMENTS,
If the set of ELEMENTS is empty, return the EMPTY-LIST.
Otherwise, return a CONS actor,
whose FIRST is the first ELEMENT,
and whose REST is a LIST of the remaining ELEMENTS.

As a simple example, the first line of the ditty *Row, Row, Row Your Boat* might be as follows.

Create an actor called MELODY, which has a LIST-OF-NOTES.

Create a MELODY actor called ROW*3-YOUR-BOAT
whose LIST-OF-NOTES is
a LIST actor, whose elements are
a NOTE actor, with PITCH C, with DURATION of a QUARTER-NOTE,
a NOTE actor, with PITCH C, with DURATION of a QUARTER-NOTE,
a NOTE actor, with PITCH C, with DURATION of a QUARTER-NOTE,
a NOTE actor, with PITCH D, with DURATION of a EIGHTH-NOTE,
and a NOTE actor, with PITCH E, with DURATION of a EIGHTH-NOTE.

If we have a simple procedure that, given a note and a key, computes a chord that harmonizes with that note, we can harmonize the ROW*3-YOUR-BOAT melody by sending it a HARMONIZE message.

If I'm a MELODY, and I receive a message asking to HARMONIZE,

Send the LIST-OF-NOTES a message asking if it is EMPTY,
if so, return the EMPTY-LIST.
Otherwise, create a list whose FIRST is
a CHORD resulting from sending a HARMO-
NIZE message to the result of
sending FIRST to the LIST-OF-NOTES,
and with the KEY of the MELODY.
And the REST of the list is
the result of sending HARMONIZE to the REST
of the MELODY.

So far, this representation of melodies is just like any list-processing language. But Act 1 gives us the freedom to define new kinds of lists that behave differently, as long as they also obey the list protocol of FIRST, REST, and EMPTY messages.

Suppose that instead of wishing to write out all the notes of a melody in advance, we want to have a performer play the melody on a clavier. The natural thing to do is to represent the played melody as a list. If we used Lisp-style lists, we could first have the performer play the whole melody, construct the list, then compute the harmony. But it would be more fun to have the harmony computed in real time so that the computer can play along with the performer. We can achieve this by defining a list whose components appear only when they are asked. When we send a message asking for the FIRST note of a KEYBOARD-MELODY, the object waits until a note is available, then returns the first note played. When a message is sent asking for the REST of the KEYBOARD-MELODY, an object is returned that will obtain the rest of the notes played. Some signal is also necessary for the performer to end the melody, perhaps by pressing a button, or by not playing for a certain length of time.

Create a kind of MELODY called KEYBOARD-MELODY.

If I'm a KEYBOARD-MELODY, and I'm asked whether I'm EMPTY:
If the performer has signaled to stop playing, say YES.
If the performer is still playing, say NO.

If I'm a KEYBOARD-MELODY, and I'm asked for my FIRST note:
Wait until the performer plays a NOTE.
Return the NOTE played by the PERFORMER, and remember it as my FIRST [in case anybody else asks later].

If I'm a KEYBOARD-MELODY, and I'm asked for my REST:
If the performer has signaled to stop playing, return the EMPTY-LIST.
Otherwise return a KEYBOARD-MELODY.

The import of defining the KEYBOARD-MELODY in this manner is that the HARMONIZE message that we wrote previously can now work on both types of melody: HARMONIZE just depends on being able to send the MELODY the messages FIRST, REST, and EMPTY, messages to which KEYBOARD-MELODY also responds. Put another way, HARMONIZE depends only on the *behavior* of melodies, not on the format of their physical representation in the machine. We did not have to rewrite HARMONIZE to reflect the fact that the simple MELODY was stored as a data structure, whereas KEYBOARD-MELODY was represented by a procedure (Fig. 3).

We need not stop here in defining alternative kinds of melodies. We could define another kind of melody that is stored on a disk. Retrieving it would require a procedure for reading it off the disk. Another type of melody could be stored somewhere else on the computer network. Any of these melodies could be substituted completely transparently.

This example illustrates an important point about Act 1. We have defined a new data type, a melody, which has the behavior of a list, which is usually a predefined system primitive data type. We can use our new data type in all contexts where the system data type is appropriate. We could not have done this in languages such as Ada that have embedded objects. A program in such a language must, in general, know whether it is dealing with a system object (through primitive procedures) or a user object (through an explicit message-passing operation).

*Fig. 3. Different represen-tations of melodies. Melo-dies respond to the ques-tions, Are you EMPTY? What is your FIRST? What is your*

*REST? In list melody, notes are stored as data. In key-board melody, notes can be represented as procedures.*

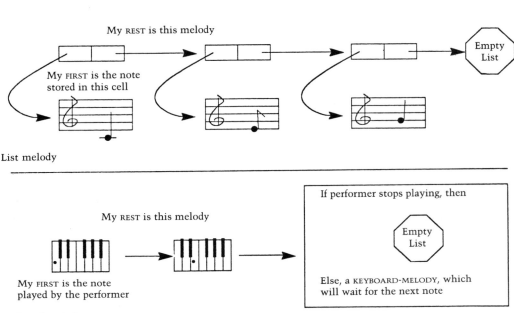

List melody

Keyboard melody

## Knowledge Sharing Through Message Delegation

As stated earlier, whenever an actor receives a message it cannot answer immediately on the basis of its own local knowledge and expertise, it delegates the message to another actor, its proxy. Delegating a message is like passing the buck. The actor originally receiving the message, the client actor, tells its proxy, "I don't know how to respond to this message; can you respond for me?"

Many client actors may share the same proxy actor or have proxies with the same script. Very general knowledge common to many actors may reside in a proxy, while more specific knowledge resides in each client actor sharing that proxy. This avoids the need to duplicate common knowledge in every client actor.

Delegation provides a way of incrementally extending the behavior of an actor. Often, actors existing in a large system will be almost correct for a new application. Extension is accomplished by creating a new client actor, which specifically mentions the desired differences and falls back on the behavior of the old actor as its proxy. The client actor gets first crack at responding to messages, so it can catch new messages or override old ones.

Delegation replaces the *class, subclass,* and *instance* mechanisms of Simula and Smalltalk. Delegation provides similar capabilities for sharing common knowledge among objects, but allows more flexibility. Other languages generally fix the pattern of sharing between objects either at compilation time or at the time the object is created. Delegation is dynamic: deciding which actor to delegate to is wholly up to the client actor that receives the message. Message passing is used for communication between client and proxy, so that a client may delegate a message dependent on some condition or may delegate a message to more than one actor.

In Act 1, there is no rigid distinction between

*classes* and *instances*. Any actor may behave like a class and manufacture new objects with similar behavior. All sectors are defined to respond to CREATE messages, which produce actors that copy the behavior of the recipient. Any actor may create actors with extended behavior by responding to EXTEND messages. Implementing *defaults* for newly created actors is accomplished by writing handlers that intercept the CREATE or EXTEND messages.

## Implementing Different Kinds of CHORDS

As a simple example of delegation, suppose we have a CHORD actor, defined to respond to a PLAY message by delegating the PLAY message to each of its constituent notes.

Create a CHORD actor
  that has a list of NOTES.

If I'm a CHORD, and I'm asked to PLAY,
  I delegate to each of my NOTES a PLAY message,
  asking them to PLAY all at the same time.

An ARPEGGIO shares all the knowledge of a CHORD, but responds to a PLAY message a bit differently. Instead of playing all the notes at the same time, it will play them one by one. Handlers for messages (such as a request for the list of notes) that are commonly passed between both types of chord need not be duplicated, because an ARPEGGIO actor will delegate to a CHORD any messages for which it does not have special behavior.

Create an ARPEGGIO
  by sending an EXTEND message to CHORD.
    Any messages not specifically intercepted by
      an ARPEGGIO
  will be delegated to CHORD.

If I'm an ARPEGGIO, and I'm asked to PLAY,
  First, delegate a PLAY message to the lowest
    note in my list of NOTES.
  The next time, play the next lowest note, and
    so on,
  until all notes have been played.

We can now proceed to define more specific varieties of CHORDS.

Create a MAJOR-CHORD, with a ROOT-NOTE [in
    root position],
  delegating to CHORD.

If I'm a MAJOR-CHORD, and I'm asked for my
    NOTES,
  return a list of my ROOT-NOTE, my MIDDLE-
    NOTE, and my HIGH-NOTE.

If I'm a MAJOR-CHORD, and I'm asked for my
    MIDDLE-NOTE,
  return the NOTE four half-steps higher than my
    ROOT.

If I'm a MAJOR-CHORD, and I'm asked for my
    HIGH-NOTE,
  return the NOTE seven half-steps higher than
    my ROOT.

A MINOR-CHORD is defined similarly.

Create a MINOR-CHORD, with a ROOT-NOTE,
  delegating all messages I don't handle myself
    to MAJOR-CHORD.

If I'm a MINOR-CHORD, and I'm asked for my
    MIDDLE-NOTE,
  I delegate the message, asking my MAJOR-
    CHORD for its MIDDLE-NOTE,
  then move that note down one half step.

The flexibility of implementing sharing via delegation allows us easily to combine unrelated but compatible extensions to the behavior of actors. For example, we might now choose to have an APPREGIATED-MINOR-CHORD, which can be built by creating an actor that shares knowledge both from MINOR-CHORD and ARPEGGIO (Fig. 4).

## Managing Parallelism

The actor model has many advantages in systems that make large-scale use of parallelism. Since knowledge is extremely localized in actor systems, it becomes easier to isolate subsystems of actors

Fig. 4. Patterns of delegation among CHORDS.

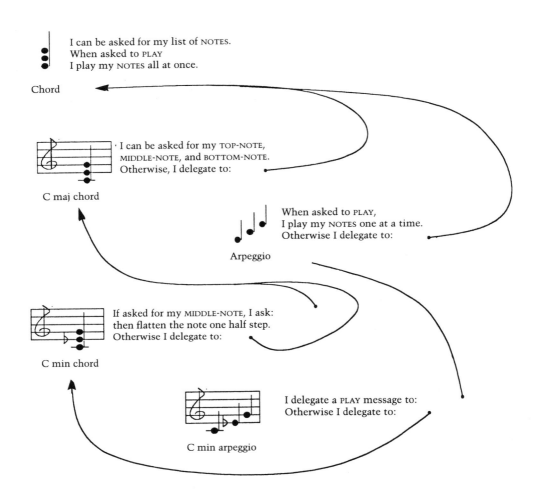

that can be run in parallel without interfering with one another. Since each actor has only the data and procedures relevant to its own operation, needless communication with global resources, which becomes a bottleneck in parallel systems, is avoided.

Actors may be distributed across many processors running in parallel, and message passing may involve communication across a network to reach actors on different processors. Since all communication is performed by message passing, a user need not know whether the actor resides on the same processor or on another.

Because of the principle that actors are defined by their behavior and are independent of representation, we can create actors that allow or restrict parallelism but otherwise behave identically to their serial counterparts. In other languages, a user program must be aware of whether it is dealing with an ordinary value, a parallel process, or a synchronized resource. This makes it more difficult to exploit parallelism.

Act 1 supplies two kinds of actors for parallel programming, which I will describe briefly before going on to consider a parallel application in music. *Futures* are actors that represent the values computed by parallel processes. Unlike parallel processes in some other languages, futures can be created dynamically and disappear by "garbage collection" when they are no longer needed.

Synchronization is provided by *serializers*. If an actor must receive messages from several parallel processes and has an internal state that is changeable, it can be protected by having a serializer actor wrapped around it. The serializer controls access to the internal actor to prevent timing errors that might otherwise occur when different processes try to change the state of the same actor simultaneously.

Both futures and serializers implement parallelism *transparently*. A program that makes use of a value computed by a parallel process, or an actor that can also receive messages from other processes, can interact with these actors just as it would if no parallelism were present. If a message is sent to a future or serializer prematurely, while it is still busy performing some computation, the sender is simply delayed until the message can be handled. This allows many serial programs to be extended easily for operation in a parallel environment.

### Adding Parallelism to a Serial Program

Let us consider the following problem, which will illustrate how future actors can be used as a convenient means of introducing parallelism to improve the performance of a serial program. Suppose, as before, we wish to define a music system that accepts a melody played by a performer on a clavier and produces sound from a synthesizer. This time, in addition, we want the system to display the score in music notation on a graphic display screen while the performer is playing.

In the interest of avoiding duplication of code, we would also like to retain the representation of melodies as lists of notes we used before. To arrange

the display of NOTE actors, we should make each NOTE actor respond to a message DISPLAY, which causes it to appear on the screen. The result of displaying a note can be a new actor called DISPLAYED-NOTE, just like the original NOTE, but including information relevant to the graphic representation of notes such as their position on the screen. We could write the program as follows.

Create an actor called DISPLAYED-MELODY, given a
KEYBOARD-MELODY:
I create a CONS actor whose FIRST is
    A DISPLAYED-NOTE that I get by
    sending a FIRST message to my KEYBOARD-
        MELODY, getting a NOTE.
    I send the NOTE a message to PLAY itself on
        the SYNTHESIZER,
    Then I send the NOTE a message to DISPLAY
        itself on the screen,
        which produces a DISPLAYED-NOTE.
and the REST of the CONS returned is
    a DISPLAYED-MELODY created from the REST of
        the KEYBOARD-MELODY.

When we actually try to run this program, we may encounter a problem. Although the process of playing the note on the synthesizer may occur almost instantaneously, analyzing the note and displaying it properly may be a time-consuming task. It might happen that before the display of one note has finished, the performer plays another note. We will not mind if the displayed score lags behind the performer a bit, but if there is any appreciable delay between the time the performer strikes a key and the time sound is heard from the synthesizer, the performer will find it impossible to play! This situation calls for parallelism. The solution is to overlap the computation of the display with the process of playing notes on the synthesizer. In Act 1, the way to achieve this is to wrap a future actor around the event in which the note is sent the DISPLAY message. A future actor is created and returned immediately, but the process of displaying the note is allowed to run concurrently with the rest of the DISPLAYED-MELODY (Fig. 5). The program should be revised as follows.

*Fig. 5. Two control struc-*
*tures for real-time perfor-*
*mance. In sequential con-*
*trol, sound from one note*

*must wait for display of*
*previous note. In Parallel*
*control, display and sound*
*can overlap.*

Sequential control

1. Performer strikes a key

2. Sound is output from synthesizer

3. Notation is displayed on screen

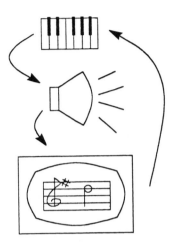

Parallel control

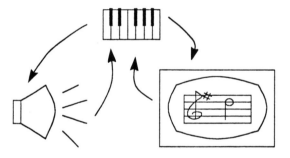

Create an actor called DISPLAYED-MELODY, given a
   KEYBOARD-MELODY:
   I create a CONS actor whose FIRST
      sends a PLAY message to the FIRST of the KEY-
        BOARD-MELODY, as above.
     Then I create a FUTURE actor that
      sends the NOTE a message to DISPLAY itself
        on the screen.
   and the REST of the CONS actor is as above.

In any program in which the DISPLAYED-MELODY
actor is used, both versions of the program behave
identically. The only difference is that the future
permits better real-time response from the program

on a parallel processor machine or sufficiently fast
time-sliced machine. This kind of parallelism
should be highly useful in programming parallel
signal processing architectures for musical applications as well.

A future is like an I.O.U. or a promise to deliver
the value when it is needed. When a future is created, it spawns a parallel process whose task it is to
compute the needed value. The future always returns immediately, though the process created may
still be running after the future is returned. The
user may pass the future around or perform other
computations, and these actions will be overlapped
with the computation of the future's value. The be-

havior of a future actor is arranged so that if computation of the future's value has been completed when some other actor requests the value, the future actor will pass the request along. If some other actor needs the value before it has been determined, the sender will be made to wait until the computation runs to completion. This is possible in an actor system because the notion of when one actor "needs" the value of another is well defined—one actor can be dependent on the value of another only when the first actor sends a message to the second.

An appealing aspect of using futures is that the future construct includes both the creation of parallel processes and synchronization of results computed by the processes. The parallelism and corresponding synchronization are always correctly *matched* with one another. This promotes more structured parallel programs than do formalisms in which we describe the creation of parallel processes and their synchronization independently, opening the possibility that there may be some mismatch between parallelism and synchronization.

## Summary

The object-oriented programming style has several unique advantages. Object-oriented programming provides a simple, clean, uniform basis for programming that allows knowledge to be distributed among active objects that can be used to represent both procedures and data. The universal communications mechanism of message passing allows the behavior of any actor in the system to be extended and allows multiple implementations of a particular concept to coexist. Delegation of messages between actors provides a flexible mechanism for sharing knowledge common to a group of actors. Actors provide a convenient means of introducing parallelism into a program, modeling concurrent processes, and taking advantage of the next generation of multiprocessor machines. Object-oriented programming is finding its way into many applications in the AI community, and I hope its importance will be recognized by the computer music community as well.

## Acknowledgments

I am grateful to Carl Hewitt, who originally developed the notion of an actor. The actor metaphor for object-oriented programming owes much to earlier work in the Lisp and Simula communities and in Alan Kay's Smalltalk. I would also like to thank Curtis Roads, editor of *Computer Music Journal*, for encouraging me to write this article.

## Bibliography

Birtwhistle, G. et al. 1973. *Simula Begin*. Philadelphia: Auerbach.

Hewitt, C. 1977. "Viewing Control Structures as Patterns of Passing Messages." *Artificial Intelligence* 8(3): 323–364.

Hewitt, C., and J. Schiller. 1980. "The Apiary Network Architecture for Knowledgeable Systems." In *Proceedings of the First Lisp Conference*, Stanford, California: Stanford University, pp. 107–117.

Krasner, G. 1980. "Machine Tongues VIII: A Smalltalk Music System." *Computer Music Journal* 4(4): 4–14.

Lieberman, H. 1980. "A Preview of Act 1." AI Memo 625. Cambridge, Massachusetts: M.I.T. Artificial Intelligence Laboratory.

Lieberman, H. 1980. "Thinking About Lots of Things at Once Without Getting Confused." AI Memo 626. Cambridge, Massachusetts: M.I.T. Artificial Intelligence Laboratory.

Liskov, B. et al. 1977. "Abstraction Mechanisms in CLU." *Communications of the ACM* 20(8): 564–576.

Roads, C. 1980. "Interview with Marvin Minsky." *Computer Music Journal* 4(3): 25–39.

Weinreb, D., and D. Moon. 1981. *Lisp Machine Manual*. 4th ed. Cambridge, Massachusetts: M.I.T. Artificial Intelligence Laboratory.

Xerox Learning Research Group. 1981. "The Smalltalk-80 System." *Byte* 6(8): 36–48.

Stephen Travis Pope

# Machine Tongues XI: Object-Oriented Software Design

## Introduction

Object-oriented programming provides a collection of new techniques for problem-solving and software engineering. Two previous articles in this "Machine Tongues" series have introduced object-oriented programming, presenting tutorials to this technology and describing its application to music modeling and software development (Krasner 1980; Lieberman 1982). This paper discusses the new problem-solving techniques that constitute the object-oriented design methodology. Object-oriented analysis, synthesis, design, and implementation are presented. The issues of design by analytical modeling, design for reuse, and the development of software packages in terms of frameworks, toolkits, and customizable applications are stressed. Numerous object-oriented software description examples and architectural structures are presented including music modeling, representation, and interactive applications.

The term "object-oriented programming" is currently a buzzword in much the same way that "artificial intelligence" was 5 years ago, or "structured programming" was 15 years ago. The parallel runs deeper in light of the fact that each of these three concepts represents revolutions in software engineering that encompass new programming languages, new types of tools, new models of what applications and interaction are, and new software description and design methodologies. In each case, there were also long periods of debate between so-called "purists" and those they deemed "impure" in the interpretation of their respective definitions and dogma. A lively debate is currently taking place in the object-oriented programming community as to definitions of object-oriented programming and object-oriented languages as well as metrics of

Computer Music Journal, Vol. 13, No. 2, Summer 1989
© 1989 Massachusetts Institute of Technology.

object-oriented programming and object-oriented software design. Research papers from the leaders in the field with titles such as "What is 'Object-Oriented Programming'" (Stroustrup 1987), "What Object-Oriented Programming May Be—and What It Does Not Have to Be" (Madsen and Moeller-Pedersen 1988), and "Dimensions of Object-Based Languages" (Wegner 1987), have surfaced in the recent literature. Another title that underscores the depth of the difference between object-oriented programming and traditional programming is "Teaching Object-Oriented Programming Is More Than Teaching Object-Oriented Programming Languages" (Knudsen and Madsen 1988).

This essay outlines object-oriented problem-solving and software design in a language-independent manner. Examples are taken primarily from the Smalltalk-80 programming system, but the reader need only refer to some of the other articles in this issue of *Computer Music Journal* for descriptions of systems based on other languages and programming environments. No basic introduction to the terms or techniques of object-oriented languages is presented here. The introductory materials found in any of several references are recommended to readers not familiar with object-oriented programming concepts and terminology (Krasner 1980; Lieberman 1982; Flurry 1989; Peterson 1987; Byte 1981, 1986; Goldberg and Robson 1983; Goldberg 1984; Stefik and Bobrow 1986; Meyer 1988).

## Dimensions of Object-Oriented Programming

According to the current lack of unity as to the definition of object-oriented programming, the most fitting initial definition should be a list of the features that describe existing artifacts that are acknowledged as being "object-oriented." This list of features can be factored into several groups related to language issues, problem-solving and design features, types and interpretations of inheritance and reuse, programming environments, and user interface management systems.

The language-related characteristics of common object-oriented systems include explicit separate descriptions of the state and behavior of objects; interaction of objects via (asynchronous or concurrent) message-passing; strict (semantically-rooted) encapsulation and modularity between objects; distinct external and internal views of abstract data structures; and late-binding of message name to method body by the receiver of a message.

The aspects of these systems that affect the problem-solving, analysis, and design phases are the description of module interfaces that describe the "what" rather than the "how"; standardized class interface description format (class lattices and diagrams); design for maximal reuse and sharing of interfaces and implementations; rapid prototype implementations and multistep incremental redesign; delegation and forwarding of protocols or roles among objects; and the viewing of protocol families as roles or local sublanguages.

The reuse of modules via inheritance in object-oriented systems has many criteria including class/instance-based versus prototype-based inheritance; inheritance via composition, refinement, factorization and abstraction in class hierarchies; abstract data types representing aspects or roles in domain modeling; single or multiple inheritance hierarchies (with trees or lattices as models); and the availability of flexible control structures based on the reification of blocks or closures as first-class objects.

Many people equate object-oriented programming with integrated programming environments. Some of the characteristics of integrated object-oriented systems are support for interaction with objects and browsing/navigating within hierarchies of classes and instances; interactive inspectors and editors for manipulating objects; instance catalogs and persistent collections; rapid development-cycle turnaround due to encapsulation and late-binding; computer-assisted software engineering (CASE) support with object-oriented notations, processes, and tools; and special support tools for redesign and reimplementation.

The higher-level features of a dynamic object-oriented user interface management system include its support for kits of pluggable user interface components and interactive view construction tools; flexible object-oriented interaction paradigms; input modeling via control delegation, selection agents, continuation-passing, or event filters; and integrated domain-specific frameworks and highly-customizable applications.

## Object-Oriented Software Design Concepts

Adele Goldberg (one of the pioneers of the Smalltalk systems at the Xerox Palo Alto Research Center in the 1970s and 1980s), drew up a list of four steps to learning object-oriented design and programming at a recent panel discussion on teaching object-oriented programming. She classifies these steps as follows: processes of decomposition and composition; recognition of similarities and differences; behavioral description of kinds of objects; and the application of metrics and examples of "good design."

The central role of decomposition and composition (related to analysis and synthesis) in the design of software systems is shared with several other disciplines in which complex systems are being constructed (e.g., musical composition). The design of modeling hierarchies involves the analysis of a set of objects in terms of the similarities and differences of their properties and behaviors. The description of objects as combinations of state and behavior permits an increased level of reuse through the sharing of protocol among classes with different state variables and different implementations of the shared protocol.

The sharing of message protocol that is found within most abstract/concrete class hierarchies (which are also known as *protocol families*) is evidenced by the fact that users tend to group these families in terms of their common protocol. For instance, one thinks of Streams as objects that can be accessed via messages such as **next** and **nextPut:** for reaching or writing to them, or of DisplayObjects as objects that can be sent **display** messages (note that we follow the Smalltalk style and capitalize the names of class). The most generally-cited among the many metrics of quality for object-oriented software has become the level of reuse or sharing. This is interesting largely because it runs counter to many traditional metrics of productivity; a programmer's productivity has often been measured by the amount of code produced, but now "less is better" and small hierarchies with *"power through reuse"* are more highly valued.

## Levels and Types of Reuse

There is already a rich literature on software reuse and techniques for improving reusability. Several special works therein relate to reuse in object-oriented systems and object-oriented design for maximal reuse (see especially Pope, Goldberg and Deutsch 1987; Deutsch 1983; Freeman 1987; Johnson and Foote 1988). For the description of object-oriented systems, four types of reuse are differentiated:

   reuse of algorithms across data structures, a form of data abstraction allowing algorithms to be shared by different data structures;
   reuse of module interfaces, a system designed to be portable as a whole to a variety of machines with modest effort, allowing reuse of the complete system across hardware environments;
   reuse of frameworks across applications, many interchangeable building blocks and conventions for implementing interactive applications; and
   reuse of tools across languages, programming tools that can be reapplied to programming in other languages.

Object-oriented systems are designed to facilitate reuse of both code and design. This reuse can take place at granularity levels ranging from individual algorithms and data structures to entire systems, and can provide sharing across a range of both hardware (which supports the system from "below"), and applications (which employ the system from "above"). The two types of reuse of design can be labeled *reuse of specification* (sharing of protocols

or roles), and *reuse of implementation* (inheritance or refinement of algorithms).

As an aside, we note that the ability of a language and a system to support reusability is meaningful only if the programmer can (1) find the objects to be reused and (2) determine how to reuse them. This changes the software development process to one of searching for information and reading about existing capability (Goldberg 1986).

## Object-Oriented Design Techniques

The process of software design and implementation is often divided into several phases, and one often hears of special techniques and tools for these phases. The development process most closely associated with object-oriented design is that of rapid prototyping and incremental redesign. The use of object-oriented languages' abstract data types and of the support for interaction found in many object-oriented programming environments also encourages phases of exploratory programming (Alexander 1985; Diederich and Milton 1987).

Many techniques for structured software design identify the phases of *analysis* and *synthesis*, whereby the analysis phase is often mapped onto the process of top-down functional decomposition. Object-oriented modeling techniques, on the other hand, encourage multistage implementation and incremental redesign rather than multistage design process preceding prototype implementation. The proponents of object-oriented design identify programming cases where no a priori decomposition or top-down design can be drawn up (i.e., "there is no top"). Other cases are cited where the abstractions that will allow maximal reuse and sharing cannot be generated from the specification, but can result from rapid prototyping and incremental redesign.

We present four central object-oriented design techniques—composition, refinement, factorization, and abstraction—in the following sections. We describe them as belonging to two passes, the prototype pass and the second (or third or *n*th) generation design and implementation refinement. Composition and refinement are the two most prevalent pass-one techniques.

Fig. 1. Composition ex-
ample: calculator class.

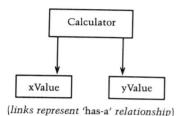

Calculator

xValue          yValue

(*links represent 'has-a' relationship*)

**Calculator Composition Diagram**

| name | Calculator |
|---|---|
| **superclass** | Model |
| **instance** | x  "a magnitude or number" |
| **variables** | y  "a magnitude or number" |
| **accessing** | getX  "answer the x value" |
| **methods** | setX:  "set the x value" |
| | getY  "answer the y value" |
| | setY:  "set the y value" |
| **operations** | addYtoX  "add the two into X" |
| | subtractYfromX |
| | multiplyYtimesX |
| | divideXbyY |

**Calculator Class Diagram**

## Composition

Composition involves the reuse of existing classes by using them as instance variables of new classes. The new composed class then forwards (delegates) protocol to its instance variables; the composed class is a client of the instance variable's external protocol. The classes involved are related by a *has-a* relationship; for example,

```
composedClass has-a
    instanceVariable Class.
```

This can also be seen as

```
composedClass delegates-to
    instance VariableClass.
```

The reuse of entire subprotocols of the instance variable's class is common; one speaks of the "mixin" of roles (e.g., Stream-ness or Magnitude-ness).

In our first example, we attack the task of designing a simple calculator model capable of responding to messages such as:

```
calc ← Calculator new.
calc x:1.34.
calc y:5.45.
calc multiplyXtimesY.
```

The design technique we use is the composition of two Magnitudes into a calculator class whose instances understand the simple calculator language as their protocol. The steps are to define a model class whose state includes *x* and *y* values and which has protocol for accessing and operating on them. Figure 1 illustrates the composition of the calculator model and shows its class diagram. In the class diagram, we can see the class and its super-class, the class's instance variables, and the protocol of the class (methods it implements). Comments describing the behavior of the class's methods are shown within double quotation marks in the class diagram.

A musical example of composition would be to start to implement a model of EventLists for simple music description formats such as

```
aNote←Event duration:(1/4 beat)
        pitch:'c#3'
        voice:'violin'
        loudness:'mezzo-forte'
        dynamic:'con legno'.
anEventList>EventList new.
eventList add:(aNote)
        at:(eventStartTime).
    . . .
eventList add:(aNoteEventDescription)
        at:(eventStartTime).
eventList play.
```

Fig. 2. Composition ex-
ample: EventList class
diagram.

(See the Music-*N*-type languages (Buxton 1978;
Dyer 1984 or Pope 1987.) The composition of an
OrderedCollection and an Event will serve quite
nicely here. One simply defines an Event subclass
that includes a Collection of events. It will inherit
Event state and protocol, and add collection state
and protocol for subevents. It can then reuse the
enumeration protocol of collections by forwarding
it to the event-collection instance variable. Figure 2
shows the class diagram for the EventList class. It
shows EventList's event protocol (e.g., **play** and **duration**) as well as its collection protocol (e.g., **add:at:** or
**select:**).

The examples of composition have shown it to be
a familiar technique for describing and constructing
interesting behaviors. The facet of the technique
that is most similar to structured programming is
the delegation of forwarding of messages (or entire
protocols) to one's instance variables.

| | | |
|---|---|---|
| **name** | EventList | |
| **superclass** | Event | |
| **instance variables** | events | "a collection of Events" |
| **accessing methods** | events | "answer the event collection" |
| | add: | "add a new event to the end" |
| | add: at: | "add an event at the given time" |
| | remove: | "remove the argument from the list" |
| **Event methods** | duration | "answer my duration" |
| | playAt: | "play my events" |
| **Collection control structure operations** | do: | "iterate over the events" |
| | select: | "select from the events" |
| | detect: | "detect from the events" |
| | reject: | "reject from the events" |

## Refinement

The technique of refinement allows one to reuse
existing system classes and specialize them via subclassing. The subclass may extend the inherited
state (add instance variables) and/or extend or refine the inherited behavior (add or override methods). The new subclass can see and/or override the
inherited class's internal state and method implementations. The two classes involved in refinement
subclassing are linked by the relationship of

subclass *is-a* superclass

or

subclass *inherits-from* superclass.

The direct inheritance of method implementations allows overriding of specific methods or protocols (e.g., reimplementation of private protocol).

The simplest example of refinement we present
is building a simple push/pop stack via refinement
of the state and behavior of OrderedCollections.
This can be accomplished by defining a new OrderedCollection that inherits its indexable instance
variables and accessing protocol such as **first** and
**addFirst:**. We then refine the implementation of the

inherited collection accessing methods providing
for different overflow and underflow behavior, and
rename them to be **pop** and **push:**. Figure 3 shows
the refinement structure and the class diagram for
the Stack class.

A musical example of refinement is the design of
a flexible framework for music description and processing using event and event list models (see the
EventList example above). The technique of refinement is applied here to make a new subclass of Dictionary that adds a new named instance variable
(duration) and flexible property-list protocol. We define a new Dictionary (property list) subclass which
inherits Dictionary's protocol for property list behavior and adds one state variable and new protocol
for accessing and scheduling. In Fig. 4 one can see
the class diagram for Events; note the different protocols it demonstrates.

Refinement is the typical inheritance-based
design technique. The reuse and refinement of
inherited state and behavior involves extension
of inherited state and protocol and/or customization (through overriding), of inherited method
implementations.

The later pass techniques are centered around
processes that transform the descriptions of class
hierarchies in order to maximize reuse and/or sharing. These two techniques are known as factorization and abstraction.

Fig. 3. Refinement example: stack refinement and class diagrams.

Fig. 4. Refinement example: Event refinement and class diagrams.

Fig. 3

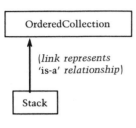

| name | Stack | |
|---|---|---|
| **superclass** | OrderedCollection | |
| **instance variables** | (none) | |
| **accessing methods** | push: | "uses inherited addFirst: method" |
| | pop | "uses inherited removeFirst method" |
| | isEmpty | "inherited" |
| | peek | "uses inherited first method" |

Fig. 4

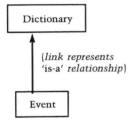

| name | Event | |
|---|---|---|
| **superclass** | Dictionary | |
| **instance variables** | duration | "my duration time" |
| **accessing methods** | duration | "answer the value" |
| | duration: | "set the value" |
| **dictionary operations** | at: | "answer a property's value" |
| | at: put: | "set a property's value" |
| **playing** | play | "play me now" |
| | playAt: | "play me at the given time" |

## Factorization

The factorization technique is applied in the case where one wants to increase the reusability by describing a complex class in terms of a hierarchy of possibly concrete aspects. The process of factorization involves reifying the roles or aspects of a class into several levels of more reusable classes; one constructs a hierarchy of refinement and composition out of a single class. The newly-defined classes normally represent abstractions from the domain of discourse that provide further opportunities for reuse. Factorization emphasizes sharing of state and accessing behavior; it leads to abstract classes less likely to have complex behavior, and to vertical hierarchies of "mixins" for further composition or refinement steps.

The train example describes the design of a model of a control system for a passenger train using the techniques of rapid prototype implementation and redesign via factorization into a one-dimensional hierarchy. The first pass (shown in Fig. 5) consists of building a monolithic class called Train with states such as capacity, passenger count, location, and velocity. In the second pass, the large and complex Train class becomes a framework for reuse, and we then split it into a hierarchy of Container (with state for capacity and contents), Vehicle (with state for location and velocity), and Train (which adds no state but overrides some inherited method implementations). The increased abstraction allows easier extension of the framework via refinement of the intermediate classes—for example, adding other Containers (such as cof-

Fig. 5. Factorization ex-
ample: two passes at
Trains.

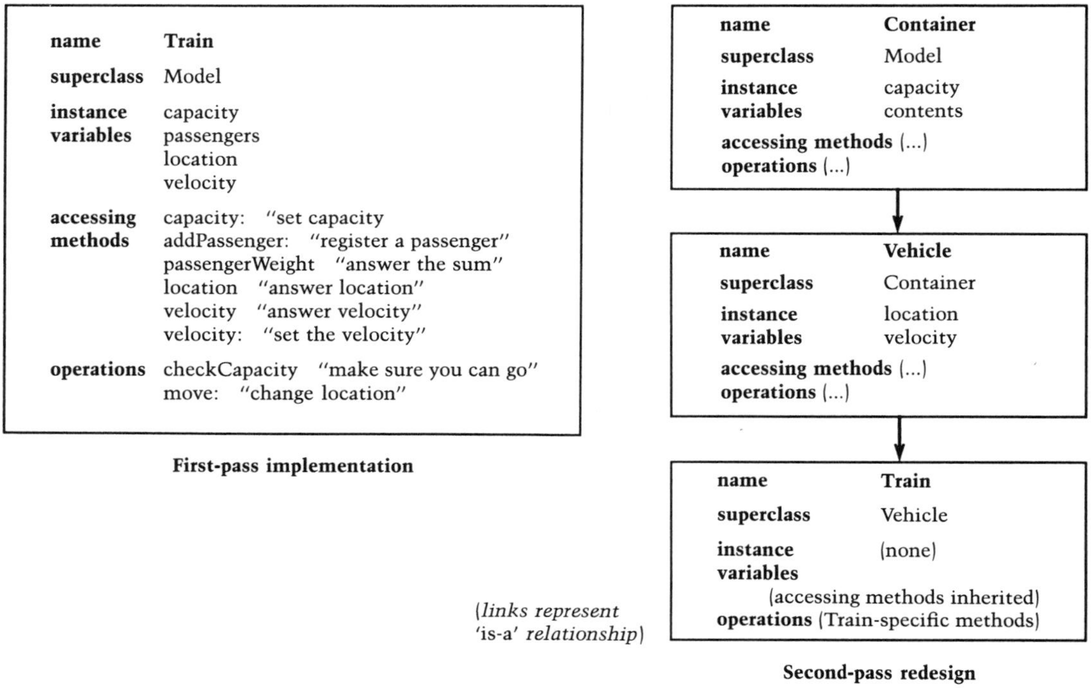

| name | Train |
|------|-------|
| **superclass** | Model |
| **instance variables** | capacity<br>passengers<br>location<br>velocity |
| **accessing methods** | capacity: "set capacity<br>addPassenger: "register a passenger"<br>passengerWeight "answer the sum"<br>location "answer location"<br>velocity "answer velocity"<br>velocity: "set the velocity" |
| **operations** | checkCapacity "make sure you can go"<br>move: "change location" |

**First-pass implementation**

| name | Container |
|------|-----------|
| **superclass** | Model |
| **instance variables** | capacity<br>contents |
| **accessing methods** (...)<br>**operations** (...) | |

| name | Vehicle |
|------|---------|
| **superclass** | Container |
| **instance variables** | location<br>velocity |
| **accessing methods** (...)<br>**operations** (...) | |

| name | Train |
|------|-------|
| **superclass** | Vehicle |
| **instance variables** | (none) |
| | (accessing methods inherited) |
| **operations** | (Train-specific methods) |

*(links represent
'is-a' relationship)*

**Second-pass redesign**

fee cups) or Vehicles (such as cars). Figure 5 shows
the before and after class diagrams for the Train example. In the first class diagram, we see the single-
class solution. The second diagram shows the
factorized version as a single-strand inheritance
hierarchy.

A musical example that demonstrates factorization well is the design of a framework for rapid
implementation of interactive user interfaces for
musical EventList editing. We again choose to do a
rapid prototype implementation and then redesign
via factorization into a rich multidimensional hierarchy. The first step is to design a catchall class for
event list editing. The EventListEditor class will
include methods for displaying staves and event
lists in some sort of music notation; for selecting,
grouping, and operating on events; for scrolling and
zooming; and for reading and writing event lists to

and from disk files. The later passes will use factorization to split this complex and nonreusable
class into a family of related classes, each of which
will model some important part of the functionality. The DisplayList and DisplayList Layout-
Manager classes form the basis of the graphical
presentation kernel. Instances of EventListEditor-
Controller, ScrollManager, and the Selection-
Manager are the central interaction objects, and
the various function-related managers (e.g., Store-
Manager) are used for delegating the many peripheral operations. By refactoring the EventListEditor,
we achieve greater readability and flexibility, and
we provide opportunities for increased reuse by
decomposing the functionality of the editor into
smaller, more domain-related chunks. Figure 6
shows the two EventListEditor class diagrams.

We see that factorization can lead to increased

*Fig. 6. Factorization example: EventListEditor refactoring for reuse and pluggability (a) and second-pass redesign, partial hierarchy (b).*

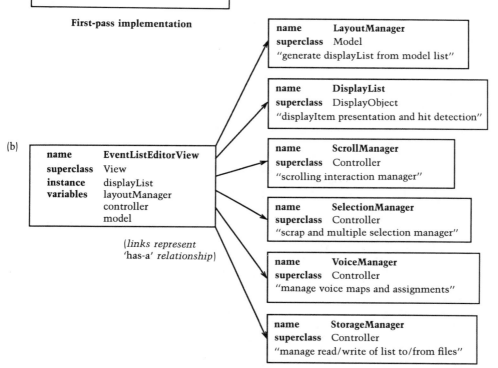

(a)

| name | EventListEditorView |
|---|---|
| **superclass** | View |
| **instance variables** | model<br>layoutProperties<br>controller<br>scrollingProperties<br>"lots more state" |
| **accessing methods** | verticalSpacing<br>staffSize<br>"lots more" |
| **operations** | hitDetectModelForPoint:<br>scrollViewBy:<br>"lots of misc. operations" |
| **displaying** | displayView<br>generateCachedView<br>"lots of code in here" |

**First-pass implementation**

| name | LayoutManager |
|---|---|
| **superclass** | Model |
| "generate displayList from model list" | |

| name | DisplayList |
|---|---|
| **superclass** | DisplayObject |
| "displayItem presentation and hit detection" | |

(b)

| name | EventListEditorView |
|---|---|
| **superclass** | View |
| **instance variables** | displayList<br>layoutManager<br>controller<br>model |

*(links represent 'has-a' relationship)*

| name | ScrollManager |
|---|---|
| **superclass** | Controller |
| "scrolling interaction manager" | |

| name | SelectionManager |
|---|---|
| **superclass** | Controller |
| "scrap and multiple selection manager" | |

| name | VoiceManager |
|---|---|
| **superclass** | Controller |
| "manage voice maps and assignments" | |

| name | StorageManager |
|---|---|
| **superclass** | Controller |
| "manage read/write of list to/from files" | |

reuse via composition or refinement in hierarchies that start out as "large objects" whose state can be factored, or as classes with complex protocols that can be split off into aspects or roles.

## Abstraction

The design technique of abstraction can be used to increase the amount of reuse within a set of classes by describing abstract classes that embody some of their shared state and/or behavior. One uses abstraction to construct a hierarchy relating several concrete classes to common abstract classes for better reuse of state and behavior. This emphasizes sharing of both state and behavior; abstract classes often implement algorithms in terms of methods that are overridden by concrete subclasses. The result of abstraction is a more horizontal hierarchy or a new protocol family.

A typical abstraction example is building model graphical objects for an object-oriented drawing package. The first pass includes several concrete classes (for the different types of displayable objects). The later passes will use abstraction to reimplement these classes as a hierarchy with significant sharing among abstract and concrete classes. One would start by prototyping a wide and shallow hierarchy of DisplayItems from a collection of classes with little reuse. The first pass implements DisplayRectangle, DisplayCircle, and DisplayTriangle with common protocol but no inheritance among them and no state or behavior sharing. The second pass adds abstract class DisplayItem with position, size, and orientation instance variables and protocol for manipulation and display; concrete subclasses now inherit all their state and reuse shared protocol specification and implementations of most algorithms. The third pass refines this, adding another level of abstract modeling for line-segment- and arc-based DisplayItems; and easy extensibility is achieved. Further passes might identify Square as a special case of Rectangle and Circle as a special case of EllipticalArc. Figures 7 and 8 show three of the possible class hierarchies for DisplayItems.

There are many approaches to the architecture of a framework for algorithmic composition or an algorithmic music description language. We illustrate the design as a multistep process that starts with the construction of an abstract class named EventGenerator as a subclass of EventList. Subclasses of EventGenerator should implement the message **generateEvents,** so we define it in the abstract class as "subclassResponsibility" (i.e., it is expected that subclasses will override it). The first-pass design's concrete classes are Chord (which might hold its root and its inversion), Roll (which has a single Event and can repeat it), Trill (repeat an EventList), Arpeggio (play with internote skew), Ostinato (repeat as a process), SelectorCloud (select from given pitch, amplitude, and voice sets), and PodCloud (select from given ranges). They share little state except what EventGenerator inherits by being a subclass of EventList. Several of them add instance variables to deal with their particular representations; and each implements its own **generateEvents** method.

Shared state and behavior among EventGenerators is often not apparent until after the first implementation; and in the implementation of further subclasses, we use some of the first-pass classes as abstract intermediate classes. We try to push as much of the method implementation as possible into the abstract class EventGenerator; protocol and method implementations such as creation, accessing, and user interface can then be shared. Increased abstraction inserts abstract classes Cluster (a more general notion for chords), and Cloud (an abstract stochastic EventGenerator), and makes Trill a subclass of Roll (that repeats a collection of notes rather than just one). In Fig. 9 one can see the first-pass class diagram for EventGenerators and one of the possible abstraction-based refinements of this design.

There are several trade-offs in using abstraction-based techniques. The DisplayItem and EventGenerator examples could each be used to demonstrate extremes of factorization or abstraction. Examining the construction of classes for the generation of many types of Chords, for example, one might implement a prototype that includes a class called Chord with many different methods for generating EventLists according to given rules and root

*Fig. 7. Abstraction example: adding abstract DisplayItem classes.*

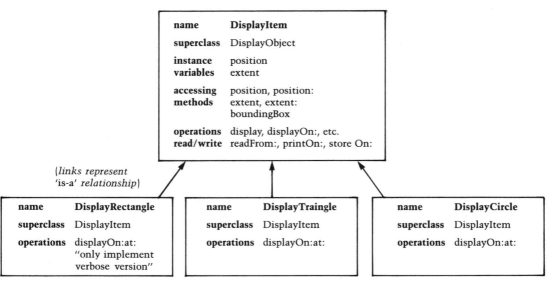

| name | DisplayRectangle |
|---|---|
| superclass | DisplayObject |
| instance variables | position extent |
| accessing methods | position, position: extent, extent: "return and set inst vars" boundingBox "return enclosing box" |
| operations | display, displayOn:at: "simple and verbose display messages" |

| name | DisplayCircle |
|---|---|
| superclass | DisplayObject |
| instance variables | position extent |
| accessing methods | position, position: extent, extent: boundingBox |
| operations | display, displayOn:at: |

| name | DisplayTriangle |
|---|---|
| superclass | DisplayObject |
| instance variables | position extent |
| accessing methods | position, position: extent, extent: boundingBox |
| operations | display, displayOn:at: |

**First-pass implementation**

| name | DisplayItem |
|---|---|
| superclass | DisplayObject |
| instance variables | position extent |
| accessing methods | position, position: extent, extent: boundingBox |
| operations read/write | display, displayOn:, etc. readFrom:, printOn:, store On: |

*(links represent 'is-a' relationship)*

| name | DisplayRectangle |
|---|---|
| superclass | DisplayItem |
| operations | displayOn:at: "only implement verbose version" |

| name | DisplayTraingle |
|---|---|
| superclass | DisplayItem |
| operations | displayOn:at: |

| name | DisplayCircle |
|---|---|
| superclass | DisplayItem |
| operations | displayOn:at: |

**Second-pass redesign (improved sharing, easy extensibility)**

*Fig. 8. Abstraction example: possible refined DisplayItem hierarchy.*

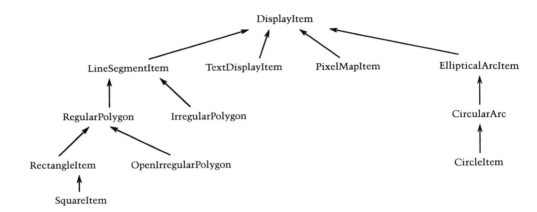

pitches. The prototype might be cleaned up so that the types of chords (e.g., major, minor, 4th, pentatonic) are grouped into protocols in class Chord. The extreme of abstraction would be to have a deep and wide hierarchy of Cluster subclasses (e.g., classes like MajorEleventh, SixteAjoute, PentatonicCluster, FourthRow, or CParker1957), each with one method (e.g., **generateEvents**). It is not always possible to say which of these solutions is better. The design that implements a single, very large Chord class (in terms of number of methods) will probably lead to a more readable system and a simpler architecture, but will have almost no reuse. The alternative implementation, with a large number of one-method classes, might be more easily extensible, but possibly also more difficult to navigate.

### Multistep Techniques for Design and Implementation

The relationship between rapid prototyping and design has become muddied in this discussion. This is intentional and is a byproduct of object-oriented design. The prototyping phase is included in several of the object-oriented design techniques because it is assumed that it is not always possible to arrive at a class hierarchy that maximizes sharing and reuse in the first pass.

The object-oriented design literature certainly includes numerous proponents of other sets of beliefs, models, terms, and methodologies than the one presented in this discussion. The other software architecture articles in this issue of *Computer Music Journal* present some similar and some alternative approaches, as do the highly-developed design methodologies used in the ADA programming language by Grady Booch (Booch 1986), in Eiffel by Bertrand Meyer (Meyer 1988), and in LISP/LOOPS by Mark Stefik and Daniel Bobrow (Bobrow and Stefik 1984). More basic design methodology references can be recommended for further study (Cardelli and Wenger 1985; Schlaer and Mellor 1988).

### Application Development in an Integrated Object-Oriented Programming Environment

The best-known integrated interactive object-oriented programming systems are Smalltalk-80 (Goldberg 1984), Lisp Machine LISP (Symbolics 1983), and INTERLISP-D (Tietelman and Masinter 1981). There are several general characteristics brought about by the mixture of a high-level integrated programming environment (along the lines described by Barstow, Shrobe, and Sandewall 1984, or Deutsch and Taft 1980) with one of these flexible interactive object-oriented programming systems. In a sense, program development by rapid prototyping and incremental refinement becomes so strongly the order of the day that the programming environment and tools themselves are malleable

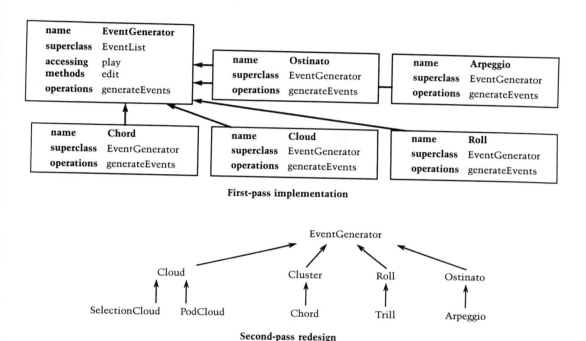

**First-pass implementation**

**Second-pass redesign**

open applications constructed as hierarchies for reuse by the techniques inherent in the host language. In general, these systems have promoted dynamic, multiphase incremental prototyping and development through the common steps of the design of abstract classes and/or reuse of existing system classes, of subclassing abstract classes to construct concrete classes, and of defining user interfaces by subclassing for new behaviors and "plugging in" existing components where appropriate.

One can group object-oriented software packages by the characterization of their external interfaces and their primary modes of reuse into three categories. We call these *frameworks, toolkits, and customizable applications.*

**Frameworks**

The examples of frameworks presented above use refinement and composition of existing classes as first-pass techniques and abstraction or factoriza-

tion in the second and further refinements to produce hierarchies of abstract and concrete classes that use common protocols and define new shared behavior. The Collection and Stream classes are two of the distinguished protocol families (i.e., frameworks) within the Smalltalk-80 systems. They each define state variables and behavior methods at several levels of abstraction and refinement. The client-side view of frameworks is often that the user uses or overrides the implementation of a few of the important methods, so the refinement-oriented user is on the inside of these frameworks, seeing the implementation of their methods.

The Event, EventList, and EventGenerator classes discussed in the examples represent a framework that is easily extensible by further refinement describing new types of behavior. Several beautiful framework architectures are presented in the other articles in this issue of *Computer Music Journal.* Kyma's sound model classes, the virtual digital signal processing (VDSP) models of data types and processors, TTrees, or the CreationStation's schedules can serve as examples.

## Toolkits

In the examples of the use of toolkits, existing code was incorporated by direct reference or by composition and delegation. The elements of toolkits tend to be reused by composition, where they incorporate their behavior into the behavior of the aggregate. The client-side view of toolkits is (very simple) message interface, such as eventGenerator or pluggableView instance creation messages. Another view is that the elements of a toolkit all are members of the same protocol family and share some small interface, for example, those same view creation messages.

The reuse of user interface components is common in integrated object-oriented systems, where applications are often modeled as model objects being displayed in view objects and being manipulated by controller objects. The view and controller components are taken from standard libraries that might include different types of screen presentation views and interaction monitors. Examples of toolkits of pluggable components for music user interfaces are the NeXT SoundKit and MusicKit (TM of NeXT, Inc.) discussed in this issue of *Computer Music Journal*, and my own HyperScore ToolKit's pluggable user interface components and event list editors (Pope 1987).

## Customizable Applications

The notion of an open application, where a high degree of end-user customization is supported, is not novel for software development tools. A significant number of object-oriented applications (especially in music-related areas) attempt to extend this openness into the range of non-programming-oriented domains.

Kyma, Javelina, Forest, and the HyperScore Tool-Kit are among the musical applications that are built as end-user application tools built into reusable environments with frameworks and/or toolkits for user customization and extension.

## Conclusions

The five most pressing problems in software applications development are software complexity, portability, development effort, user interface flexibility, and maintainability. It is the goal of object-oriented software design to address these problem areas by providing support for the process of rapid prototyping and incremental design, and improved reuse and sharing.

We have described object-oriented problem-solving and analysis in terms of modeling of abstract/concrete description structures, and have discussed the object-oriented design methodology. In several examples, the problem-solving techniques of decomposition/composition, behavioral analysis, and the development of special-purpose protocols or languages were presented, and four specific techniques that can be applied during a multistep specification/design/implementation cycle were demonstrated. The use of exploratory programming techniques can be supported in programming environments through integrated systems with very-fine-grain incremental development and high levels of interactivity.

The analysis of, and design for, reuse of several kinds on several levels is central to many of these techniques, and is a theme running through the other articles in this issue of *Computer Music Journal*.

## Acknowledgments

Many of the ideas expressed in this article come from discussions the author had with L. Peter Deutsch, Adele Goldberg, Glenn Krasner, and Kenny Rubin. Adele Goldberg, Kenny Rubin, Glenn Krasner, and Cliff Hollander also read early versions of this article and provided valuable comments.

## References

Alexander, J. H. 1985. *Exploratory Programming Using Smalltalk.* Beaverton, Oregon: Computer Research Laboratory, Textronix.

Barstow, D., H. Shrobe, and E. Sandewall. 1984. *Interac-*

tive *Programming Environments*. New York: McGraw-Hill.

Bobrow, D., and M. Stefik. 1984. *The LOOPS Manual*. Palo Alto, California: Xerox Palo Alto Research Center.

Booch, G. 1986. *Software Engineering with ADA*. Menlo Park, California: Benjamin/Cummings Publishers.

Buxton, W., et al. 1978. "The Structured Sound Synthesis Project (SSSP): An Introduction." Technical Report CSRG-92, University of Toronto.

*Byte*. 1981. Special Smalltalk-80 Issue. *Byte, The Small Systems Journal* 6(8).

*Byte*. 1986. Special Object-Oriented Programming Issue. *Byte, The Small Systems Journal* 11(8).

Cardelli, L., and P. Wenger. 1985. "On Understanding Types, Data Abstraction and Polymorphism." *ACM Computing Surveys* 17(4).

Deutsch, L. P. 1983. "Reusability in the Smalltalk-80 Programming System." In *Proceedings of the ITT 1983 Workshop on Reusability Programming*. Reprinted in P. Freeman, ed. 1987. *Tutorial Software Reusability*. New York: IEEE Press.

Deutsch, L. P., and E. Taft. 1980. "Requirements for an Experimental Programming Environment." Report CSL-80-10. Palo Alto, California: Xerox Palo Alto Research Center.

Diederich, J., and J. Milton. 1987. "Experimental Prototyping in Smalltalk." *IEEE Software* May, pp. 50–64.

Dyer, L. M. 1984. "Toward a Device Independent Representation of Music." In *Proceedings of the 1984 International Computer Music Conference*. San Francisco: Computer Music Association, pp. 251–256.

Flurry, H. S. 1989. "An Introduction to the CreationStation and Its Design." *Computer Music Journal*, this issue.

Freeman, P., ed. 1987. *Tutorial: Software Reusability*. New York: IEEE Press.

Goldberg, A., and D. Robson. 1983. *Smalltalk-80, The Language and Its Implementation*. Reading, Massachusetts: Addison-Wesley (also available in Japanese).

Goldberg, A. 1984. *Smalltalk-80, The Interactive Programming Environment*. Reading, Massachusetts: Addison-Wesley.

Goldberg, A. 1986. "Programmer as Reader." In J. H. Kugler, ed. *Proceedings of the IFIP Information Processing Conference 1986*. Amsterdam: Elsevier Publishers.

Johnson, R., and B. Foote. 1988. "Designing Reusable Classes." *Journal of Object-Oriented Programming* 1(2):22–35.

Knudsen, J., and O. Madsen. 1988. "Teaching Object-Oriented Programming Is More Than Teaching Object-Oriented Programming Languages." In *Proceedings of the Second European Object-Oriented Programming Conference*. Berlin: Springer Verlag, pp. 21–40.

Krasner, G. 1980. "Machine Tongues VIII: The Design of a Smalltalk Music System." *Computer Music Journal* 4(4):4–22.

Lieberman, H. 1982. "Machine Tongues IX: Object-Oriented Programming." *Computer Music Journal* 6(3):8–21.

Madsen, O., and B. Moeller-Pedersen. 1988. "What Object-Oriented Programming May Be—and What It Does Not Have to Be." In *Proceedings of the Second European Object-Oriented Programming Conference*. Berlin: Springer Verlag, pp. 1–20.

Meyer, B. 1988. *Object-Oriented Software Construction*. New York: Prentice-Hall.

Peterson, G. E.; ed. 1987. *Tutorial: Object-Oriented Computing* (in two volumes). New York: IEEE Press.

Pope, S. T. 1987. "A Smalltalk-80-based Music Toolkit." In *Proceedings of the 1987 International Computer Music Conference*. San Francisco: Computer Music Association, pp. 166–173. Excerpted in *Journal of Object-Oriented Programming* 1(1):6–11.

Pope, S. T., A. Goldberg, and L. P. Deutsch. 1987. "Object-Oriented Approaches to the Software Lifecycle Using the Smalltalk-80 System as a CASE Toolkit." In *Proceedings of the 1987 IEEE/ACM Fall Joint Computer Conference*. New York: ACM Press, pp. 13–20.

Shlaer, S., and S. J. Mellor. 1988. *Object-Oriented Systems Analysis: Modeling the World in Data*. New York: Yourdon Press/Prentice-Hall.

Shriver, B., and P. Wegner, eds. 1987. *Research Directions in Object-Oriented Programming*. Cambridge: MIT Press.

Stefik, M., and D. Bobrow. 1986. "Object-Oriented Programming: Themes and Variations." *AI Magazine* 6(4):40–62.

Stroustrup. B. 1987. "What Is Object-Oriented Programming?" In *Proceedings of the 1987 European Object-Oriented Programming Conference*. Paris: AFCET.

Symbolics. 1983. *Symbolics 3600 Technical Summary*. Cambridge: Symbolics, Inc.

Tietelman, W., and L. Masinter. 1981. "The INTERLISP Programming Environment." *IEEE Computer* 14(4).

Wegner, P. 1987. "Dimensions of Object-based Language Design." In *Proceedings of the 1987 ACM Conference on Object-Oriented Programming Systems, Languages and Applications*. New York: ACM Press, pp. 168–182.

# II

# Music Representation
# and Processing Tools

**C. Fry**
Cambridge, Massachusetts, USA

# Flavors Band: A Language for Specifying Musical Style

## The Problem

One of the tasks of music composition is the precise expression of a tremendous number of sonic events. Traditional notation does not permit composers to communicate precise sonic details to the performers of their works. The composer uses the performers to interpret the unwritten details of the score. Composers who use computers must somehow teach the computer-performer exactly what to play. For a large score this is a burden.

Many operations on scores are conceptually simple yet difficult to realize using conventional music media. Transposing of whole sections, global articulation modifications, insertion of several bars in all parts, and filling in harmonies are all examples of processes that are easy to specify, yet hard to implement using pen and paper or even scores typed into a word-processor-like musical interface. More difficult to specify but still imaginable are operations that generate original melodies and harmonies, and produce variations on themes.

## The Goal

*Precision of specificity* is a term I use to describe the degree of detail in the plan for a final product (which could be a musical score, a building, or anything). The composer should be able to choose the precision of specificity for each piece. Some pieces may require every nuance of every sonic event to be described exactly from the beginning. Alternatively, the composer might want to start with a very sketchy description by specifying a composition whose only important qualities are a duration of five minutes and a common time signature. Values for tempo and amplitude, as well as note durations and pitches could come from default values. (De-

faults are preset values that are used in the absence of a composer's explicit specification.) Incremental modifications could be made to the entire score, refining it from the top down, rather than making hundreds of separate, local changes to achieve the same end.

Typically the composer would want to specify certain sections very carefully, while other sections need not have the same accuracy. The precision of specificity would vary throughout the piece as well as from part to part.

## Features of Languages

Completely general composition programs are impossible to design because the problem space of composition is unbounded. The programmer can't know in advance what algorithms a composer would like to use, even if the programmer is the composer (as in my case). However, for certain styles of music, the programmer can guess the functionality of some likely to be desired compositional algorithms. These algorithms should be configurable in a wide variety of juxtapositions. The program should also allow hooks to a general-purpose programming language to aid the construction of new algorithms.

## Flavors Band: A Solution

Flavors Band is a language for specifying jazz and popular musical styles procedurally. The procedural representation allows the generation of a large number of scores in a specified style by making only minor changes to a score specification. A style can be specified very narrowly such that all tunes generated by a style sound similar (Levitt 1981, 1984). A broader specification allows more diverse compositions to come from the same specification. Since the precision of specificity is easily controlled in Flavors Band, styles often have some tightly con-

Fig. 1. Hardware block
diagram.

Fig. 2. Flavors Band Score
topology. (PP = Phrase
Processor)

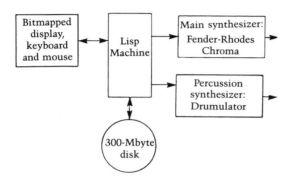

Fig. 1. Hardware block diagram.

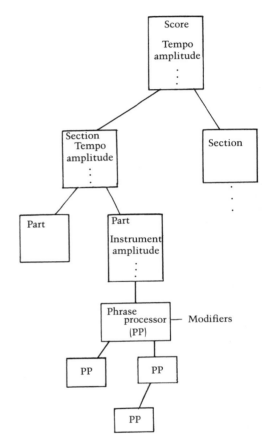

Fig. 2. Flavors Band Score topology. (PP = Phrase Processor)

trolled aspects and some loosely described aspects that can provide musical scores with a predetermined amount of self-similarity. (For a fascinating discussion of musical styles and their relationship to natural language, see Moorer 1972.)

Flavors Band is embedded in Lisp. The languages are entwined such that each may call the other in a structured but flexible way. A Flavors Band construct can explicitly evaluate a composer-specified Lisp expression that itself uses a second Flavors Band construct, and so on.

## System Overview

The essential hardware of Flavors Band consists of a Lisp Machine with a bitmapped display, alphanumeric keyboard and mouse, and a sound synthesizer for realizing scores. I also use a drum synthesizer in addition to the main synthesizer (Fig. 1).

Inside the Lisp Machine, Flavors Band organizes musical structure into a tree topology (Fig. 2). Modifiers of musical structure can be applied to each level of a Flavors Band score, from the entire score, to its sections, parts, and phrase processors.

A musical style is represented as a *phrase-processing network*. Each phrase processor exhibits a particular low-level musical behavior. By interconnecting phrase processors in various ways, different higher-level musical behaviors are specified. Currently about 60 kinds of phrase processors are

implemented in Flavors Band. Since all phrase processors conform to the same input/output (I/O) conventions, a new phrase processor can be added to Flavors Band and used in conjunction with the existing phrase processors without modification.

## Pitch-time Events

Phrase processors manipulate *event streams*. In Flavors Band, a note is specified by two events, an "on" event and an "off" event. Each event has a time (in

Fig. 3. Phrase processor
input types. (a) Single
event stream input. The
normal case. (b) Multiple

event stream input. (c) No
event stream input. An
event generator.

Fig. 4. Phrase processing
networks.

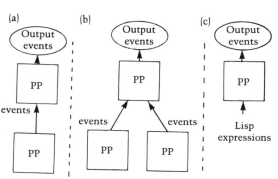

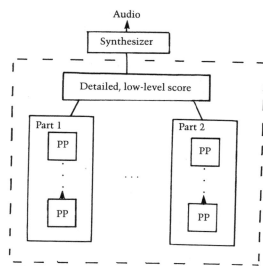

beats), a flag indicating whether the event is an
"on" event or an "off" event, a pitch-class (0–11),
an octave (0–10), another flag indicating whether it
is a rest or not, and a note identification number
(ID). The two events of a note travel independently
through a phrase processing network. The only way
a phrase processor can tell whether two events are
for the same note is to check if they have the same
ID. IDs are manufactured in such a way as to guar-
antee that each note's ID is unique.

An optional characteristic of an event is a property list that can hold any number of additional
properties. (Read any text on Lisp for an explanation of property lists.) Properties may be added, deleted, and read by phrase processors as an event
progresses through a network.

Flavors Band deals primarily with the pitch-time
structure of a score. The property list could be used
to hold timbre modifications, but the synthesizers
in the current system support few such modifications. Frequently the property list is used to hold
amplitude, and sometimes scales, or voicings of
chords. Two languages that go beyond Flavors
Band from the standpoint of timbre modifications
are FORMES (Rodet and Cointe 1984), and Pla
(Schottstaedt 1983).

## The Anatomy of a Phrase Processor

Each phrase processor produces an event stream
that becomes the input to another phrase processor.
Most phrase processors have one input event stream

and act like a black box whose behavior depends on
the kind of phrase processor used, and the parameter values used to refine the behavior of the phrase
processor. Some phrase processors have more than
one input event stream, where the output events
are some combination of the input events. Other
phrase processors have no event streams as inputs.
This kind of phrase processor acts more like a generator than a filter (Fig. 3).

## Phrase Processing Networks

A connected set of phrase processors forms a network. Scores are specified in terms of such networks.
When a score specified by a network is computed,
an array of events suitable for performance by a synthesizer is created (Fig. 4). These events are stored
in the *events* slot of the part that made them. Thus
the output of Flavors Band is stored in the same
data framework used for input and computation.
This insures the association between a score specification and the computed score, as well as facilitating inheritance (described later).

The input and output behavior of a phrase-

Fig. 5. Macro phrase pro-
cessor. (a) Complex net-
work. (b) Simplified
network.

processing network is no different in syntax from
that of a single phrase processor. A sophisticated
user can build a small network containing several phrase processors that can then become a construct in the language. This new construct performs semantically just as the subnetwork it was
constructed from and syntactically just like other
single phrase processors (Fig. 5).

## Kinds of Phrase Processors

Phrase processors fall logically into three categories: *note modifiers*, *control flow modifiers*, and
*accessors* to precomputed event arrays. Phrase processors typically have several arguments, one of
which is a phrase processor from which to get the
input event stream, and the rest of which are Lisp
expressions that customize the phrase processor for
each particular use. Any number of a particular
kind of phrase processor can be used in a network,
as can any mix of phrase processor types. In the rest
of this section, I describe some of the more interesting phrase processors.

### Note-Modifier Phrase Processors

**notes** is a phrase processor that allows the specification of the begin-end pairs of events that make up
a note. Each of the *characteristics* of a note (duration, pitch, octave, and rest) has a Lisp expression
associated with it that is evaluated to yield the
value for the characteristic. For example, the value
for pitch must be a number, typically between 0
and 11. The specification for pitch could be any of
the following:

| | |
|---|---|
| 3 | The pitch E-flat |
| e- | A Flavors Band global variable representing the pitch E-flat |
| my-favorite-pitch | A user-declared global variable |
| (+ 1 my-favorite-pitch) | One greater than the above |

The important point here is that all of the expres-

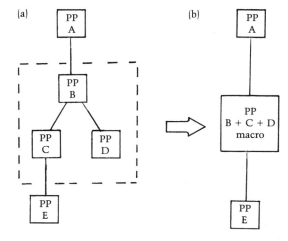

sive power of Lisp can be used with little effort on
the part of Flavors Band. **notes** allows the specification of the start time as either an absolute time (in
beats) or as the ending time of the previous note.
The ending time of a note may be specified either as
a duration from the starting time, or as an absolute
time. **notes** is an event generator rather than a filter
since it has no event stream as input. It creates
events as they are requested from the phrase processor controlling **notes**.

Several phrase processors use pitch modes and
scales (Coker 1964; Russell 1959). Modes are formal
objects in Flavors Band. Each mode contains a set
of intervals in semitones specified by integers between 0 and 11 inclusive. Certain mode objects include just the chord tones of seventh chords while
others include more than seven intervals that represent altered jazz modes (Fig. 6). Additional modes
are easily specified by the user.

A scale in Flavors Band is a mode with an associated pitch class that is designated as the root of the
scale. Scales with any defined mode containing any
root are easy to specify.

**transpose** has the arguments of *interval*, *scale*,
and an *input phrase processor*. It requests events
from its *input phrase processor* and adds *interval* to
the pitch of the incoming events before returning
them. The interpretation of *interval* depends on

Fig. 6. The Flavors Band
modes menu. From this
menu, you can modify the

current root; then see,
hear, or edit the intervals
in any mode.

```
┌─────────────────────────────────┐
│ FLAVORS BAND Defined MODES      │
│       Current Root = C          │
│CHROMATIC                        │
│DIMINISHED          (DIM)        │
│DIM-HALF-STEP-1ST                │
│LYDIAN              (LYD)        │
│IONIAN              (ION MAJOR)  │
│MIXOLYDIAN          (MIX)        │
│DORIAN              (DOR)        │
│AEOLIAN             (AEO MINOR)  │
│PHRYGIAN            (PHR)        │
│LOCRIAN             (LOC)        │
│MELODIC-MINOR                    │
│HARMONIC-MINOR                   │
│HUNGARIAN                        │
│LYD-AUG                          │
│LYD-DIM                          │
│LYD-NO-4TH                       │
│DORIAN-NO-6TH                    │
│WHOLE-TONE                       │
│PENTATONIC          (PENT)       │
│PENT-NO-3RD                      │
│PENT-MINOR                       │
│BLUES-9             ×            │
│BLUES-7                          │
│BLUES-6                          │
│MAJOR-7-CHORD                    │
│DOM-7-CHORD                      │
│MINOR-7-CHORD                    │
│4THS                             │
│1-SCALE-DEGREE                   │
│            EXIT                 │
└─────────────────────────────────┘
```

*scale.* If the interval is 1, the scale is C Chromatic, and the input pitch is D, the output pitch will be D-sharp. However, if the scale is C Ionian, the output pitch will be E. Since *interval* is evaluated for each event, the transposition need not be by a constant value throughout the life of an instance of the **transpose** phrase processor.

**harmonize** is similar to **transpose** except that it takes a list of intervals rather than just one interval as an argument. For each input event, **harmonize** puts out an event for each of the intervals in the list transposed by that interval from the original input event. Thus with the intervals of (0 2 4 6) and the scale D Lydian, **harmonize** will output a major seventh chord for each input event. The root of the chord will be the same pitch as the incoming event (transposed by the 0 interval), and the rest of the pitches will be above that root using every other scale degree in D Lydian.

**coerce-into-scale** takes as arguments a *scale* and

an *input phrase processor.* If the pitches of the input events are not in the *scale,* they are modified by the smallest amount to make them be in the *scale.* This phrase processor can correct the output of a previous phrase processor that plays "out of key."

**shift-time** adds one number to the time of an ending event and the time of the next starting event. The number may be negative and expressed as a floating point number or as a rational ($-0.5$ and $1/3$ are legal values). Shifting the onset times of a melody by varying amounts can cause it to lag behind the original, then get ahead of the original, a technique used frequently in jazz performance.

**swing** represents a more specialized functionality. It adds the value of its *time-increment* argument to the times of events that occur halfway between beats. For example, with a time-increment of $1/6$, an event at beat 2 1/2 will be shifted to 2 2/3. Events on the beat (such as events at time 2 or 3) will be unmodified.

**phrase-gap** makes it easy to insert rests periodically in a long phrase. One motivation for this phrase processor is to give the effect of a horn player taking a breath.

**context-mapper** is a very general phrase processor. It takes as its arguments a *Lisp expression* and an *input phrase processor.* The *Lisp expression* is evaluated during the processing of each input event. Before evaluation of the *Lisp expression,* certain variables are bound to the characteristics of the current event as well as the two previous and two next events (the event's context). The *Lisp expression* can read and/or modify these variables. In computing the characteristics for the current event, **context-mapper**'s ability to read the values of the surrounding events' characteristics gives it a limited context within which it can operate.

For example, **context-mapper** could be used to limit melodic leaps in the input event stream by coercing the pitch of the current event to be no more than a certain interval from the previous event. A smarter use of **context-mapper** might choose to smooth out leaps by placing the current pitch between the previous pitch and the next pitch. The *Lisp expression* can access both the previous events from its input stream and the previous events in its output stream. The **context-mapper** can generate precisely one output event for each input event.

**embellish** initializes and runs an entire subnetwork of phrase processors for each input event. The phrase processors in the subnetwork can read the values of characteristics in the input event as well as a limited context surrounding it. When the subnetwork is done, a new input event is acquired and the subnetwork is computed all over again. One of my uses for **embellish** is to add off-beat eighth notes to a walking bass line that originally contained only quarter notes.

### Control Flow Phrase Processors

**concat** is used to put together serially two or more event streams. This permits phrase processors to generate events with a time base of zero, and yet still have their output appended onto that of another phrase processor rather than played concurrently with it.

**repeat** allows its argument *phrase processor* to be reinitialized and run a specified number of times. (Without **repeat**, most phrase processors finish when their input stream is used up.) If **repeat** is given an argument of *forever* instead of a number, it will continue reinitializing and running its input phrase processor until either the machine's memory is full, the user kills the process, or a controlling phrase processor somewhere up the network kills the **repeat**.

**coerce-time** passes events from its *input phrase processor* until an event more than a *specified time* is produced. **coerce-time** then kills its input phrase processor and returns an event equal to the *specified time*. **coerce-time** can also be used to pad short phrases with rests, should the input processor die a natural death before it reaches the specified time. **repeat** *forever* phrase processors are often limited by a **coerce-time** processor. For example, the user could have an ostinato bass figure that he or she wanted to repeat many times. If the user didn't know the number of times to repeat, but did know how long the entire bass line must be, a **repeat** *forever* controlled with a **coerce-time** phrase processor is called for. This does more than simply save the

user from doing some arithmetic. If the duration of the ostinato figure is not a whole number multiple of the entire bass line duration, or the user simply can't figure out the duration of the ostinato figure before the score is computed, the functionality of **coerce-time** is needed.

**gate** behaves like a transistor. It takes two arguments, both of which are phrase processors. The event stream from one phrase processor (the *control stream*) allows the events from the other phrase processor (the *main stream*) to pass through the gate only when there is an ongoing note in the control stream that is not a rest. The control stream can be modified just like any other event stream. The **invert** phrase processor was initially designed to invert the control stream to a **gate** phrase processor, allowing events from the main stream to pass when there are no ongoing notes in the control stream. These phrase processors used in conjunction with **filter** (which conditionally removes events based on a Lisp expression) and **merge** (which combines two event streams into one) allow a user to construct phrase processing networks analogous to the networks that synthesizers use for generating sound.

### Event Array Accessors

Event array accessors are designed to store intermediate event streams to be used and modified in numerous other places.

**set-events** passes its input unmodified, but has the side-effect of storing copies of the events that go through it into an array. These events may be accessed with the **use-events** phrase processor from anywhere in the network after the **set-events**, or by the phrase processing network of another part.

As an example of the use of event array accessors, a bass part might generate roots of chords in its early processing. These roots could be saved, and the bass part could go on to transpose its events such that it played only the thirds and fifths of the roots. Meanwhile a melody part could extract the roots from the saved array and embellish them to form a melody. Both parts used a musical skeleton that was never explicitly output by any part. For accessing the final score of a part, **use-events** can be applied since the data format for storing a part's completed score is an array of events.

## Lisp Functions

Most of the arguments to most of the phrase processors can be passed by arbitrary Lisp expressions. Some of the more commonly used expressions have been coded into Lisp functions and made available for use in constructing a network. Currently there are about 30 of these functions. Like phrase processors, these functions can be added to Flavors Band with no modification to the rest of the language. Calls to these functions can occur everywhere that Flavors Band calls the Lisp evaluator, which is just about anywhere within a network. Here are descriptions of two particularly interesting user functions.

**make-line-envelope** makes line-segment envelopes from specified points. It is used by sending it a value (the *address* or *x* value). It returns a value (the *y* or *data* value). The address can come from anywhere, but usually comes from the time of an event. A melody with a particular pitch contour can be generated by making an envelope of the desired contour, generating an event stream, using the events' times as addresses into the envelope, and assigning the events' pitches to the output of the envelope. Only the rhythm of the input event stream is important, which can come from anywhere, for instance from another part. Inputs and outputs of the envelope generator can be scaled and offset with common Lisp functions.

**sequencer** is used because sometimes an application calls for a series of numbers that are not easily specified as an envelope, or may require a series of objects which are not numbers. **sequencer** can contain a list of any number of objects to sequence through. Each object has a *count* and a *value specification*. Each time the sequencer is asked for a value, the *count* of the current object is decremented, and its *value specification* is evaluated and returned. When the current object's *count* reaches 0, the next object is made the current object. The evaluation of an object's *value specification* can

modify the *count* of the object. Thus the sequencer can modify itself as it is run. **sequencer** is an experiment in sequencer autonomy.

## Use of Indeterminacy

The user can allow Flavors Band to choose from among a constrained set of values to generate arguments to phrase processors or other Lisp functions. This makes it possible to construct a network that has bounded indeterminacy, permitting the specification of a potentially wide range of musical styles with a comparatively short and simple syntax.

**fb-random**, the Flavors Band random number generator, takes as its arguments a *minimum output value*, a *maximum output value*, a *granularity*, and a *seed*. If this were used for note duration, a composer could say, "I want the duration of each note to be between 1/4 and 1 with a granularity of 1/8." The possible values would all be multiples of 1/8. Changing the seed would change the sequence of numbers, but not their other specified characteristics.

Another Flavors Band generator allows the user to specify the probability that a particular value will be returned. In the previous example on duration, the user might wish to specify that half of the durations be 1/4, and assign correspondingly smaller probabilities to the remaining possible durations. The value returned from this probability generator could be any Lisp object, not simply a number. The value could even be a phrase-processing subnetwork, effectively allowing Flavors Band to choose a composition strategy based on user-supplied probabilities. An extension to this probability generator allows the user to specify the number of times a particular value is returned once it is selected. This lends consistency to the output values.

**random-segment** allows the network to determine which one of a number of subnetworks is to be used, based on user-supplied probabilities. A **repeat** wrapped around a **random-segment** phrase processor allows the generation of event streams that are composed using the variety of techniques specified by the phrase processors selected by **random-segment**.

*Fig. 7. Deriving pitch from envelope. (a) Block diagram of the network. (b) Network specification in the Flavors Band language. (c) A random melody generated by the network in (a) and (b). (d) The random melody modified by a pitch envelope.*

A

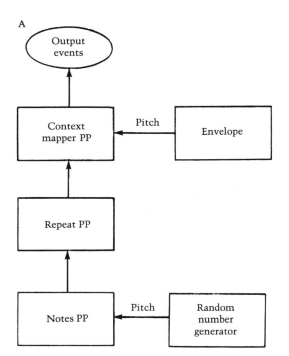

B

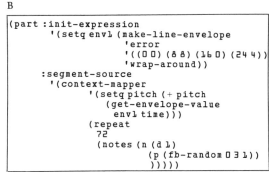

```
(part :init-expression
        '(setq envl (make-line-envelope
                        'error
                        '((0 0) (8 8) (16 0) (24 4))
                        'wrap-around))
      :segment-source
        '(context-mapper
             '(setq pitch (+ pitch
                  (get-envelope-value
                     envl time)))
             (repeat
                72
                (notes (n (d 1)
                       (p (fb-random 0 3 1))
                       )))))
```

C

D

## Phrase Network Architectures

An instance of a phrase processor with its arguments could be thought of as a sentence in the Flavors Band language. Most sentences can be placed adjacent to most other sentences permitting an unlimited variety of paragraphs. However, as in natural languages, only a small subset of such paragraphs are likely to be coherent and/or interesting. This section examines how meaningful paragraphs are constructed in the Flavors Band language.

### Example 1: Deriving Pitch from Envelope

An interesting pitch generation technique is to get a value from an envelope and add a slight amount of deviation to it. If the deviation comes from a random number generator, then each pass through the

envelope will produce a phrase with a similar pitch contour as the previous pass, but not exactly the same (Fig. 7). Figure 7a is a block diagram of such a network; 7b gives the actual code; 7c is an unmodified random melody; 7d is a random melody modified by a pitch envelope.

In Fig. 7b a random number between 0 and 3 (with a granularity of 1) is generated with **fb-random** and assigned to pitch in the **notes** phrase processor. Seventy-two of such notes are made by the **repeat** phrase processor. In **context-mapper**, the starting time of each note is used as an index into the envelope generator specified in the **init-expression** of this part. The output of the envelope generator is added to the pitch that was assigned in **notes**. Since the envelope is just 24 beats long, and the last note will end on beat 72, three groups of notes will have the general pitch contour specified by the envelope. Each of the three groups will be slightly different due to the deviation from the **fb-random** function.

Fig. 8. Phrase library
example.

```
(shift-time 1/8 ;minimum-duration
            (random-alist '((.8 0) (.9 -1/4) (1 1/4)))
            (REPEAT 32 ;number of repetitions
                    (random-segment
                     13 ;seed
                     ;phrase library with probabilities
                     '((.3 (NOTES (N (S 0.))
                                  (N (S 0.5))
                                  (N (S 1.) (E 2.))))
                       (.6 (NOTES (N (S 0.))
                                  (N (S 0.5))
                                  (N (S 1.))
                                  (N (S 1.5) (E 2.))))
                       (1. (NOTES (N (S 0.))
                                  (N (S 1.) (E 2.)))))))))
```

## Example 2: Phrase Libraries

Long phrases can be constructed out of short phrases whose notes are specified directly. The particular combination of the short phrases to form longer phrases can be determined by a Flavors Band network. I call a group of fully specified phrases a *phrase library* from which a network may borrow. There can be any number of phrase libraries in Flavors Band, each of which can contain any number of phrases. In my use of this technique, each library rarely contains over 20 phrases. Phrase libraries allow a user to precisely specify the details while imprecisely specifying the higher-level structure of the phrase being constructed (Fig. 8).

The phrase library contains three phrase processing subnetworks each made from **notes** phrase processors. (Syntactically, any one of these could be replaced by an arbitrary network.) Each of the three **notes** phrase processors has about an equal probability of occurring. (Actually the probability for the third is 1.0 − 0.6 = 0.4.) Thirty-two times during this score, **random-segment** selects one of the three subnetworks and returns the events generated by it. The times of these events are subject to possible modification by **shift-time**. Eight percent of the events' times go unmodified, while 10% are retarded by 1/4 and 10% are advanced by 1/4. Since this net doesn't vary pitch at all, it would most likely be used as a drum part or the rhythm generator in a larger net.

## Nonstandard Communication

Typically, the topology of a phrase-processing network is a tree where the highest processor on the tree is the processor between the rest of the network and the output event stream of the network (Fig. 9). The flow of control is from the later, higher phrase processors to the earlier processors near or at the leaves of the tree.

Events move opposite to the direction of control; from the earlier processors (at the bottom of the tree) through the later processors. A surprising variety of composition algorithms can be supported with this architecture, but not all. For example, many levels of nested repeats work well in the Flavors Band treelike topology. However, some kinds of networks whose control-flow branches dynamically are difficult to implement as a treelike topology. Such an architecture might occur if you wanted to design a network containing subnetworks that are not yet fully specified at the time of initialization of the whole network. Branching based on events to be computed is also a difficult architecture. You might want to do this if the technique to be used next depends on the last note of the previous technique.

For miscellaneous communication between processors, Lisp global variables can be used. A processor can set a flag during the course of computation of an event. That flag can be read by any other processors that choose to at any time after the flag is set. Sometimes I pass starting times or indicate the

*Fig. 9. Control flow.*

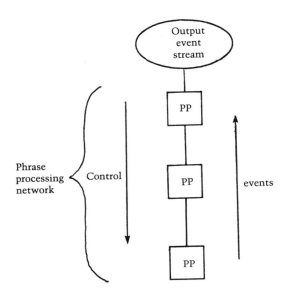

## Defaults and Inheritance

Scores, sections, and parts have ten to fifteen characteristics each. For a score of several sections with several parts each, a large number of parameters must be specified. To automate this task, all parameters have default values. A human composer can start with a procedural outline of a score and then fill in particular characteristics as desired, some of which are available via menus.

There is still a complexity problem with default values that must be explicitly overridden. Frequently a new score will have characteristics in common with previously computed scores. Flavors Band takes advantage of this by permitting inheritance of characteristics between scores.

The entire score, individual sections, or whole parts can be inherited from a previously computed score. The user can specify that only particular characteristics are inherited. Most importantly, the set of defaults can come from other scores, sections, or parts. This permits easy construction of a new score that behaves just like a previous score except for certain characteristics. Being able to use pieces of existing scores facilitates the specification of a new musical style that has similarities to a previously-coded style.

The entire description of a phrase-processing network can be inherited from one part to another. But if the new part is really supposed to behave exactly as its parent did, it can inherit the output events of that part as well. This saves redundant computation and facilitates building very large scores by combining smaller, previously debugged, and computed scores.

current pitch mode (e.g., Ionian or Dorian) via a global variable. A variable can contain a subnetwork.

As previously mentioned, *Event Array Accessors* can conveniently store and retrieve event arrays. The reading phrase processor can be placed anywhere in the network (before as well as after the writer) or in the network of a different part. Thus event streams, as well as control information may move nonhierarchically within a score's phrase processing networks.

Event arrays can be used to store themes to be read by another phrase processor in order to generate a variation. A subnetwork whose output is fed back into its input constitutes a *phrase-locked loop*. A predecessor to Flavors Band, the program called Computer Improvisation (Fry 1980), could create original phrases but didn't have the ability to make variations on them.

Within a section, parts are computed in parallel such that no part computes far ahead or behind the other parts. This permits parts to share recently computed events among themselves.

## User Interface

Flavors Band uses a careful interaction between custom menus (Symbolics 1984a) and a text editor (Symbolics 1984b) as its user interface. A user remains continually in the text editor while constructing and performing Flavors Band scores. Over 20 menus are used in Flavors Band (Fig. 10). All of them are accessible through the Flavors Band Command Menu, which pops up on the screen via a key-

*Fig. 10. Some of the menus in the Flavors Band user interface. (a) Flavors Band Command Menu. (b) Phrase processors sub-* *menu. [See (d).] (c) Instrument menus for the parts of a section. (d) Phrase processors menu.*

A

B

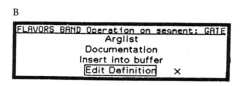

C

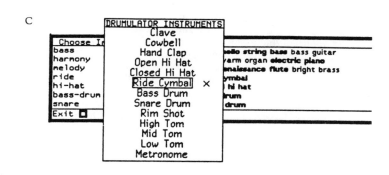

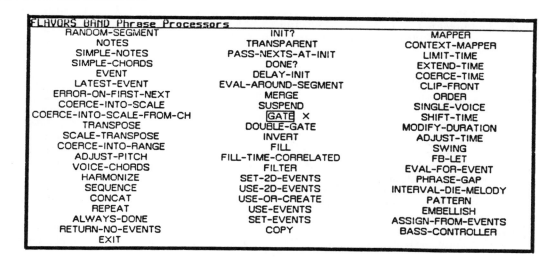

stroke. The Flavors Band Command Menu allows access to the following:

Documentation (including this article on-line)
Examples of score descriptions
Menus of phrase processors and user functions
Evaluation of the current score description
Performance of computed scores
Modifications to computed scores
Debugging aids

For each phrase processor type and user function, the user can get via menu: documentation, the argument list, the source code, or insert the name of the processor or function into the current text buffer. Examples of the use of every phrase processor can be found in the examples file that is accessible via menu. For beginning users, two simple examples can be inserted directly into the current buffer via menu.

Once a score has been computed, it can be played as many times as desired via menu. Certain parts of the score can be modified without complete recomputation. Instruments can be assigned to parts via menu; approximately a hundred instruments are available. The amplitude of each part can be modified via a simple "mixing console" menu. Each part can also have its octave offset modified via menu without recomputation of the whole part.

A history list of the previously computed scores during the current terminal session is maintained. Any previously-computed score can be selected via menu as the current score and have all of the aforementioned operations performed on it.

## Implementation

I started coding Flavors Band in the fall of 1982. The core of the program is fairly stable, although extensions occur regularly. Currently about 35 source code and peripheral files contain over 10,000 lines of code. I'm the sole programmer up to now. Flavors Band is written entirely in Lisp Machine Lisp (Symbolics 1984c; Symbolics 1984d). It runs on both the Symbolics LM-2 and 3600 systems.

A Fender-Rhodes Chroma synthesizer is connected to the Lisp Machine for sound output. The Chroma is a digitally-controlled analog synthesizer. It can produce eight voices (with eight different instruments) in real time, with each voice consisting of several oscillators, filters, and envelopes (Fender-Rhodes 1982). An E-mu Drumulator synthesizer (E-mu 1983) provides realistic percussion sounds.

The Flavors Band software takes advantage of numerous Lisp Machine system features making the code both powerful and unportable. Flavors, the Lisp Machine mechanism for object-oriented programming, is used extensively (Cannon 1982). (The "Band" part of "Flavors Band" is a pun on the term *band* used to refer to a disk partition on the Lisp Machine.) Each phrase processor is implemented as a flavor. Most communication between phrase processors occurs via message-passing.

Each musical part is implemented as a process with its own stack. The scheduling of these processes is determined by a combination of the Lisp Machine scheduler and a special scheduler inside the Flavors Band interpreter.

## Musical Applications

I am still at an early stage of musical application. So far, most of the scores made with Flavors Band have been developed for experimentation with compositional algorithms and for diagnostic purposes. A few short works have been produced and are described in this section.

### My Favorite Things

In the Flavors Band arrangement of *My Favorite Things* (written by Richard Rodgers and adapted from John Coltrane's arrangement) the melody and chords were coded directly. One verse of the melody was constructed by merging the rhythms from a phrase library with the pitches from the original melody. Another verse used **shift-time** on the original rhythms with sporadic applications of **transpose** to pitches. The piano part used **harmonize** on the supplied chords with nonmetrical starting times for the chords. The bass player arpeggiated the chords with a certain amount of deviation rhythmically and harmonically. For drums I used only a brushlike sound. The drummer played a traditional ride cymbal figure by attacking on every beat and playing a high percentage of the swing eighth notes between beats.

### Norwegian Wood

As an experiment, I decided to reuse the score description of *My Favorite Things* to arrange *Norwegian Wood* (written by John Lennon and Paul McCartney). I changed only the input melody and chords. Both pieces are in related meters (*My Favorite Things* in 3/4 time and *Norwegian Wood* in 12/8) and have a two-part structure (A and B sections). The similarities between the two pieces end there. The chord structures and melodies are very different. Recorded versions of the compositions also have very different arrangements and instrumentation.

What I had really done in arranging *My Favorite Things* in Flavors Band was to specify a style in machine-readable form. One way to observe the essential characteristics of that style was to listen to more than one piece in the style. I do not consider the Flavors Band version of *Norwegian Wood* as played in the style of the Flavors Band version of *My Favorite Things* to be a musical success. *My Favorite Things* sounds better. Perhaps this is primarily due to the fact that I developed this style with *My Favorite Things* in mind.

Regardless of this result, the technique of using a style adapted from one piece to realize another piece is still a fascinating concept. For once, the phrase "as played in the style of" is not ambiguous. Moreover, the building of libraries of networks, each of which concretely describes a style, is both technically feasible and conceptually powerful as a composition technique.

### Light My Fire

The longest piece I have produced with Flavors Band is an attempt to capture the style of the guitar solo section of the long version of *Light My Fire*

(written by The Doors). The bass plays an embarrassingly consistent one-measure line throughout on the record, so I simply used **repeat** on those notes. The organ part uses numerous two-measure licks selected from a phrase library. The drummer plays both a bass drum and a snare drum. The snare drum part is minimally conscious of phrasing: a short fill is played every four measures, and a longer fill is played every sixteen measures.

The lead guitarist knows eight one-measure licks. They are coded in scale degree rather than chromatic notation. As a lick is selected, it is transposed based on previous transpositions and the location of the current measure in the current four-measure phrase. Quite a bit of the code is devoted to making certain that phrasing over four-measure periods is consistent with the style being imitated.

### Giant Steps

The most advanced use of Flavors Band is an arrangement of *Giant Steps* (by John Coltrane). *Giant Steps* is a classic, fast (285 beats per minute) jazz composition with many II-V-I chord progressions. The most interesting parts of the Flavors Band arrangement are the bass line and the improvised solo, played on the Chroma synthesizer.

To create a walking bass line, I use a special phrase processor called the **bass-controller**. The **bass-controller** sets up a context in which a bass style computes. The **bass-controller** provides its bass style with the current chord, the next chord, the pitch of the expected first bass note to be played during the chord, and the pitch of the expected first bass note for the next chord.

It is the responsibility of each bass style to choose the notes to be played during the chord. For walking bass, Flavors Band uses a bass style that makes a trajectory of pitches aiming toward the expected first note of the next chord. The pitches are usually constrained to be within the scale indicated by the current chord. Constraining the legal scale degrees to the root, the third, the fifth, and the seventh produces a more conventional-sounding bass line.

Although the improvised solo does not occur in

the bass register it uses the **bass-controller** and a bass style that is similar to the one mentioned in the previous paragraph. The main difference is that the expected first pitch of each chord is not the root of the chord as it is in the bass part. It is rather a pitch that is a small interval from the last pitch of the previous chord. This causes the solo to wander more freely through the chord changes than the bass part.

Not surprisingly, the resulting score did not sound as good as the John Coltrane Quartet. However, except for the unnatural sound of the Chroma synthesizer, it is conceivable that the piece could have been performed by a human jazz band.

### Original Compositions

Flavors Band has also been used to produce original pieces. Chord progressions, melodies, and rhythms can be made via complex use of phrase libraries, envelopes, sequencers, probability functions, and other phrase processors.

### Conclusions

The core of Flavors Band is a framework upon which many kinds of phrase processors can be hung in a wide variety of configurations. The architecture has proven successful with respect to extensibility.

Flexibility is more difficult to measure. When constructing compositional algorithms, it is much easier to build them from the bottom up based on the tools immediately available. If you attempt to build them to conform to an existing style, as I chose to in the aforementioned compositions, the task is considerably more difficult. Deficiencies in the toolkit become apparent and suggest the need for new constructs in the language.

For each of the pieces described previously, I built new phrase processors or adopted new styles of using the language. Flavors Band was able to accommodate concepts I had not considered before completing the majority of the code. Given the impossibility of predicting future uses, this is a necessary characteristic of any flexible language.

Throughout the implementation of Flavors Band, flexibility had a higher priority than ease of use. Consequently, despite my efforts at user interface, Flavors Band is not simple to use. Maintaining the ability to have a widely variable precision of specificity means that when a high level construct is built, all of the obvious levels below that high level must be accessible. This increases generality at the expense of complexity and size of the language. No doubt simplifications could be made to Flavors Band that would both increase flexibility and reduce complexity to the user. Such elegant solutions are difficult to discover. If they are not found, Flavors Band will continue to have the trait of complexity in common with the domain it attempts to describe.

### Acknowledgments

Tom Trobaugh is to be credited with random theoretical insights. Jim Davis developed key parts of the Flavors-Band-to-synthesizer software interface. Curtis Roads, Jim Davis, and Gareth Loy made comments on drafts of this paper. John Coltrane and The Doors provided musical inspiration. David Clark and John Voigt gave me insights into jazz bass theory. Most importantly, my thanks to David Levitt and Bill Kornfeld for Lisp Machine tutorials over the last three years along with essential friendship.

### References

Cannon, H. 1982. "Flavors: A Nonhierarchical Approach to Object-oriented Programming." Cambridge, Massachusetts: Symbolics.

Coker, J. 1964. *Improvising Jazz*. Englewood Cliffs, New Jersey: Prentice-Hall.

E-mu. 1983. *Drumulator Service Manual*. Santa Cruz, California: E-mu Systems Inc.

Fender-Rhodes. 1982. *Chroma Programming Manual*. Fullerton, California: Fender-Rhodes.

Fry, C. 1980. "Computer Improvisation." *Computer Music Journal* 4(3):48–58.

Jackson, C. P. 1980. *How to Play Jazz Basslines*. Boston, Massachusetts: Hornpipe Music Publishing.

Levitt, D. 1981. "A Melody Description System for Jazz

Improvisation." M. S. Thesis, Cambridge, Massachusetts: Massachusetts Institute of Technology.

Levitt, D. 1984. "Machine Tongues X: Constraint Languages." *Computer Music Journal* 8(1):9–21.

Moorer, J. A. 1972. "Music and Computer Composition." *Communications of the Association for Computing Machinery* 15(2):104–113.

Rodet, X., and P. Cointe. 1984. "Formes: Composition and Scheduling of Processes." *Computer Music Journal* 8(3):32–50.

Russell, G. 1959. *The Lydian Chromatic Concept of Tonal Organization.* New York, New York: Concept Publishing.

Schottstaedt, B. 1983. "Pla: A Composer's Idea of a Language." *Computer Music Journal* 7(1):11–20.

Symbolics. 1984*a*. "User Interface Support." *Symbolics 3600 Documentation, Release 5.0 version.* Cambridge, Massachusetts: Symbolics.

Symbolics. 1984*b*. "Program Development Tools." *Symbolics 3600 Documentation, Release 5.0 version.* Cambridge, Massachusetts: Symbolics.

Symbolics. 1984*c*. "Lisp Language." *Symbolics 3600 Documentation, Release 5.0 version.* Cambridge, Massachusetts: Symbolics.

Symbolics. 1984*d*. *Symbolics 3600 Technical Summary.* Cambridge, Massachusetts: Symbolics.

## Xavier Rodet and Pierre Cointe

IRCAM
31, rue Saint-Merri
F-75004 Paris, France

# FORMES: Composition and Scheduling of Processes

## Introduction

> Trouver une forme qui accomode le gachis,
> telle est actuellement la tâche de l'artiste—
> Samuel Beckett

For some time, it has been recognized that the development and use of complex systems has been stifled by the inadequacy of ordinary programming languages (Winograd 1979). Music composition and synthesis (MCS) by computer offers a particularly clear example of this "complexity barrier." In the 1970s, a new generation of interactive languages appeared (Cointe 1983), establishing the concepts of *active objects* and *message passing* as a control structure for computation. It is significant that object-oriented programming matches most of the requirements of MCS.

Toward a solution to problems of complexity in computer music, an object-oriented programming environment called FORMES has been developed and implemented at IRCAM. It supports a new language with original features for composition and scheduling of objects. FORMES "processes" are obviously not in exact correspondence with musical processes as perceived by the listener.

FORMES is an interactive system first intended for MCS. However, by virtue of its unique architecture, its flexibility, and its ease of use, it should find applications in a large number of domains such as graphics animation and speech synthesis. Composers use FORMES for score development and sound synthesis. As an example, *Chreode*, a piece composed with FORMES by Jean-Baptiste Barrière, won

the International Bourges Festival award in 1983 (Barrière 1983).

Why is MCS one of the most interesting fields for testing advanced technology for computing? In MCS, perhaps even more than in artificial intelligence, programs have to be tested, modified, and rewritten very often. This modification must be effected quickly and easily; otherwise, the continuity between musical ideas and results gets lost. The complexity usually involved in human composing activity is far beyond what we are nowadays able to code in a few weeks or months. At the same time, scientists and musicians cannot be hampered by esoteric or "hairy" programs in the course of sophisticated musical research. Thus, "friendly" interaction is not a wish but a necessity. Finally, the system must be interactive and fast enough to control a real-time synthesizer.

## Requirements of MCS

We developed FORMES after several years of experience in MCS research and production, including our CHANT system (Bennett 1981; Rodet and Bennett 1980; Rodet, Potard, and Barrière 1984). In MCS, the aim of a musician is to capture a certain musical image. An MCS program is an attempt to find and realize this image—using models that implement our knowledge about sound production and perception—within a particular compositional context. Consequently FORMES provides a framework to manipulate and integrate these models as basic building blocks or objects. These models are characterized by their contribution to synthesis and by their (temporal) behavior irrespective of implementation details.

Desirable properties of MCS models include the following, all of which are goals of the FORMES system:

1. Generality: Apart from a specific application a model should not be a portrait of a

particular sound or note but should be as general a representation of a process as possible (e.g., a model of a crescendo or an attack pattern should apply to as many different sounds as possible).

2. Universality: A model should try to be independent of a particular synthesis technique and should refer to universal concepts as found in acoustics and psychoacoustics.

3. Compatibility: Models should be applicable in any context in which they are placed. In any combination they should gracefully cooperate and interact in the universe created by the composer.

4. Simplicity of program text: Models will be much simpler if they follow common human communication conventions and presuppositions (e.g., default values everywhere).

5. Ease of use: For certain interactions, (close to) natural language communication constructs facilitate the apprenticeship and use of that system. Otherwise simple and clear symbolism should be used. Invocation, modification, and integration of models should be direct and easy.

6. Modularity and hierarchical construction: The complexity of models necessitates that they be built from submodels. By such a construction, it is also possible to integrate different specific behaviors into a new and more general one.

## Objects and Message Passing

The concepts of objects (actors) and message passing were introduced in computer science by O. Dahl, A. Kay, and C. Hewitt, and first developed by the languages Simula, Smalltalk, and Plasma (Birtwistle and Dahl 1973; Kay 1969; Hewitt 1976). These concepts constitute a very apt response to MCS demands.

Simula introduced the concept of a hierarchical organization of *classes*: a class describes the set of functions that operate on its instances. This is adequate for properties 1, 3, and 6, mentioned above.

Simulation by the management of several processes also appears in Simula.

Plasma (Planner) introduced the concept of *actor*. Each entity of the language is an actor communicating with other actors by a message-sending mechanism using a selective reception of messages by pattern matching (Hewitt and Smith 1975; Hewitt 1976, Pomian 1980; Durieux 1981). An offspring of Plasma called Act 1 perfected message sending by allowing inheritance properties with *delegation*: instead of refusing a message an actor can delegate it to another actor (Lieberman 1981). Plasma and Act 1 made possible the definition of complex control-structures such as backtracking, coroutining, and simultaneous activation of the same actor (Durieux 1981). This is a great help in managing complex musical structures and tasks (Lieberman 1982).

The development of Smalltalk systems (Kay and Goldberg 1976; Ingalls 1978; Goldberg and Robson 1983) and office machines such as the Xerox Star system (Smith 1983) with a bitmapped screen and mouse pointer has motivated the development of interactive software tools using graphic devices (Cointe 1982a, 1982b). With its syntax and structure, Smalltalk is particularly adapted to properties 4–6.

Implementation of multiple windows, graphics editing, and menu systems is greatly facilitated by the use of objects, classes, and inheritance. Several newer-generation Lisp dialects include the concept of objects. A prime example is the Lisp Machine Flavor system (Moon and Weinreb 1980; Cointe 1981, 1982a, 1982b; Novak 1982; Rees 1982; Steels 1983).

## Object-oriented Programming and MCS

The power of object-oriented programming is now well known (Lieberman 1982), but let us underline how its properties match MCS requirements. From a user point of view, object-oriented languages have the following properties:

Extensibility: It is always possible to increase the language domain in developing new control structures. This property complements requirements 1–3, mentioned above.

Interactivity: Dialogue with the machine is essential for ease of use and for research purposes.

Modularity: The inheritance concept allows one to describe a situation in terms of elementary subsituations (property 6).

Suitability for multiple representations: The object notion allows for multiple implementations and representations of a particular concept (properties 1–3). This is important since our understanding of a phenomenon depends upon the way it is presented to us. Multiple representations favor properties 4–6.

## FORMES Guidelines

Keeping MCS requirements in mind, the guidelines for the development of the FORMES system follow.

### Accessibility

Our experience in teaching and using FORMES shows that users wish to have access to each component of the system, in order to study, understand, and modify every piece of the global architecture. This wish is satisfied by two features. First, FORMES is an interactive environment, and second, each entity of the FORMES universe is actually an object.

### Message-Passing Operation

Each object is a potential receiver of messages linked with functions (methods). Each method embodies the behavior corresponding to a particular message. The set of methods can be read, written, expanded, or contracted by the user. Users can dynamically observe modifications in a family of objects, and they have the choice of keeping or modifying the default behaviors. In this way, we have at our disposal an incremental and self-documented system, the present state of which is always accessible.

### Processes

In order to represent the complexity of musical models, we have to deal with time-dependent objects that we call *processes*, built from subobjects called *offspring*.

### Implementation

FORMES was developed in Vlisp, first on a DEC PDP-10 then on a DEC VAX-11/780. It is presently available in Vlisp (Greussay 1982) and Le Lisp (Chailloux 1984). Lisp allows a great flexibility in the development of such a complex prototype system. However, production versions of the FORMES system for other machines could be developed in other languages.

## Main Features

### Processes

A FORMES process is a named entity that groups together *rules* (procedure bodies), a *monitor* (a kind of scheduler), an *environment* (local variables or fields), and *offspring* (or *children*). A FORMES process has typical process capabilities (like a *script* in Plasma), such as the ability to "sleep," "wakeup," "wait," and "synchronize" when asked. In general, a FORMES process behaves according to the messages passed to it.

The role of each process is to ensure the calculation of a particular musical characteristic, such as an aspect of phrasing, vibrato, loudness control, or timbre. This calculation takes place during a precise duration (called a *span*), that extends from a begin time (*btime*) to an end time (*etime*). (These times are not necessarily explicitly specified.)

In FORMES, computation is accomplished through rules (as in *synthesis by rule* [Rodet 1977; Sundberg, Askenfelt, and Fryden 1983]). It is performed in the specific environment of the process. The environment consists of static *local variables* that keep their value unless they are explicitly changed. A process starts to execute its rules when

Fig. 1. The span of a
CHILD process is included
in the span of a PARENT
process.

it is activated. Thus, the span of a process is the time segment during which it is *active*.

In synthesis, several processes are activated. The role of the monitor is to maintain the *activity* of the process (execution of the rules) during the span, and to maintain the correct sequencing and collaboration of different processes (e.g., the calculation of a general loudness contour, then calculation of the local loudness of a motive, then calculation of the amplitude envelope of a note). Monitors are explained in more detail later.

From a synthesis point of view, the calculation periodically feeds the inputs or controls of a synthesizer with a set of new values or commands. Thus, running a process should start a sound output, and the value of the variable **time** in FORMES (a logical clock) stays close to physical time. However, running a process can result in other effects like screen display, and patch loading.

### Process Definition

A process is defined by instantiation of an original generator called **process**. The definition should not be confused with the activation of the process that takes place at its begin time. The definition or creation of a process as an instance of a generator can occur at any time before its begin time. For example, instantiation of process **foo** from a generator can be accomplished by the construct:

(process new 'foo)

This expression passes a message **new** to **process** with the argument **foo**. It is interesting to notice that new processes can be defined from **foo**, or more precisely, derived from **foo** through some changes. For example,

(foo new 'bar
    env: '(partial1 440.0))

defines a new process named **bar** which is the same as **foo** except for the value of the variable **partial1** in its environment.

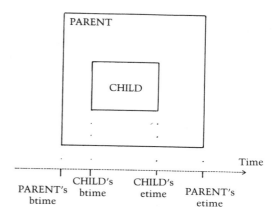

### Sequential, Parallel, and Hierarchical Structure

As with any complex system, a computer music system should be modular. To this end, processes can be organized in a structure that reflects some aspects of the desired musical structure, by combination in sequence, in parallel, and hierarchically. A process may be built from subparts, themselves built from subparts, and so on. Thus, a process may have children and a *parent*. The hierarchical relationship "**Process-PARENT** is the parent of **Process-CHILD**" encompasses several aspects. These include the span of **Process-CHILD**, which is included in that of **Process-PARENT** (Fig. 1).

It also includes the respective sequencing of **Process-PARENT** and **Process-CHILD** rules at a precise instant $t$. The "pre-rules" (denoted by the identifier **each-time:**) of **Process-PARENT** are executed before the pre-rules of **Process-CHILD**, and the "post-rules" (denoted by the identifier **each time*:**) of **Process-PARENT** are executed after the post-rules of **Process-CHILD** (Fig. 2).

Let us take a simple example of a hierarchical structure. Suppose that the process **PARENT** has three children named **CHILD1**, **CHILD2**, and **CHILD3**. This lineage will be indicated within the process **PARENT** definition by the list definition construct:

children: (CHILD1 CHILD2 CHILD3)

*Fig. 2. Sequence of rule execution for a PARENT process and its CHILD.*

*Fig. 3. Sequential children.*

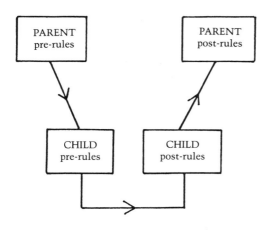

*Fig. 2. Sequence of rule execution for a PARENT process and its CHILD.*

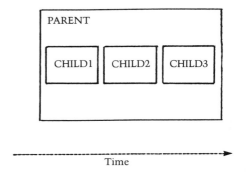

From there, the scheduling of the children is defined by the **PARENT**'s monitor. Let us briefly describe two cases of monitors. With the monitor called **sequential-node** denoted in **PARENT** by the construct

    monitor: sequential-node

the three children are simply juxtaposed in time, the first starting its activity at **PARENT**'s btime, and the others starting when the preceding one is finished (Fig. 3).

With the monitor called **parallel-node**, denoted in **PARENT** by the construct

    monitor: parallel-node

the three children start together at **PARENT**'s btime (Fig. 4).

However, with the parallel monitor, a list of lists of sequential children are started, so that we have to add extra parentheses:

    children: ((CHILD1) (CHILD2) (CHILD3))

The second monitor shows how some processes (and eventually their descendents) may not be hierarchically related, from the standpoint of temporal

span. This is what we call *parallelism*, and it is essential for representing many aspects of musical structure, for instance when different voices are "not necessarily synchronized," but processes from different voices can communicate and interact with each other.

**The Calculation Tree**

The structure in which processes are organized can be represented as a (genealogical) *tree*. The root of this tree is a process, the span of which covers all its offspring. But at a precise instant $t$, the only active processes are those that include time $t$ in their span. These represent a cross-section in the tree that we call the *calculation tree* (Fig. 5). At a specific time, only the rules of active processes are executed, in the order determined by the cross-section corresponding to that time.

At present, the calculation tree is a list of the rules of active processes in the proper order. The reason for calling it "tree," however, is that, in a forthcoming implementation, it will really be organized as a tree.

**Communication with Processes**

Users converse with processes by passing or sending messages. They send a message when they want to query a process on its "nature," "state," or "capabilities," and when they want it to do something

*Rodet and Cointe*

Fig. 4. Parallel children.          Fig. 5. A calculation tree.

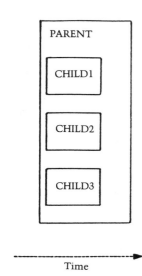

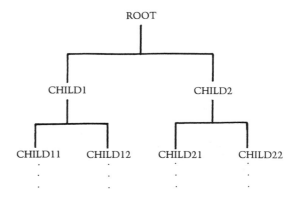

For example, the expression (**Process help**) asks the process to display documentation about itself. (**Process selectors**) asks the process to display the list of all messages it knows about.

like activate a process or display a graph on the screen. In order to pass a message to a process, the user types: (**Process ⟨message⟩**) where ⟨**message**⟩ consists of a message name (the selector) optionally followed by some arguments, as shown in the Backus-Naur Form (BNF) notation below. In BNF, the left side of an expression is replaced by one of the phrases on the right side of the expression.

| | |
|---|---|
| ⟨message⟩ | ::= ⟨selector⟩ [ ⟨argument_list⟩ ] |
| ⟨argument_list⟩ | ::= ⟨arg⟩ |
| | ::= ⟨arg⟩ ⟨argument_list⟩ |
| ⟨selector⟩ | ::= help |
| | ::= selectors |
| | ::= play |
| | ::= understands |
| | ::= name |
| | ::= kill |
| | ::= sleep |
| | ::= wake-up |
| | . |
| | . |
| | . |

## Portability of Rules

As underlined in the introduction, generality, compatibility, and modularity are essential. In FORMES, it is nearly always the case that a rule refers to the process in which it is placed, for example to access its environment. To fulfill these requirements, rules have to be independent of the name of the process in which they are embedded, so that they can be copied and transferred without modification from a library into any process.

Thus an important construct is the one that refers to the actual active process that calls the rule, without explicitly naming that process. This is the role of the construct **fself**, which refers to the process whose rules are being evaluated. Thus, referring to the process **bar** defined above which has a variable **partial1** of value 440, in its environment, the construct (**fself ? 'partial1**) appearing within **bar** returns 440. The question mark (**?**) is the selector of a message passed to the process **fself** (**bar** in that context), and asks for the value of the variable **partial1** in its environment. Similarly, (**fself ?← 'partial1 'A4**) asks process **bar** to change the value of its **partial1** to A4. In the same vein (**fself ? 'PARENT**) returns the **PARENT** of the designated process. For a certain class of processes called *transition processes*, discussed later, the expressions

(fself ? 'left-sibling)
(fself ? 'right-sibling)

return the **left-sibling** and the **right-sibling** of **fself** in their common parent's list of children. For example, the construct **(fself ? 'left-sibling)** appearing in a rule within process **CHILD2** (as defined above) would designate **CHILD1**. Finally, in **PARENT**, the expression **(fself ? 'active-children)** gives the rest of the list of successive children beginning at the first presently active.

### Execution of FORMES Programs

FORMES programs and commands may be prepared in files and then loaded into the system, or typed on-line. A FORMES program is a *structure of processes*. The execution of such a structure involves the repetition at successive times of the following two steps, called the *FORMES System Loop*: (1) update the list of rules that constitute the calculation tree and (2) execute (evaluate) the rules of the calculation tree. The execution of the program (structure) is started by sending the message **play** to the process at the root of the structure (let's call it **Root-Process**):

(Root-Process play)

Note that any process can be considered as the root of a substructure. (If it has no child, the substructure reduces to the process alone.) Execution ends when the root process finds a condition that was given by the user as an exit condition, like a duration elapsed.

The "current time" is found in a variable called **time**, incremented by the message **next-tick**. The expression

(while (Root-Process end?)
  (tree evaluate))

means the following. Repetitively, message **end?** is passed to **Root-Process**. According to its monitor and some other conditions, **Root-Process** updates the calculation tree and returns "false" if it has not yet finished or "true" if it has. Thus we see that the **while** loop is repeated until **Root-Process** decides the end has occurred.

The evaluation of the calculation tree caused by the message **evaluate** passed to **tree** is also repeated. The last rule that appears in the tree is **(clock next-tick)**, where the message **next-tick** passed to **clock** causes **time** to be incremented (**time = time + quantum**). By default, **time** is incremented by the default value of **quantum**, which is 0.01 sec.

Hence the FORMES System Loop can be sketched in an Algol-like form:

WHILE (Root_Process_not_ended)
  DO BEGIN
      Update_the_tree;
      Evaluate_the_tree;
  END

### Programming (Composing) in FORMES

FORMES involves the composer in playing (running), and listening to processes and modifying their environment. This can be a simple but very fruitful activity. This is especially the case for beginners who can learn by literally "playing" with the already defined objects (processes and rules of the library) like in an Adventure game, without having to first succeed at building a "hairy" error-free patch. This is also true for expert programmers who sometimes prefer to modify an old program rather than writing a brand new one. Ultimately, this mode of working fulfills our requirements that FORMES be an environment in perpetual evolution, where abstraction and the power of objects grows with the benefit of past experience.

Users can also create rules. Creating processes that incorporate new rules is a second stage of interaction with FORMES, slightly less simple but still accessible to people who are not computer experts.

Creating new monitors is a rarer mode of interaction, since it can sometimes require knowledge of the details of the system.

*Rodet and Cointe*

Fig. 6. FORMES code to
build an envelope for
notes and phrases.

```
; Processes:
                    (process new 'CHILD1
                      each-time: '((envelope))
                      env: '(duration 0.2))

                    (CHILD1 new 'CHILD2 env: '(duration 0.3))

                    (process new 'PARENT
                      each-time: '((envelope))
                      children:      '(CHILD1 CHILD2 CHILD1))

; Rules:
                    (de envelope ()
                      (*= amplitude (envelop.fun (tnorm))))

; Initialization:
                    (setqq each-quantum (amplitude 1.))

; Load breakpoint functions:
                    (bitpad envelop.fun)
```

## Elementary Example of Working with FORMES

This example treats a well-known problem: describing the amplitude envelope for a note model, and using this model to build the amplitude envelope for a monophonic phrase. The code is shown in Fig. 6. (Comments start with a semicolon.)

As can be seen in Fig. 6, the rule **envelope** appears without modification after the identifier **each-time:** in **PARENT** and in the children (this demonstrates the portability of the rules). The envelope rule is a Lisp function defined by the (**de envelope** () . . .) construct. Using the prefixed Lisp notation, this function sets the global variable **amplitude** to its previous value multiplied by that of the function **envelop.fun** with argument **tnorm**. This last expression stands for "time normalized," which means that its value is proportional to **time** but goes from 0 to 1 during the span of the process using it. In other words,

$$\text{tnorm} = \frac{\text{time} - \text{btime}}{\text{duration}}$$

or more precisely, **tnorm** is defined in FORMES as follows:

```
(setq tnorm '(div (sub time (fself ? 'btime))
  (fself ? 'duration)))
```

The construct (**envelop.fun (tnorm)**) is like an envelope generator, with the time of the envelope scaled to the process span, and with the **quantum** as the sampling period. The actual envelope definition is obtained by the construct (**bitpad envelop.fun**), where the argument **envelop.fun** is the name of a file that contains the description of a breakpoint function entered by typing or by drawing a curve on a bitpad tablet, for example:

| Value | Time |
|-------|------|
| 0 | 0 |
| 1 | 1 |
| 6 | 2 |
| 4 | 7 |
| 0 | 10 |

Values and times are normalized to the interval [0, 1].

Fig. 7. Amplitude envelope
created by the envelope
rule.

The way rule **envelope** is written (using *=) necessitates that **amplitude** be initialized at each step of the loop and before **PARENT**'s rule. The reason for this apparent complication is to ensure rule portability. A global variable like **amplitude** carries information from one process to the other at low cost. Furthermore, rules may be written with explicit reference to global variables like fundamental-frequency, vibrato-excursion, or tempo. This allows processes to be easily inserted into or deleted from the larger structure, since the global variables are common to most structures.

In defining amplitude at each quantum, we use the following command:

(setq each-quantum '(amplitude 1.))

which has the effect of setting **amplitude** to the value 1 at the beginning of each tree evaluation.

At this point, one can play with the system. First, we send the message **play** to **CHILD1**:

(CHILD1 play)

This starts the FORMES System Loop on the root process **CHILD1**. Its rules ((**envelope**) after the identifier **each-time:**) are executed repetitively at times 0, 0 + **quantum**, 0 + (**2 * quantum**), and so on, (0, 0.01, 0.02 . . .) up to the **CHILD1** end (0.2, which is its duration). Thus the variable **amplitude** samples values of the previously mentioned envelope, and can be sent to a synthesizer amplitude control input.

The result can be checked with the command (**amplitude screen**), which displays successive amplitude values on the screen in the form of a graph that plots amplitude versus time (Fig. 7).

(Actually, this picture was generated by the command (**amplitude plot**), which draws it on a plotter.) Now, we send the message **play** to **PARENT**:

(PARENT play)

**PARENT** is set "active" from time 0 to time 0.8 (the sum of the durations of its three children). Within the time interval [0, 0.2] only **CHILD1** is also active, and in the calculation tree the rule of **PARENT** is followed by the rule of **CHILD1**. PAR-

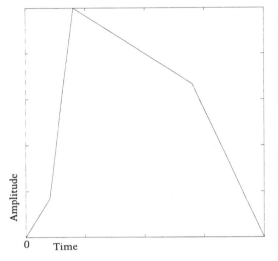

ENT's rule sets amplitude to values corresponding to Fig. 7 scaled on a [0, 0.8] interval. But then the **CHILD1** rule multiplies the amplitude by the same form scaled on [0, 0.2]. Similarly, during the time interval [0.2, 0.5] only **PARENT** and **CHILD2** are active, and the amplitude is the product of the corresponding portion of **PARENT**'s amplitude setting by a [0.2, 0.5] **CHILD2** setting, and similarly for [0.5, 0.8] with **CHILD3**. Finally, the message (**amplitude screen**) results in curve shown in Fig. 8.

Through this elementary example, we have demonstrated several points. Modularity allows one to extend the musical environment by increasing the domain of existing objects, and to test elementary objects independently of each other before grouping them in higher-level objects. The rule we used would be found in a generally accessible library of rules. It is usable in other objects, so that it can be exploited in different contexts by different musicians and researchers.

Notice that a new object, just created, can be tested immediately by sending **play** and listening to the corresponding sound. The value of a process parameter (like duration) is held in the process itself. The user may see it in the process definition code,

Fig. 8. *Interaction between PARENT process and CHILD processes modifies the original envelope.*

Fig. 9. *GRAND-PARENT envelope.*

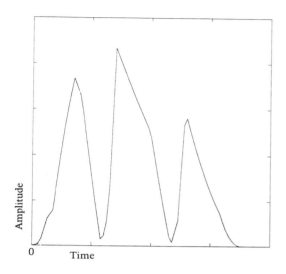

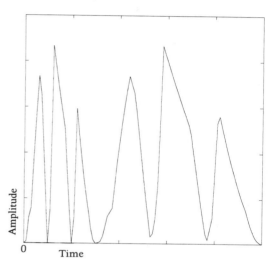

not in a separate list. It is not referenced by its position but is pointed at by a mnemonic identifier, insuring that you can consult or change it easily.

The correctness of a program is quickly checked on a graphic display; we have often recognized that a picture of parameter values could immediately indicate not only the presence of a bug but exactly where and how it occurred within a complex program! Since any process can be played (if it makes sense) in the course of building and experimenting with a structure, one can follow a bottom-up procedure as we have done here. That is, build a *leaf process* (e.g., describing details of the sound), and when you are satisfied with it, embed it in a **PARENT**, then tune the structure **PARENT-child**, and so on.

One can also follow a top-down approach, that is, build the highest level element of the structure, and then fill it in with more and more detailed refinements. Naturally one can start from any intermediate level of structuring, for instance by appropriating it from another structure stored in the library.

The flexibility and adaptability afforded by this scheme are especially favorable to artistic creativ-

ity. Furthermore, even this simple example would not be easy to write in other languages.

**Further Extensions of the Example**

We could benefit from the hierarchy within FORMES and type the following commands:

(PARENT new 'UNCLE 'duration 0.3)
(process new 'GRAND-PARENT
    children: (PARENT UNCLE))

Then the expression **(GRAND-PARENT play)** would result in the amplitude evolution shown in Fig. 9.

In working with an envelope, you might want to change its basic curve. FORMES gives you the power to effect major changes through simple instructions. For example, we can shift to a much more flexible form by giving the following command that redefines the function **envelope**:

(de envelope ()
  (*= amplitude
      (* (power (tnorm) gamma)
         (power (− 1. (tnorm)) (− 1. gamma)))))

Fig. 10. Result of adjusting
gamma to redefine the
envelope.

Fig. 11. Insertion of a part
of GRAND-PARENT into
an existing envelope.

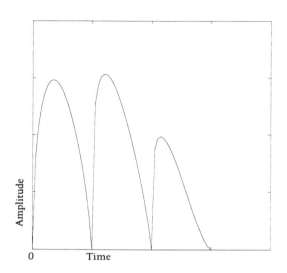

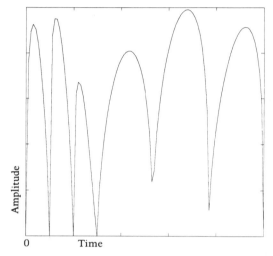

This means that the previous value of the amplitude is multiplied by

$$tnorm^{gamma} * (1 - tnorm)^{1 - gamma}$$

Now if you set **gamma** to the value, 0.25 and play **PARENT**, the amplitude evolution will look like Fig. 10.

Finally, suppose we want to modify the value of the parameter **gamma** during the span of **GRAND-PARENT**. To simplify the explanation, we chose a ramp from 0.2 to 0.8 during **GRAND-PARENT**'s span. Then we can insert this rule between those already linked with its **each-time:**

(GRAND-PARENT insert 'each-time: '(set-rampq
   'gamma 0.2 0.8))

After **GRAND-PARENT** is run, the amplitude evolution looks like Fig. 11.

We hope this shows how a relatively simple user program can result in rather complex and powerful results such as amplitude envelopes controlling a synthesizer. The example also shows how rules can be easily modified, and how message passing and the modify-and-test procedure can make the devel-

opment of a composition faster and more intuitive than previous languages have allowed.

## The Role of Monitors

A monitor defines a temporal control structure. The monitor of a process is the scheduler of its children. It has three tasks:

Determine the start time (btime) for each child and activate it.

Update the calculation tree when the state of a process is modified.

If possible, determine the duration of the root process (the difference between etime and btime). Different duration algorithms are available. For example, the duration of a sequential process can be defined as the sum of its children's durations, or on the contrary, it can be defined by scaling its children so that their sum equals its explicit duration.

For each monitor those tasks are implemented by three generic Lisp functions called respectively: **init, end?**, and **duration**.

In order to define a new monitor the user can

*Fig. 12. Example of FOR-
MES used to generate
high-level musical process.*

```
; Some function definitions appear in Appendix 1

; PROCESSES:

(process new 'PARENT
   monitor: 'parallel_node
   children:   '((VOICE1) (VOICE2)))

(process new 'VOICE1
   monitor:     'seq-node
   first-time: '((fself change 'children:
                    (derive '<following>
                        '(short short s_asc Ef4)(fself ? 'phrase_number)))
                 (transition?))
   each-time: '((rest? in_n_notes))
   children:     '((???)
   env:          '(phrase_number 14))

(process new 'VOICE2
   monitor:     'seq-node
   each-time: '((rest? in_n_notes))
   children:     (bass))

(process new 'Ef4
   first-time: '((tempo))
   each-time: '((envelope) (warp) (my-pitch)))

(Ef4 new 'Ff4)

(Ef1 new 'Gf1)

;            .
;            .
;            .

; DECLARATIONS:
(synthesizer f0 coefamp freq1 freq2 freq3 freq4 freq5)

(setq each-quantum '(coefamp 1.))
```

choose between redefining it completely (by sending the message **new** to the meta-generator monitor), or by redefining only some methods (generic
Lisp functions associated with the monitor). In this
latter case, the message **new** is also sent but to an
existing monitor.

## Utilities in the FORMES Environment

The FORMES environment provides a number of
tools that aid the user in developing programs and
compositions. During execution of a FORMES program, the current value of **time** and the calculation
tree are always displayed on the screen.

The messages **print** and **print:** respectively display the internal (Lisp) and external (as given by the
user) representations of objects.

On-line documentation is provided by the message **help** passed to objects. Furthermore a help program (called Aid, written by Patrick Greussay) may

be called at any time. Another program, written by
Harald Wertz, keeps track of all mail and news concerning FORMES from implementers as well as
users.

A file address is linked with each function in the
system, allowing access to the file that defines the
function if needed. Objects and functions created or
modified by the user can also be interactively saved
in a file. Finally, users can ask for a *trace* of parts of
the FORMES System Loop.

## Another Example

In this example (Fig. 12) we describe a FORMES solution to a musical problem. One of the purposes of
the example is to study a "real-life" synthesis problem. Another is to demonstrate FORMES ability to
include the "high-level" or compositional aspects of
the synthesis process. We think there is much to gain
if the "high-level" and the "pure synthesis level"
are developed with the same formalism in the same
program (Rodet, Potard, and Barrière 1984).

Before looking at the synthesis procedure itself
and at the compositional aspects (even though the
separation into "high" and "low" levels is mislead-
ing), let us explain some additional FORMES constructs that we use in the example.

### Additional FORMES Constructs

In order to produce simultaneously two "unsyn-
chronized" voices, we use in **PARENT** the monitor
**parallel_node** described earlier. Here, the children
are **VOICE1** and **VOICE2**, each one representing an
independent voice. Thus, both sequences of the
children of **VOICE1** and **VOICE2** will be executed
in parallel.

We also use the function **trelative**, which is a
time relative to the beginning of the current process. The definition of **trelative** is as follows:

```
(de trelative ()
   (sub time (fself ? 'btime)))
```

In the preceding example, the rules of a process appeared after the identifier **each-time:**, and they were executed at each quantum during the process activity, that is, "each-time" the process was executed. Obviously, it is desirable to benefit from rules that are executed once only, at activation of the process (identified by **first-time:**) or at end of the process (identified by **last-time:**).

Finally, the construct

```
(fself change 'children: '(CHILD1 CHILD2
  CHILD3))
```

changes the list of children of the process presently pointed at by **fself**, into the list **(CHILD1 CHILD2 CHILD3)**. In the code below, it appears in the form:

```
first-time: ((fself change 'children:
             (derive '(following)
                '(short short s_asc Ef2)
                (fself ? phrase_number))))
```

which means that at the initialization of the process **(VOICE1)**, its list of children is changed to the result of the evaluation of the form **derive**, explained later.

## A FORMES Program

The children of **VOICE2** are in a list named **bass** that we do not explain in detail. For each note process in Fig. 12 (**Ef1**, etc.), we apply an envelope to the parameter **coefamp**, which is a loudness input of the CHANT synthesizer (more precisely, the spectrum slope, and hence the sound richness, varies also with the value of **coefamp**). Also for each note we use the same envelope as in the preceding example.

Here, the function **warp** (in the **each-time:** section of **Ef4**) is in charge of timbre variations. It warps the envelope spectrum by modifying the formant frequencies (Rodet, Potard, and Barrière 1984). (Note that formant frequencies can be used to set a formant filter or to control another synthesis technique. The point is that this rule is relatively independent of the synthesis technique used.) The fundamental frequency of each note process

is calculated by the function **my_pitch** according to the name of the process.

The note list is *self-generated* in **VOICE1**, and is substituted for the **???** that appears after the identifier **children:**.

The other important point to observe is the interaction between the two voices. Due to slightly varying tempos (function **(tempo)** in **Ef1**, **Ff1**, and so on) the two voices are not synchronous. But, at any instant, one of them is in *master mode* and looks ahead in its children list. Specifically, it tests if a rest is coming in **in_n_notes** notes. This is done by the function called **(rest?)** in the **each-time:** section of **VOICE1** and **VOICE2**. If a rest is coming, the master voice modifies the duration of the forthcoming processes in the other voice in order that both are synchronized with the note following the rest. Furthermore, when such a resynchronization occurs, the master voice may decide to reverse the roles so that the other voice becomes the master. This kind of easy communication between two or more voices is generally very difficult to achieve in most other music languages.

The last important point is that we want to allow a legato articulation between two notes, in the form of a continuous pitch contour from one note to the following note, in place of the two fixed pitches of the note. For this, we use a kind of process called a transition process, whose span covers a time segment before and after the transition between two processes.

The role of the transition is to take information simultaneously from both processes in order to generate a new pattern by combining them with a *transition rule*. Transitions are also a very important class of processes in musical applications, including attacks of successive notes, legatos, and the articulation of successive phrases. Transition processes implement the concept of *anticipation* since they can take information concerning the "future state" of the second process and use it in order to behave in a way that was not originally implemented in the "non-transitional" processes. Note that it is not very easy to deal with such transition effects in music languages that separate the world into patches and note lists.

In our example (Fig. 12), the transition processes

are introduced dynamically in the list of children by the function call **(transition?)** in the **first-time:** section of **VOICE1**.

### Generation of the List of Children

We now explain the function call used in **VOICE1** to generate its list of children. The idea of this musical sketch is to use a very simplified and modified version of rules found in the study of jazz improvisation. (We thank Andre Hodeir and Philippe Gautron for communicating these rules.) We have formalized them in terms of rewriting rules. A classical rewriting rule in BNF form is as follows:

⟨identifier i⟩ ::= ⟨list_of_identifiers_1⟩
::= ⟨list_of_identifiers_2⟩
.
.
.
::= ⟨list_of_identifiers_n⟩

Such a rule means that ⟨**identifier_i**⟩ is rewritten as the list of identifiers ⟨**list_of_identifiers_1**⟩ or as ⟨**list_of_identifiers_2**⟩, and so on. But when using such rules for production of a phrase, it is necessary to specify which of the alternatives is chosen for any derivation. Therefore, each alternative or derivation is accompanied by a condition of application of the derivation:

⟨identifier i⟩ ::= condition_of_application_1 ⟨list_of_identifiers_1⟩
::= condition_of_application_2 ⟨list_of_identifiers_2⟩
.
.
.
::= condition_of_application_n ⟨list_of_identifiers_n⟩

Let **expression_i** be an expression which, when evaluated, returns the same alternative that would be chosen according to the conditions. Then, the above rule can be simply expressed as follows:

⟨identifier i⟩ ::= expression_i

This means that when the identifier **i** is found, it is rewritten into the list of identifiers returned by the

evaluation of the expression **i** (a function call), the role of which is to choose among the different possibilities and to return one of them explicitly.

### Rewriting Rules

In this example, without any loss in generality, a very short set of rules has been chosen:

⟨following⟩ ::= derive_following
⟨rest⟩     ::= derive_rest

In rule 1, **derive_following** is the function called to rewrite ⟨**following**⟩ into:

⟨rest⟩ ⟨list_of_notes⟩ [⟨following⟩]

where the brackets [ ] mean that ⟨**following**⟩ is optional. The **list_of_notes** is chosen among several possibilities, according to the previous phrase's features. The previous phrase's features constitute a quadruple:

{**start_beat end_beat class pivot**},

where **start_beat** is the beat (long or short) on which the phrase starts, **end_beat** is the beat on which the phrase ends, **pivot** is the last note of the phrase, **class** corresponds to the pitch contour constituted by the three last notes of the phrase—one of the following forms: descending and ascending is called *ascendant* or *asc*, ascending and ascending is called *super-ascendant* or *s_asc*, ascending and descending is called *descendant* or *desc*, descending and descending is called *super-descendant* or *s_desc*. These features are used by the function **derive_following** to choose the next phrase in the class of the previous one according to the pivot note.

The function **rest** rewrites ⟨**rest**⟩ into **long_rest**, **short_rest** or nothing, in order to ensure that beat alternation (long, short) is respected, and that the next phrase starts on a beat of the same type as its **start_beat**.

The code for deriving the rules and the code of these functions is given in Appendix 1. For phrases and classes, they use the following structure of data (a portion of real data appears also in Appendix 1):

$\langle$class$\rangle ::=$
 $(($pivot_1 $\langle$phrase_1_data$\rangle$ . . . $\langle$phrase_i_data$\rangle)$
 $($pivot_2 $\langle$phrase_1_data$\rangle$ . . . $\langle$phrase_j_data$\rangle)$
.
.
.
 $($pivot_h $\langle$phrase_1_data$\rangle$ . . . $\langle$phrase_m_data$\rangle))$
$\langle$phrase_x_data$\rangle ::=$
 $( |\langle$start_beat$\rangle\langle$end_beat$\rangle\langle$class$\rangle|$
 $($note_1 note_2 . . . note_p$) )$

As an example, suppose that we choose (**short short asc Ef4**) as our initial "previous phrase's features" and that we want the derivation to stop after four phrases are produced. Then the evaluation of the expression

(derive '$\langle$following$\rangle$ '(short short asc Ef4) 4)

returns the following:

(Gf4 G4 Bf4 C5 Ef5 C5
 long_rest Gf5 Bf4 A4 Ef5
 short_rest Gf5
 short_rest F5 Ef5 C5)

In this example, we have shown that complex procedures can be embedded in FORMES to realize a compositional task. The main benefit is that high-level procedures may interact easily with the details of the synthesis procedures since they are implemented not only in the same environment but even in the same program.

## Interconnection with Synthesizers

One of the fundamental aims in the FORMES project is to build a library of "models of the processes brought into action in musical production" (Rodet, Potard, and Barrière 1984). As mentioned previously, we try to design these models to be independent of a particular synthesis technique.

FORMES is used to represent both discrete and continuous (i.e., sampled at a high rate) events and control parameters, which describe acoustic, physical, and musical characteristics. In its structure, it makes no assumption about the device that will calculate a signal corresponding (as closely as possible) to those characteristics. As a consequence, FORMES is interfaced to different types of synthesizers. Suppose **PARENT** is the root process of a structure described in Fig. 12. The command (**PARENT chant**) asks process **PARENT** to format the program outputs for the CHANT sound synthesis system. Similarly (**PARENT 4X**) lets this same FORMES program (without any modification) drive a given patch of the 4X synthesizer (built at IRCAM by G. DiGiugno). Any other device can be controlled in the same way, for example (**PARENT ap**) sends the parameters of the program to our Floating Point Systems array processor, and (**PARENT symbol**) draws a symbolic representation (e.g., a score) of the piece.

This kind of versatility guarantees a more uniform access to different devices. It allows use of one device in place of another when the first device is not available or when it is not adequate for musical or technical reasons. (For example, some synthesis devices have a greater number of voices or more precision in the calculations or better control facilities than some others.) Finally, and most importantly, it opens the way to a standard representation or formalization of musical structures and processes, which would be of great use to the computer music community.

## The FORMES Environment and Workstation

The environment we want to build for FORMES should have the capability to execute FORMES programs in real time. This requires a fast host computer with floating-point arithmetic in hardware and about 1 Mbyte of main memory—nothing more than current workstations provide. A high-resolution, bitmapped display is indispensible, as are control devices like a mouse, a joystick, and potentiometers.

The host computer should be connected to a floating-point synthesizer (this is presently the rarest component). The synthesizer should embody as few restrictions as possible in terms of its internal control structure. For example, it should be able to handle subroutines and coroutines, as well as the buffering of any input, output, or internal data flow. The synthesizer should also possess a large input/output capacity between FORMES programs and signal-processing programs, in order to ensure rapid updates from the host computer.

The workstation environment should also include a variety of signal and data analysis programs, including sophisticated signal-processing techniques such as multiple pulse analysis and synthesis, algorithms for psychoacoustic data extraction, and good graphic displays (three-dimensional displays, and color displays of symbolic representations).

But the most essential part that we want to build is a library or database of models implemented in predefined processes and rules, which can be accessed through perceptual ("richer," more "grain") and musical terms, as well as through terms concerning physical models of sound production (e.g., G. Weinreich's models of piano and violin [1983]). A fundamental point is that this library should constantly grow richer in processes and rules due to the contributions of composers and scientists working on the station.

## Acknowledgments

We thank Yves Potard for his essential contribution to the conception of FORMES, Bernard Serpette and Jean-Pierre Briot for participating in the implementation of the FORMES system, and Jean-Baptiste Barrière for suggestions and musical tests of the FORMES environment. We also thank Patrick Greussay, Jerome Chailloux, Jean-François Perrot, Harald Wertz, Eugen Neidl, Christian Queinnec, and Daniel Goossens for providing the Lisp environment. Finally, we thank Pierre Boulez, Tod Machover, Philippe Manoury, Marco Stroppa, and everyone at IRCAM for their encouragement and comments on the musical aspects of the FORMES system.

## References

Barrière, J.-B. *Chreode.* 1983.

Bennett, G. 1981. "Singing Synthesis in Electronic Music." In *Research Aspects of Singing,* ed. J. Sundberg. Report 33. Stockholm: Royal Swedish Academy of Music, pp. 34–50.

Birtwistle, G., and O.-J. Dahl. 1973. *SIMULA BEGIN.* New York: Petrocelli/Charter.

Chailloux, J. 1984. *Manuel Le Lisp.* Second edition. Paris: Institut National de Recherche en Informatique et Automatique.

Cointe, P. 1981. "Fermetures dans les λ Interprètes: Application aux Langages LISP, PLASMA, et Smalltalk." Thèse de troisième cycle. Laboratoire d'Informatique Théorique et Pratique. Paris: Université de Paris 6.

Cointe, P. 1982a. "Vlisp: un langage objet?" In *Actes de l'Ecole de Printemps d'Informatique Théorique.* Paris: Laboratoire d'Informatique Théorique at Pratique, pp. 143–164.

Cointe, P. 1982b. "Une réalisation de Smalltalk en Vlisp." *Techniques et Sciences de l'Informatique* 1(4):325–340.

Cointe, P. 1983. "Evaluation of Object-oriented Programming from Simula to Smalltalk." In *Proceedings of the Eleventh Simula User's Conference.* Paris: Simula Information, pp. 17–24.

Cointe, P., and X. Rodet. 1984. "FORMES: An Object and Time Oriented System for Music Composition and Synthesis." To appear in the conference record of the 1984 ACM Symposium on LISP and Functional Programming, Austin, Texas, 5–8 August 1984.

Durieux, J. L. 1981. "Sémantique des liasons nom-valeur: application à l'implémentation des λ langages." Thèse d'Etat. Toulouse: Université Paul Sabatier.

Goldberg, A., and D. Robson. 1983. *Smalltalk-80: The Language and Its Implementation.* Reading, Massachusetts: Addison-Wesley.

Greussay, P. 1982. "Le Système Vlisp-Unix." Département Informatique. Paris: Université Paris 8, Vincennes.

Hewitt, C. 1976. "Viewing Control Structures as Patterns of Message Passing." A.I. Memo 410. Cambridge, Massachusetts: M.I.T. Artificial Intelligence Laboratory.

Hewitt, C., and B. Smith. 1975. "A Plasma Primer." Draft. Cambridge, Massachusetts: M.I.T. Artificial Intelligence Laboratory.

Ingalls, D. H. 1978. "The Smalltalk-76 Programming System Design and Implementation." Presented at the Fifth Annual ACM Symposium on Principles of Programming Languages, Tucson, Arizona.

Kay, A. 1969. "The Reactive Engine." Ph.D. diss. Salt

Lake City: Department of Computer Science, University of Utah.

Kay, A., and A. Goldberg. 1976. "Smalltalk-72 Instruction Manual." SSL-76-6. Palo Alto: Xerox Palo Alto Research Center.

Lieberman, H. 1981. "A Preview of Act 1." A.I. Memo 625. Cambridge, Massachusetts: M.I.T. Artificial Intelligence Laboratory.

Lieberman, H. 1982. "Machine Tongues IX: Object-oriented Programming." *Computer Music Journal* 6(3):8–21.

Moon, D., and D. Weinreb. 1980. "Flavors: Message Passing in the Lisp Machine." A.I. Memo 602. Cambridge, Massachusetts: M.I.T. Artificial Intelligence Laboratory.

Novak, G. S., Jr. 1983. "GLISP: A Lisp-based Programming System with Data Abstraction." *AI Magazine* 4(3):37–47, 53.

Pomian, C. 1980. "Contribution à la définition et à l'implémentation d'un interprète PLASMA." Thèse de troisième cycle. Toulouse: Université Paul Sabatier.

Rees, J., and I. Adams. 1982. "T: A Dialect of Lisp, or Lambda: The Ultimate Software Tool." In *Proceedings of the 1982 Symposium on Lisp and Functional Programming*. New York: Association for Computing Machinery, pp. 114–122.

Rodet, X. 1977. "Analyse du signal vocale dans sa representation amplitude-temps. Synthèse de la parole par regles." L.I.F. Thèse d'Etat. Paris: Université Paris 6.

Rodet, X., and G. Bennett. 1980. "Research in Musical Synthesis Using a Model of Vocal Production." Presented at the 1980 International Computer Music Conference, Queens College, New York.

Rodet, X., Y. Potard, and J.-B. Barrière. 1984. "The CHANT Project: From the Synthesis of the Singing Voice to Synthesis in General." *Computer Music Journal* 8(3):15–31.

Smith, D. C. et al. 1983. "Designing the Star User Interface." In *Integrated Interactive Computing Systems*, ed. P. Degano and E. Sandewall. Amsterdam: North-Holland, pp. 297–313.

Steels, L. 1983. "ORBIT: An Applicative View of Object-oriented Programming." In *Integrated Interactive Computing Systems*, ed. P. Degano and E. Sandewall. Amsterdam: North-Holland, pp. 193–206.

Sundberg, J., A. Askenfelt, and L. Fryden. 1983. "Musical Performance: A Synthesis-by-Rule Approach." *Computer Music Journal* 7(1):37–43.

Weinreich, G. 1983. "Violin Sound Synthesis from First Principles." Presented at the 106th Meeting of the Acoustical Society of America.

Winograd, T. 1979. "Beyond Programming Languages." *Communications of the Association for Computing Machinery* 22(7):391–401.

## Appendix 1

```
(de derive (ident S ns)
   (let-named self ((rules rew_rules) (rule* ()))
      (cond
          ((null rules) indent)
          ((setq rule* (apply_rule ident (next1 rules) S ns))
           (if (eq rule* 'no_rest) '* rule*))
          (t (self rules ni1))))))

(de apply_rule (ident (ident1 ::= frule) . args)
   (when (eq ident ident1) (apply frule args)))

(de vcons (elt list) (⟨cf elt (cons elt list) list))

(de following (S ns)
   (lets ((next_data (next_phrase_data S ns))
          (rest (derive '⟨rest⟩ S ns)))
```

```
    (append
      (vcons rest (cadr next_data))
      (when () ns 0) (derive '⟨following⟩ (car next_data) (1 − ns))))))

(de rest (S ns)
  (letvq (? cb . r) S
    (cond
      ((neq cb (caar next_data)) 'no_rest)
      ((eq cb 'short) 'long_rest)
      (t 'short_rest))))

(de next_phrase_data ((? ? class pivot) n)
  (car (find (cva1 class) pivot))))

(de find (1 pivot)
  (when 1
    (letvq ((p . phrases) . r) 1
      (if (eq p pivot) phrases (find r pivot)))))

; REWRITING RULES
(setq
  rew_rules  (
              (⟨following⟩ ::= following)
              (⟨rest⟩       ::= rest)
              )
  )

; DATA
(setq
  s_asc
    '(
    (Ef4
      ((short long asc Bf4)
       (Ef4 Gf4 G4 F4 A4 Bf4 r))
      ((long long s_asc Bf4)
       (Ef4 Gf4 long_rest G4 long_rest Ef long_rest A4 Bf4))
      ((long short asc Ef4)
       (Ef4 Gf4 G4 Gf4 G4 Ef long_rest Ef A4 Bf4 A4 Bf4 Ef4 short_rest))
      )
    (Gf4
      ((long short asc Gf4)
       (Gf4 Ef4 Gf4 G4 Bf4 C5 Gf4 short_rest))
      ((long short asc Gf4)
       (Ef4 Gf4 Ef G4 Ef Bf4 Ef C5 Ef C5 Gf4 short_rest))

      )
    )
  asc
    (
```

```
(Ef4
  ((long short desc C5)
   (Gf4 G4 Bf4 C5 Ef5 C5))
  ((long long desc Bf4)
   (Ef4 Af4 Gf4 A4 Ef5))
      .
      .
      .
```

## Appendix 2

```
(de rest? (in_n_notes)
  (when (eq master (fself name))
    (let ((notes (fself ? 'active-children)) (t_sum 0))
      (let ((a_note (nthcdr in_n_notes notes)))
        (when (memq a_note '(short_rest 'long_rest))
          (repeat in_n_notes (+ = t_sum ((next1 notes) ? 'duration)))
          (ajuste (alter master) in_n_notes (plus time t_sum))
          (when (gt (random 0 6) 3)
            (setq master (alter master)))))))))

(de alter (voice)
  (if (eq voice 'VOICE1) 'VOICE2 'VOICE1))

(de ajuste (voice in_n_notes the-time)
  (let ((reste ((car (voice ? 'active-children)) ? etime))
        (tsum ()) (list-t ()) (list-o ())
        (r-s (cdr (voice ? 'active-children))))
    (setq tsum reste)
    (let ((r-s r-s))
      (when (and (lt tsum the-time) r-s)
        (setq tsum (plus tsum (new1 list-t
          (apply (get new1 list-o (next1 r-s)) 'duration:)))))
        (self r-s)))
    (if (setq aux (sub tsum reste))
    (setq fact (div (sub the-time reste) (− tsum reste))))
    (mapc list-o (lambda (o) (put o 'duration: [lambda ()
                                (mul fact (next1 list-t))])))
)))
```

Stephen Travis Pope

# Introduction to MODE: The Musical Object Development Environment

The MODE (Musical Object Development Environment) is the result of several iterations of design, implementation, and evaluation of Smalltalk-80-based tool kits for musical score and sound processing and performance. The application areas of the software include sound and score editors, real-time algorithmic composition, and music performance front ends. One of the goals of this design is to offer a portable and open system for experimentation in composition and performance software design using techniques borrowed from the fields of artificial intelligence, computer graphics, and simulation. The system is also designed to support interchangeable ("pluggable") interactive front ends (e.g., graphical editors, or musical structure description languages) and back ends (e.g., MIDI output, sampled sound processing commands, sound compiler note-lists, or DSP coprocessor control). The current system achieves both power (real-time algorithmic composition systems and interactive score editing) and portability (the above systems running in compatible versions on several different hardware/OS platforms).

This document presents the design and implementation of the MODE and discusses several examples of its usage. It does not attempt to be a complete reference manual or to be a tutorial to the Smalltalk-80 Programming System or to the use of the MODE, both of which are beyond the scope of this format. Throughout this article, we assume the reader has some familiarity with the concepts of object-oriented programming (classes, inheritance, message-passing) and with the Smalltalk-80 programming system.

## What Is the MODE?

The MODE is a collection of software modules (object-oriented classes), for general sound, event, event list, and score processing as well as a music-

oriented user interface tool kit, embedded in the Smalltalk-80 Programming System (Goldberg and Robson 1989; Goldberg 1983)—a powerful, interactive, integrated programming environment. The MODE is designed to ease the implementation of music processing software and graphical sound, score, and musical structure editors. It is a re-implementation of the author's earlier package, the HyperScore ToolKit (Pope 1987), itself son of DoubleTalk (Pope 1986), son of ARA (Pope 1984). The types of applications envisioned for the MODE range from traditional score editors to experimental music structure editors, real-time hardware control, and non-real-time sound compiler kits.

The MODE is a software tool kit, i.e., a set of flexible and reusable components that are designed for extension and customization. It cannot and does not attempt to be "all things to all people" or to be any specific music-related software application. It is intended to be used by Smalltalk-80 programmers for building music representation languages, real-time performance systems, or new user interfaces for music applications. As the name implies, the MODE carries with it a "way of thinking" about music and composition much more strongly than its predecessors did. Whereas the previous systems strove for extreme generality, even at the expense of additional complexity and decreased power, the current MODE system makes the various decisions along the generality/power continuum much differently.

The MODE and its predecessors all stem from music software that was developed in the process of the author's realization of compositions using computer tools for the representation of the score. ARA was an outgrowth of the Lisp system used for *Bat out of Hell* (1983); DoubleTalk was based on the Smalltalk-80-based Petri net editing system used for *Requiem Aeternam dona Eis* (1986); and the HyperScore ToolKit's various versions were used (among others) for *Day* (1988). In each of these

Fig. 1. Representations for
music magnitudes.

| Magnitude model | | | |
| --- | --- | --- | --- |
| | **Pitch** | **Amplitude** | **Duration** |
| **Integer** | 36—key number | 64—MIDI velocity | 500—msec |
| **Float** | 440.0—frequency (Hz) | 0.7071—ampl. ratio | 1.0—sec. |
| **String** | 'a5'—note name | 'mf'—dynamic name | '1/2'—'beats' |
| **Fraction** | 3/2—ratio to 'root' | 1/3—ampl. ratio | 3/4—'beats' |

**Implementation model** (label at left of table, rows Integer/Float/String/Fraction)

cases, some amount of effort was spent—after the completion of the composition—to make the tools more general-purpose, often making them less useful for any particular task. In the MODE, which is based on the representations and tools used in the author's recent realization entitled *Kombination XI* (1990), this effort was minimized; the new package is much more useful for a much smaller set of tasks and attitudes about what music representation and composition are. If the MODE works well for other composers, it is because of its idiosyncratic approach rather than its attempted generality.

The system consists of Smalltalk-80 classes that address five areas: (1) the representation of musical parameters, sounds, events, and event lists; (2) description of middle-level musical structures; (3) real-time performance scheduling; (4) user interface components for building music processing applications; and (5) built-in end-user applications. I will address each of these areas in the sections below, introducing them in the object-oriented style according to their external behavior and internal state. As in Smalltalk-80 programming, class names are capitalized in this text.

## Smalltalk-80 Classes for Event and Score Processing

The intention of the MODE is to provide comprehensive note-, score-, and sound-processing functions, and tools for the rapid prototyping of new graphical or command-oriented user interfaces to music processing software packages built in an extensible programming environment. Using inheritance among Smalltalk-80 classes—the facility to

specify software modules (classes) as specialized versions of other modules (their superclasses)—one first defines very general (abstract) classes for the tool kit, then more specific (concrete) subclasses of these that have more specialized messages for their particular behavior. There are several sets of classes involved in the MODE kernel. They are organized into class meta-categories named *Magnitudes*, *Events* and *EventLists*, *Schedulers*, *Interfaces*, etc. Each of these categories of classes is introduced below.

### Music Magnitudes

MusicMagnitudes are a set of extensible abstract representations for the properties of musical events. The models include pitch, duration, and loudness. Examples of the use of music magnitudes are shown in Fig. 1. For each type of magnitude, we have shown some of the possible representations that are available. Note that each MusicMagnitude model (e.g., Pitch) can have several representations or units (e.g., MIDI key number, Hertz frequency value, or symbolic name). The central requirement of the MusicMagnitude classes is that they allow flexible use of these various representations within scores, providing a variety of declaration formats and conversion methods. The primary behavior of MusicMagnitude objects is provided by their inherited Magnitude protocol—the arithmetical and coercion messages of Magnitudes.

The objects used to represent these magnitudes can freely translate between their respective representations; for example one can define a note event to have the symbolic pitch of 'c3' (a note name) and, if this event is performed on a MIDI output device, the pitch can be transformed into MIDI key number 60. If one later decided to generate a Music-V format notelist file from this event list, the pitch could be transformed into the floating-point string value '261.623 Hz'. Only the drivers used for "playing" events ever have to be concerned with the actual representation of voice parameters, as will be described below. By using these types of abstract representations in scores, one can move towards portability of music representations.

After evaluating the previous implementations of MusicMagnitude classes, a new implementation strategy was decided upon (see Pope 1991a for an in-depth discussion of the design issues). The MODE defines two dimensions of class hierarchy called *model* and *representational* abstractions. The model types (e.g., Pitch or Loudness) are present as abstract classes which are not subclassed but which serve as the *species* for a family of concrete magnitudes. The new representational abstractions introduce assumptions about the type and range of the magnitude object's value, as shown in Fig. 2.

Concrete music magnitude classes (e.g., Hertz-Pitch) are now subclasses of one of the representational abstraction classes (e.g., NumericalMagnitude), and answer one of the model abstraction classes (e.g., Pitch) as their species. All mixed-mode arithmetic is now performed by defining a most general form for each species for use in cases where coercion is necessary, rather than using a scale of generality as was common in older Smalltalk systems. This kind of two-dimensional approach via separate superclass and species hierarchies (i.e., the model and representational abstraction layers) is seen as superior to a more traditional design using a multiple inheritance lattice. It results in a much simpler and cleaner MusicMagnitude implementation with more flexibility (Pope 1991a).

The OrdinalMagnitude classes shown in Fig. 2 are called *order-only* magnitudes. This means that they have no discernible values, but can be ordered in groups. One could, for example, define a magnitude called Length, which represents the experiential length of an event. Given a collection of named Length objects, one could define binary comparison relationships such that (e.g.) blink > inhale; inhale

> sigh, snap < blink; etc. The system maintains a table of these relationships so that one can sort or compare OrdinalMagnitude objects, e.g., asking whether blink > sigh (it is). OrdinalMagnitudes were used quite heavily in the realization of *Kombination XI* (Pope 1991b).

Functions of one variable are yet another type of MusicMagnitude (after a fashion). The MODE Function hierarchy includes line segment, exponential segment, spline segment, and Fourier summation Functions. Examples of the use of Function objects are presented below.

### Basic Event Classes

The classes whose instances are used for describing musical structures are Event and EventList. An event is simply an object that has a duration and possibly arbitrary other properties. The property list is accessible as a dictionary (i.e., by a symbolic key). EventList objects hold onto collections of events, sorted by start time; they are themselves types of events and can therefore be hierarchical (i.e., one event list can have another (sub-) event list as one of its event elements).

Events do not know their start time, which is always relative to some outer scope. This means that events can be shared among many event lists, the extreme case being an entire composition where one event is shared and mapped by many different event lists (Scaletti 1989). There is a small number of event subclasses, such as NoteEvent and EventList, rather than a large number of them for different types of input or output media (as in systems with MIDI, *cmusic*, and DSP event types). The primary messages that events understand are **duration: someDurationObject**—to set the duration time of the event to some Duration-type music magnitude—and property assessing messages such as **color: someColorObject**—to set the "color" (an arbitrary property) to an arbitrary value.

NoteEvent objects are like generic Events that represent musical notes with the default parameters *pitch*, *amplitude*, and *voice*. They understand messages for setting and querying their pitches, amplitudes, and voices, and the class NoteEvent

*Fig. 2. MODE Music-*
*Magnitude class hierarchy.*

Object—"root" of the inheritance hierarchy

    Magnitude—Smalltalk-80 abstract library class for scalar magnitudes

      Music Magnitude (value)

            (behavior for accessing, comparing, arithmetic, etc; coercion in terms of *mostGeneral*)

        Pitch—class creation message is a case statement which answers a species instance

            depending on value's class (e.g., SmallInteger -> MIDIPitch, Float -> HertzPitch,

            String -> SymbolicPitch (Concrete classes can of course be created explicitly.))

        Loudness—model for loudness species

        Duration—model for duration species

        NumberMagnitude—abstract class for MusicMagnitudes with numerical values

           IntervalMagnitude—abstract class that provides bounds-checking

              MIDIPitch (e.g., key 36) species = Pitch; mostGeneral = HertzPitch; range = 1..127

              MIDIVelocity (e.g., vel. 100) species = Amplitude; mostGeneral = RatioLoudness;

                    range = 0..127

           HertzPitch (e.g., 261.623 Hz.) species = Pitch, mostGeneral = self

           MSecondDuration (e.g., 254 ms.) species = Duration, mostGeneral = self

           RatioMagnitude—abstract class with instance variable for relative (anotherMagnitude)

              BeatDuration (e.g., 1/4 of aWholeNoteDuration)

               RatioPitch (e.g., 9/7 of aGivenCPitch)

              RatioLoudness (e.g., 1/21 of mySectionsLoudness)

        NominalMagnitude (class table)

           SymbolicPitch (e.g., 'c#3') species = Pitch; mostGeneral = HertzPitch

           SymbolicAmplitude (e.g., 'mp') species = Loudness; mostGeneral = RatioLoudness

        ConditionalDuration (value is a block e.g., [ :x | x > 40]) overrides arithmetic to compose blocks

        ParameterField (name) (e.g., PField name: #position field: 11 type: #Float4)

        OrdinalMagnitude (instance table)

           Sharpness (e.g., 'nasal' < 'sharp')

           Length (e.g., 'breath' > 'blink')

Fig. 3. State of a typical
EventList.

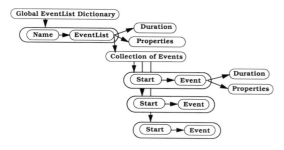

understands compact creation messages such as

**NoteEvent dur: 1.0 pitch: 'c#3' amp: 'mf'**

which will create and answer a new note event
with the given arguments as its parameters.

## Event Lists

Event lists are composite events; they hold onto a
collection of associations whose keys are durations
(the duration from the start of the event list to the
start of the association's event) and whose values
are events. Event lists can map their properties onto
their events (e.g., to use their pitch to transpose
their events). This structure is illustrated in Fig. 3.

Event lists can be hierarchical in that they can
contain sub-lists as elements to any depth. For large
compositions, the event list hierarchies can grow
quite large and deep. Event lists are named; that
is, they are given symbolic names and stored in a
global dictionary keyed by these names. This
makes them fundamentally persistent. Expressions
such as **EventList newNamed: 'scale'** for creation
and **EventList named: 'riff'** for later reference are
meaningful.

The primary messages to which event lists respond (in addition to the behavior they inherit by
being events), are **add: anEvent at: aTime**—to add
an event to the list (sorted by start time); **play**—
to play the event list on its voice; **edit**—to open a
graphical editor in the event list; and Smalltalk-80

collection iteration and enumeration messages such
as **select: [someBlock]**—to select the events that
satisfy the given block closure.

It is important to stress the uniformity of event
lists here. There are no fixed notions of scores, parts,
sections, tracks, measures, or voices in MODE;
they are all various compositions of parallel or
sequential event lists.

## Hierarchical Event Lists

Using the messages outlined above, I will now present an example of the creation of a simple event list
that contains several events and one sub-list. The
messages that one would send to create a simple
list consisting of an arpeggiated C-major triad followed by the C-major chord are shown in Fig. 4.
The structure of the resulting objects is similar to
the hierarchy example shown diagrammatically in
Fig. 5.

There are of course more comfortable and compact declaration formats for event lists, as well as
graphical editors for manipulating them and parsers
for reading and writing several popular storage formats, such as MIDI data streams, *cmusic* note lists
(CARL 1983), or Adagio scores (Dannenberg 1986).

## Links Between Events and Event Lists

Because events—and therefore event lists—can
have arbitrary properties attached to them, it is possible to describe links between events and event
lists that have some symbolic description. This is
done by adding a property whose symbolic name
is a relationship and whose value is another event
or event list. Just as we can send messages to assign values to arbitrary properties, e.g., **someEvent
color: #blue** to define the given event (the receiver
of the message) as being of the color blue, we can
also write **someEventList isVariationOf: some
OtherEventList** or **eventList1 isTonalAnswerTo:
eventList2**. Using these properties as a kind of
general-purpose link (in the hypermedia sense), one

Fig. 4. Example of Event
and EventList creation.

Fig. 5. Structure of an exemplary hierarchical
EventList.

```
el ← EventList newNamed: #demo1.                          "create a named event list"

el    add: (NoteEvent duration: 1000  pitch: 36  ampl: 100);   "add an event to it at time 0"

      add: (NoteEvent duration: 1000  pitch: 40  ampl: 100);   "add an event after the first..."

      add: (NoteEvent duration: 1000  pitch: 43  ampl: 100);

      add: (EventList new                          "add a sub-list to it with 3 simultaneous events"

            add: (NoteEvent  duration: 1000  pitch: 36  ampl: 100)  at: 0;

            add: (NoteEvent  duration: 1000  pitch: 36  ampl: 100)  at: 0;

            add: (NoteEvent  duration: 1000  pitch: 36  ampl: 100)  at: 0)
```

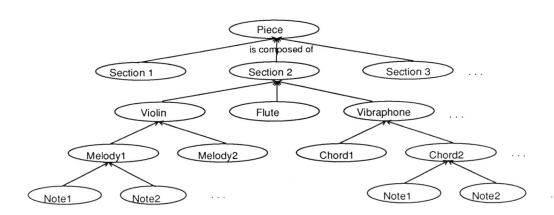

can build very powerful structures of events and event lists. Two of the most common uses of this facility are to create event lists that contain multiple types of structural or analytical information in their links (as implied by the two example messages shown above—**isVariationOf:** and **isTonal-AnswerTo:**) and to create event lists that include their previous version (using link types such as **used-ToBe:**). An example of the use of this facility is demonstrated by the EventList structure shown in Fig. 6. Note that the blurring of the distinction between properties of events and event lists and links within an event list hierarchy is intended.

**Support for Sampled Sounds**

The MODE has simple classes to support sampled sounds as properties of Events. The Sound class permits the reading and writing of a number of sound file formats, and maintains a list of named cue points within a sound. The various editors for Sounds provide the basic *cut/copy/paste/resample* functionality. Instead of building a large sound mixing and signal processing library, the MODE currently generates scripts in the form of note lists in the cmusic language for larger sound processing tasks (Pope 1991b).

Fig. 6. *Structure of links*
*within an EventList.*

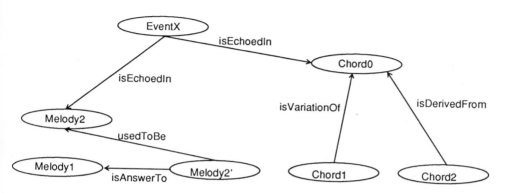

## Representing Middle-Level Musical Structures

The event hierarchy of the MODE has evolved to encompass classes that describe what we call "middle-level" musical structures (Pope 1989a, 1989b). These are representations of the nouns that are used in the musical jargon to describe musical structures—e.g., cluster, chord, ostinato, mordent, crescendo, or rubato. These objects are extremely useful for characterizing musical structures that fall into the categories provided in the system (or added by a user) in very compact formats. One can, for example, describe a chorale using the chord classes or a popular song using the ostinato classes in a few lines of declarative statements (see Pope 1989a for examples).

### Event Generators and Event Modifiers

In order to represent simple musical structures as special types of event lists, we define two abstract classes—EventGenerator and EventModifier—for creating objects that are capable either of generating event lists upon demand, given some algorithmic description, or of effecting the performance or properties of other event lists.

Most of the description examples in the vocabulary list above can be implemented in a simple set of event generator classes. The challenge is to make an easily extensible framework for composers whose compositional process will consist of enriching the event generator hierarchy for a specific composition. Event generators can generally either return an event list, or behave like processes and be told to play or to stop playing. We view this dichotomy between views of event generators as event lists versus event generators as processes as a part of the domain, and differentiate on the basis of the musical abstractions. It might, for example, be appropriate to view an ostinato as a process that can be started and stopped, or to ask it to play thrice and return an event list.

### Abstract Event Generators

The list-like event generators have messages such as **eventList** for returning an event list (which can be edited, played, etc.). The process-like event generators are more likely to have **start**, **stop**, and **playTimes:** messages. The abstract classes we choose for modeling the most abstract categorization of EventGenerators are *Cluster*—a description of the pitch or rhythm set of a one-dimensional group of events; *Cloud*—a pitch-time surface for stochastic or procedural selection; and *Ostinato*—a repetition of an event list as a process.

Fig. 7. Exemplary hierar-
chy of Cluster Event-
Generators.

Cluster—create with an arbitrary pitch set given a pitch or an event

        primary behavior: answer an event list

  Chord—create with a root and an inversion

    ... any number of chord classes (one method each for instance creation) ...

  Arpeggio—give it a cluster or chord and a delay time

  Roll—give it a note and it will repeat it

   Trill—give it an event list

   Mordent—melismatic embellishment of a note

   ... any number of embellishment description classes ...

## Clusters

The Cluster classes describe a one-dimensional collection of pitches or rhythms (i.e., their events occur simultaneously or are repetitions of the same event). The instance creation messages of these classes allow users to describe clusters in terms of their pitch set, or their structure (e.g., root, type, and inversion). Concrete types of Clusters include chords and arpeggii. An exemplary class hierarchy of Clusters is shown in Fig. 7.

Clusters also have instance creation messages for managing pitch and/or time lists separately; a Cluster will usually have one of these without the other and thus represent either a pure pitch set or rhythm. There are standard event list messages for mapping pitch and time among event list types, so that Clusters with pitch only or time only can be quite useful.

## Clouds

The notion of Clouds comes from aleatoric music, in which collections of notes can be described by their contour or selection criteria. Aleatoric generators that select notes from a given range or set of pitches can be modeled as types of Clouds. The class hierarchy of Clouds might resemble the tree shown in Fig. 8.

Cloud objects are quite useful in the composition style called *rapid prototyping and incremental refinement* or *composition by refinement* (Pope 1989a); they can be used to generate weakly structured material which is later refined or filtered through a multi-step process.

## Ostinati

Process-oriented generators usually take the form of Ostinati, repeating versions or variations of a given set of material or process input parameters. The simple Ostinato repeats an event list as long as it runs; the other two types (Markhov- and SelectionOstinati) make variations based on either transition tables or controlled random selection. More complex processes can be used for writing algorithmic composition classes as event generators. Mark Lentczner's bell peal classes—which implement the rules of ringing the changes—fit nicely into the hierarchy here. The class hierarchy of Ostinati might look like the example displayed in Fig. 9.

The process of composing with the MODE often includes defining new, composition-specific types of event lists, generators, and/or modifiers by specializing existing classes (e.g., inventing new kinds of special chords and progressions).

## EventModifiers

The MODE provides an EventModifier class in order to model objects that hold onto a Function ob-

Fig. 8. Exemplary hierar-
chy of Cloud Event-
Generators.

Fig. 9. Exemplary hierar-
chy of Ostinato Event-
Generators.

Cloud—abstract class

    PodCloud—give it pitch, amplitude and voice ranges for selection

                (à la Barry Truax's POD system)

      DynamicPodCloud—give it starting and ending ranges

    SelectionCloud—give it pitch, amplitude and voice sets for selection

      DynamicSelectionCloud—give it starting and ending pitch/rhythm sets


Ostinato—general repeater

    MarkhovOstinato—uses transition tables for repetition

    SelectionOstinato—selects notes from the given event list

    ... any number of algorithmic EventGenerators here ...

BellPeal—Generators that ring the changes (courtesy of Mark Lentczner)

ect and a property name so that they may apply the function to the specified property of an Event or an EventList. EventModifiers may be defined as *eager* or *lazy,* meaning that they should apply their functions as soon as they are given an EventList (eager) or that they should wait until scheduling time to perform their operation (lazy). No meaningful subclasses of EventModifier have been discovered as yet. Figure 10 concludes with an example of the application of a function to a property of an EventList, as might be encapsulated by an EventModifier.

## Examples Sending Event and EventList Messages

Using the messages to the basic classes described above, one can make scripts (programs) of messages to Events, EventLists, and Functions to describe simple musical processes. It is important to note that the complete protocol of these classes is rich and that only a few exemplary messages are listed here.

The Smalltalk-80 environment provides many useful messages to all objects, such as **inspect** (open an interactive inspector window on an object), **storeOn:** (write an object out on a stream in source format), **printOn:** ("pretty-print" an object on a stream), **edit** (use default editor), do: (iterate over an object's components), and **browse** (open a source

code browser on messages available to object). Figure 10 illustrates several commented usage examples of Event and EventList objects in the MODE.

## Example Hierarchical EventLists

Figure 11 shows a simple hierarchical event list—the one created by the program fragment in Fig. 4. Note that the hierarchy could easily be much deeper (having special levels to represent voices, parts, measures, instrument families, and the like) and/or wider (e.g., a large-scale piece modeled down to the note-event level), and that there is no limitation to this figure's treeness; it can be an arbitrarily dense lattice, and it often is quite dense in practice.

## Event Scheduling and Performance

Two areas that merit special attention are the real-time scheduling of event input/output and the generation of timbre parameters. The MODE uses special classes for representing schedulers and voices.

The EventScheduler class developed by Mark Lentczner is quite straightforward. Instances of

Fig. 10. Examples of the
use of Events and Event-
Lists.

```
"Demonstrate MusicMagnitudes"
    (Duration value: 1/16) asMS          "answers 62"
    (Pitch value: 36) asHertz            "answers 261.623"
    (Amplitude value: 'ff') asMidi       "answers 106"


"NoteEvent creation examples"
    (NoteEvent dur: 1/4 pitch: 'c3' ampl: 'mf') inspect
    ((NoteEvent dur: 1/4 pitch: 'c3' ampl: 'mf') color: #green; accent: #sforzando) inspect



"Smalltalk-80 program to make a list called 'random1' with 20 random notes"
    | pattern rand |
    pattern ← EventList newNamed: #random1.
    rand ← Random new.
    20 timesRepeat:
        [pattern add:
            (NoteEvent
                dur: 50 + ((rand next * 100) truncated)      "50-150 ms duration"
                pitch: 30 + ((rand next * 30) truncated)     "pitch range = MIDI 30-60"
                ampl: 50 + ((rand next * 60) truncated))]    "amplitude range = 50-110"


"Now make random1 legato (double the durations)."
    (EventList named: #random1) notesDo:
        [ :anEvent |
        anEvent duration: (anEvent duration * 2)]



"EventGenerator examples: A simple progression—C Major cadence."
    (EventList newNamed: #progression1)
        add: ((Chord majorTetradOn: 'c4' inversion: 0) duration: 1/2);
        add: ((Chord majorTetradOn: 'f3' inversion: 2) duration: 1/2);
        add: ((Chord majorTetradOn: 'g3' inversion: 1) duration: 1/2);
        add: ((Chord majorTetradOn: 'c4' inversion: 0) duration: 1/2)
```

"A Trill example—play 2 seconds of 40 msec. long notes on c5 and d5."
    ((Trill length: 2.0 rhythm: 40 notes: #(48 50))  ampl: 100) play

"A static stochastic wave/cloud."
    (Cloud dur: 2.0  "duration"
            pitch: (48 to: 64)      "pitch range—an interval"
            ampl: (80 to: 120)    "amplitude range—an interval"
            voice: (1 to: 8)       "voice range—an interval"
            density: 15)         "density per second = 15 notes"

"A static selection cloud."
    (SelectionCloud dur: 2
            pitch: #('c3' 'f3' 'g3' 'a4' 'c4')    "select from this pitch array"
            ampl: #('f' 'f' 'mf')          "and this array of amplitude values"
            voice: #(0 1 2 6)           "and these voices"
            density: 16)            "rate per second"

"Pentatonic selection that makes a transition from one chord to another."
    (DynamicSelectionCloud dur: 9
            pitch: #( #(40 43 45) #(53 57 60))    "starting and ending pitch sets"
            ampl: #(80 80 120)          "static amplitude set"
            voice: #(1 3 5 7)            "and voice set"
            density: 20)

"Function usage example—make a roll-type eventList and apply a crescendo/decrescendo to it."
    | temp fcn |
    temp ← EventList newNamed: #test3.    "Create a new named EventList."
    (0 to: 4000 by: 50) do:         "Add 20 notes per second for 4 seconds."
        [ :index |              "Add the same note"
        temp add: (NoteEvent dur: 100 pitch: 36 ampl: 100) at: index].
    fcn ← LinSeg from: #((0 @ 0) (0.5 @ 1) (1 @ 0)).   "Create a line segment function."
                           "x@y is Smalltalk-80 point creation short-hand"
    temp apply: fcn to: #loudness.       "Apply the function to the loudness of the EventList."

Fig. 11. Example inspector on a hierarchical Event-List.

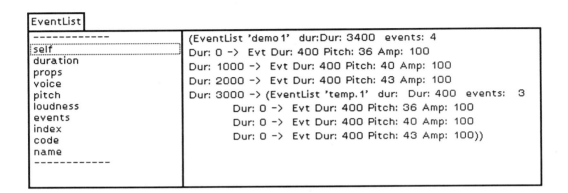

```
┌─────────────┐
│EventList│
├─────────────┬────────────────────────────────────────────────────┐
│------------ │(EventList 'demo1'  dur:Dur: 3400  events: 4         │
│self         │Dur: 0 -> Evt Dur: 400 Pitch: 36 Amp: 100           │
│duration     │Dur: 1000 -> Evt Dur: 400 Pitch: 40 Amp: 100        │
│props        │Dur: 2000 -> Evt Dur: 400 Pitch: 43 Amp: 100        │
│voice        │Dur: 3000 -> (EventList 'temp.1' dur: Dur: 400 events: 3│
│pitch        │        Dur: 0 -> Evt Dur: 400 Pitch: 36 Amp: 100   │
│loudness     │        Dur: 0 -> Evt Dur: 400 Pitch: 40 Amp: 100   │
│events       │        Dur: 0 -> Evt Dur: 400 Pitch: 43 Amp: 100)) │
│index        │                                                    │
│code         │                                                    │
│name         │                                                    │
│------------ │                                                    │
└─────────────┴────────────────────────────────────────────────────┘
```

EventScheduler can be sent appointments to queue in time-sorted order. Each appointment is a Small-talk-80 association object whose key is a time (a Duration object) and whose value is an Event or an EventList. When running, the scheduler sends scheduling messages to its clients (the appointments' values) at their key times. All Event subclasses know how to play themselves in response to scheduling messages.

Event objects that wish to be scheduled multiple times (such as event lists or event generators) can return duration objects to the scheduler in response to the scheduling messages that will cause them to be re-added to the appointment list. Executing a schedule is now reduced to the act of selecting the next event (or event list or event generator) in the appointment book, sending it the **scheduleAt:** message (which will cause it to be played), and possibly adding it to the appointment book again (if it wants to be rescheduled).

## Voices and Parameter Mapping

One of the shortcomings of many modern computer music systems is that scores are not portable among composition software packages. This means that a score that was generated using a MIDI-oriented score editor will probably not be playable with a sound compiler such as *cmusic*. This is often caused by the encoding of instrument-specific or synthesis-method-specific information in the score or note list. Another related issue is the existence of several widely used standard machine-readable music representations, including Music-V-style or SCORE-style note lists, the CMU Adagio language, DARMS, and several different MIDI-data formats. Modern music software should be expected to adapt well to input and/or output data in these formats.

One way to get around this is to encode the properties of events in an abstract symbolic form and to expand these into device-specific or output-format-specific parameters at the last possible moment. The solution worked out for the MODE (originally suggested by Lounette Dyer) is to have notes hold onto their voices and to have voices played on their respective instruments. The voice and the instrument will then take over the tasks of mapping the note's symbolic parameter information (such as being *mezzoforte* or being bowed *con legno*) onto concrete synthesis parameters for the specific instrument driver used. This allows the same score to be performed on a real-time MIDI synthesizer or on special-purpose synthesis hardware (such as the sound chips found in many personal computers today), or to be translated into a notelist for a non-real-time software sound synthesis language. The object state for scheduling a NoteEvent object onto a MIDI output port is shown schematically in Fig. 12, which shows an example of the state of a NoteEvent that is holding onto a MIDIVoice object.

*Fig. 12. State of the note-voice-port mapping for MIDI voices.*

*Fig. 13. Concrete example of playing a flute note onto a MidiPort.*

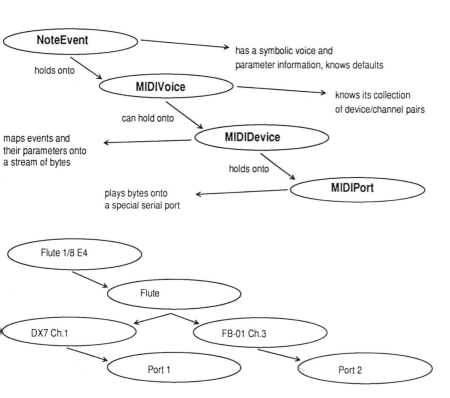

This in turn holds onto a MIDIDevice, which holds onto a MIDIPort object. Figure 13 shows a concrete example for a flute note whose voice uses channel 1 of the DX7 synthesizer on port 1 and channel 3 of the FB-01 synthesizer on port 2. In Fig. 14, the same flute note is being "played" onto a *cmusic*-format notelist file. Here, the voice holds onto one or more instrument objects (for parameter mapping) and a Stream object (for writing its output to a file).

### Examples of the Use of Voices

Figure 15 illustrates an example of the use of Voice objects for the performance of a Chord object over several output devices. The actions that are necessary to play an event list within the MODE are shown in Fig. 16. In it, the message-passing stack that leads from the event list editor controller's receiving the message **play** (presumably sent from a menu message) all the way down to the MIDI port sending out an array of three bytes for the note-on command is presented with comments describing the intermediate-level messages. These levels include the user interface messages, the Event-Scheduler operations, and the event-voice-device mapping.

## User Interface Tools for Music Software

The Smalltalk-80 programming system includes software classes that facilitate the design of interactive, graphics-based, and menu-based software user

*Introduction to MODE*

*Fig. 14. Voice output mapping for cmusic voices.*

*Fig. 15. Examples of the use of the Voice and Device classes.*

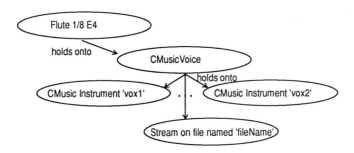

aDX7 ← MidiDevice onPort: (MidiPort newOn: 1).    "Set up a new device driver for a DX7."

anOboe ← MidiVoice onDevice: aDX7 channel: 6.    "Open a voice on it."

aChord ← Chord majorTriadOn: 'C4' duration: 2.    "Define a new chord (EventList)."

aChord playOn: anOboe.    "Play it on the given voice."
aChord voice: anOboe; play    "Set its voice and play it."

anFB01 ← MidiDevice onPort: (MidiPort newOn: 1). "Set up a new device driver for an FB01."
anOboe addVoiceOnDevice: anFB01 channel: 3.    "Add another device to the voice."
aChord play.    "Play the Chord again."

    "Create a named formatted file voice."
CmusicVoice newNamed: #k11 onStream: ('k11.2a.sc' asFilename writeStream)
aCmusicFile ← Voice named: #k11.
aChord playOn: aCmusicFile.    "Play the chord on it."
aCmusicFile close.    "Close the File."

Fig. 16. Message-passing
for playing an EventList on
a MIDIDevice.

A Controller receives the play message (e.g., from a pop-up menu or button).

EventListEditorController >> play

It forwards the message to its model, an EventListEditor.

EventListEditor >> play

It forwards to its model, an EventList.

EventList >> play

The EventList plays its Events on its default voice.

EventList >> playOn: aVoice at: startTime

This is passed on to the EventScheduler.

EventScheduler class >> runAppointments

Who starts running by calling the appointments of the shared global schedule.

EventScheduler >> callNextAppointment

The Schedule plays the Events in the Queue.

NoteEvent >> scheduleAt: startTime

Who schedule themselves on their voices.

MidiVoice >> playEvent: someEvent at: startTime

Who pass the events on to their (the voices's) devices.

MidiDevice >> play: someEvent on: aPort

Who decide what MIDI commands to generate (e.g., noteOn, noteOff).

MidiDevice >> playNoteOn: someEvent on: aPort

Who finally send some bytes out the MIDI port.

MidiPort >> sendBuffer: someMIDICommandByteArray

Fig. 17. Three-part MVC
structure.

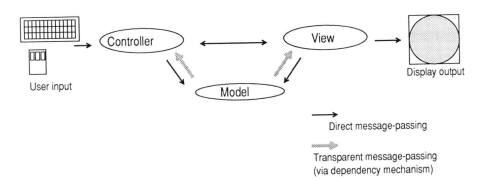

Fig. 17. Three-part MVC
structure.

interfaces. The system's Model/View/Controller (MVC) application framework (Krasner and Pope 1988) is a methodology for implementing flexible, easily configurable (pluggable) user interfaces using the interaction paradigms of browsing, editing, and inspecting. The division of a software package into a *Model* (main domain-specific objects and algorithms), a *View* (display presentation procedures), and a *Controller* (user interaction and manipulation components) aids in the rapid development and evaluation of experimental integrated applications.

The user interface side of the MODE is based on the use of the MVC framework to provide abstract and concrete tools for the design of graphical score, event, and structure editors and interaction panels. Users develop and configure new event and event list editors by selecting and "plugging together" components from a library of view and controller objects to create their own customized applications tools.

**Three Versions of MVC**

The traditional three-part MVC architecture is illustrated in Fig. 17, which shows a model object representing the state and the behavior of the domain model. The view object presents the state of the model on the display, and the controller object sends messages to the model and/or the view in response to user input. Note the separation of modeling, presentation, and interaction, and the loose

coupling (via the Smalltalk-80 dependency mechanism) between the model and the view/controller.

Many Smalltalk-80 applications extend this structure somewhat by adding a fourth object to separate the selection state of the application from the model, as shown in Fig. 18. These intermediary objects are normally called *browsers, inspectors,* or *editors.* This separation has the important effect of allowing "multiple viewing," whereby more than one browser, inspector, or editor may operate on a given model, because the model does not know about the selection or the viewing state.

A further extension of the MVC architecture, developed by Adele Goldberg, David Leibs, and the author, is Navigator MVC (Pope, Goldberg, and Leibs 1988; Pope, Harter, and Pier 1989). The fundamental feature of this architecture is that all interactive applications are modeled as display list (i.e., structured graphics) editors with some method of translating the model structure into a graphical display list representation and of translating display list interaction into model manipulation. The generic application is now seen as a "smart version of MacDraw."

The central structure is then like that shown in Fig. 19, with the view holding a display list (and probably also a cached bit map of the view's contents). The Editor holds the model (subject), a LayoutManager (for generating the display list from the model's structure), and a StructureAccessor (for accessing the model via a well-known protocol such as tree-like or graph-like messages). Navigator

*Pope*

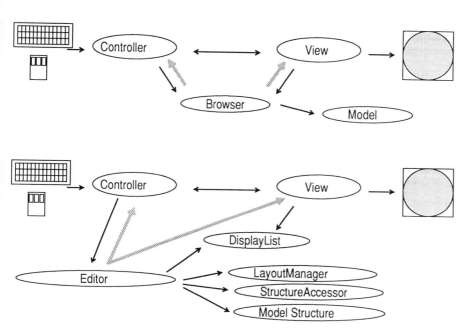

MVC has been used for the construction of user interfaces for a wide variety of application areas and has been demonstrated to be very powerful and extensible, with the added cost of its complexity and its library size.

### The MODE Implementation of Navigator MVC

The implementation of the Navigator framework in the current MODE system includes several class hierarchies. The classes DisplayItem, DisplayList, DisplayListView, PagingDisplayListView, DisplayListEditor, and DisplayListController support abstract structured graphics display lists and editing. The rich hierarchy of LayoutManager classes supports list, outline, tree, sequence, pitch/time, and other layouts, as is illustrated by the hierarchy tree shown in Fig. 20.

The relevance of the Navigator MVC architecture to users of the MODE is that a wide range of graphical user interfaces to structured information models can be constructed with a relatively small amount of customization of LayoutManager and DisplayListController classes. A LayoutManager must simply be able to take a data structure and a corresponding structure accessor and generate a structured graphics display list for the desired visualization of the structure. Tree-like structures can, for example, be viewed and edited as indented lists (outlines), or as left- or top-rooted trees, with very little additional programming effort. The examples in Pope, Harter, and Pier 1989 demonstrate this in more detail.

The use of the Navigator framework in the editors for *Kombination XI* is demonstrated by the class hierarchy as shown in Fig. 21. The primary branches of this hierarchy are event-oriented time lines, sample-oriented time lines, and tree structure editors. The event-oriented time-line representations assume that the x-dimension is a time scale; in the usual case, the y-dimension is used to show the pitch of events—as in common-practice Western music notation. Figure 22 shows a MODE Pitch-

LayoutManager (view orientation itemAccessor)—the abstract class

    HierarchyLayoutManager (length xStep yStep treeAccessor)—assumes model understands tree-style accessing messages

        BinaryTreeLayoutManager—assumes a binary tree

            LeafLinearTreeLayoutManager—lays out leaves in a line

                TRTreeLayoutManager (sequenceView)—special knowledge of TRTree node types

            TreeLayoutManager—general-purpose tree layout

        IndentedListLayoutManager—lays out hierarchies as outlines

            IndentedTreeLayoutManager (list)—outline-tree layout

    SequenceLayoutManager (timeScale timeOffset)—assumes left-to-right sequential layout in time

        GroupingLayoutManager (levelScale)—shows hierarchical grouping of events

        PitchTimeLayoutManager (pitchScale pitchOffset)—shows pitch as the y-coordinate

            CMNLayoutManager (stepArray staffTop)—approximated common-practise Western music notation

        PositionTimeLayoutManager—shows left/right position as y-coordinate


SequenceViews—display list view where x = time

    PitchTimeViews—SequenceView where y = pitch

        Hauer-Steffens, CMN, other subclasses...

    PhraseViews—spoken utterance editing, derivation of prosidic stress trees

    GroupingViews—display hierarchy of event lists

SampledSoundEditor classes

    Mix/Fade/Cross-fade sampled sound files, optionally generate sound file mixing scripts for cmusic

Location Editors

    PositionTimeViews, Panning EventGenerators and cmusic output

T-R EventList Editors for Sampled Sounds

    Support for TreeNodes, TRTree creation, derivation and application

Fig. 22. MODE Pitch-Time
view.

Fig. 23. MODE Hauer-Stef-
fens view.

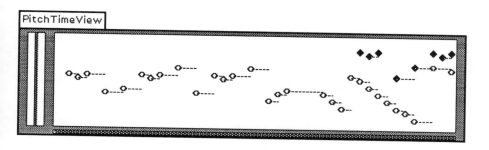

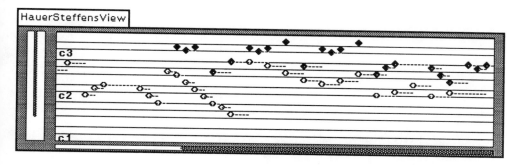

TimeView which displays an example of a Bach fugue. Figures 23 and 24 show other examples of pitch-time representations; in Fig. 23, one can see an example of the notation developed in the 1920s by Josef Matthias Hauer and Walter Steffens (Vogt 1972). Figure 24 is an example of a simple editor for common-practice Western music notation. The SampledSound views and PositionTime views are other time-line oriented representations, as shown in Figs. 25 and 26.

The power of the system becomes more apparent when one looks into the more advanced structure editors, such as the so-called phrase editor displayed in Fig. 27. In this example, a prosodic stress tree is shown above the event list of the phrase it is derived from. This example from *Kombination XI* shows the processing of the word *Dunkelkammer-gespräche* in order to change its inflection using the phrase vocoder. The prosodic stress tree shown in Fig. 27 is presented in the style of prolongational reduction trees as defined in Lerdahl and Jacken-

doff 1983. Its weights and branch types are derived from the assignment of "strength" magnitudes (an OrdinalMagnitude subclass) to the syllables of the word. In order to generate and display a concrete tree, the system maps these valueless strength magnitudes to integers in the range 0–100. These weights can be edited by dragging nodes of the tree in the editor view. The tree and/or its value array can then be stored for further use, e.g., to select weights or positions of another event list via mapping of the weights onto another parameter.

**Extensions to interaction and "Look and Feel"**

Much of the customization work of building a new event list editor within the MODE often goes into customizing the interaction and manipulation mechanisms, rather than just the layout of standard pluggable view components. Users can easily extend the range of interaction paradigms, building

*Fig. 24. MODE CMN view.*     *Fig. 25. MODE Sampled-*
*Sound view and inspector.*

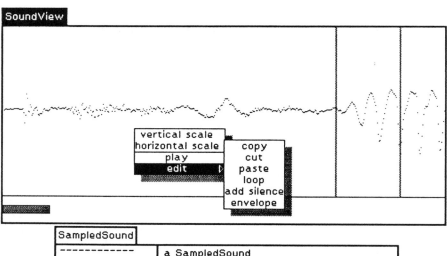

*Fig. 26. MODE Position-
Time view*

*Fig. 27. MODE Phrase-
Editor with TRTree and
Phrase views on* Dunkel-
kammergespräche.

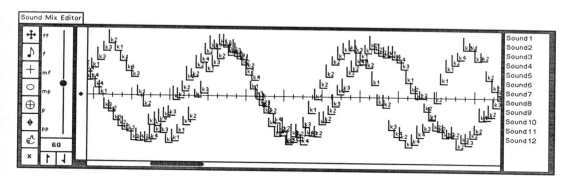

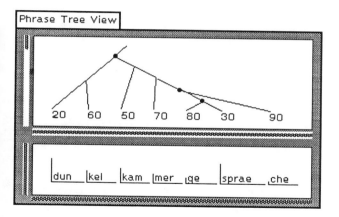

editors with powerful "accelerators" or macro capabilities, or mixed editor/inspector views.

To reiterate: the interesting feature of these editors is not that they represent state-of-the-art user interfaces, but rather that they are "soft" user interfaces based on a highly customizable framework, and that non-expert programmers can design and implement their own notations using this framework.

There are three primary extension mechanisms for MODE user interfaces: building new structure representations, customizing the interaction in existing editors, and providing new "look and feel" for existing editors. The steps for constructing new structure representations were outlined above and

usually consist of the specialization of existing LayoutManager and StructureAccessor classes. Customizing the interactive behavior of existing applications typically means changing the interaction methods in an application's DisplayListController class. Moving an application to a new "look and feel" consists of changing the DisplayListView subclass's instance creation method to use different subview layout and user interface "widget" objects.

## Applications and Composition Methodologies

Using MODE for composition has an effect on the composer just as is the case for any other instrument or tool. The three major features of the MODE that have some effect on the user's mode of application of the system are its basic data structures (the MusicMagnitude, Event, and EventList abstractions), the support for "composition by refinement" of musical structures using extensions to the set of EventGenerator and EventModifier classes, and the related issue of the dynamicity of representation possible in the system. As was stated at the beginning of this article, the model MODE user is a composer with some Smalltalk-80 programming experience who is willing to learn a new system and library in order to be able to customize his or her environment in terms of the basic music representation language and structure visualization tools.

## Related Work

The realm of music representation languages and high-level composer's software tools has advanced greatly over the six-year development history of the MODE and its predecessors. Several systems warrant mention because of their influence on various aspects of the MODE, their visibility in the literature, or their availability in the community.

Mark Lentczner's 1985 SoundKit tools (Lentczner 1985) were Smalltalk-80-based sampled sound processing classes which ran on Apple Macintosh computers with real-time sound and event I/O. This impressed me and convinced me of the possibility of real-time performance using Smalltalk —which I had not attempted until then. SoundKit also provided novel user interface ideas, several of which I "borrowed" over the next few years.

The various IRCAM MIDI-Lisp systems (Boynton et al. 1986a) provided examples of large-scale, general-purpose, relatively portable systems for composition in a wide range of styles. This goal was taken over for the five versions of the HyperScore ToolKit, and was maintained (with the exception of relaxing the constraint of "general-purposeness") in the MODE. The more recent systems built on top of this environment, such as PREFORM (Boynton et al. 1986b) and Esquisse (Baisnee et al. 1988), extend the range of representation to higher levels and in-

tegrate much of the behavior of the earlier FORMES package/environment. One of the most interesting elements of the design Esquisse, which I am still trying to understand and apply in a meaningful way, is the effort to bridge the synthesis/processing and timbre/event barriers with powerful and scalable models. FORMES (Rodet and Cointe 1984) was the first system I knew of that allowed a strictly hierarchical description of large musical structures in an object-oriented message-passing environment. Many of the ideas present in FORMES, as well as numerous discussions with its developers and hours spent playing with it, had major effects on the development of the ARA/DoubleTalk/HyperScore/MODE family of systems.

The other well-known Lisp-based music description languages and real-time processing systems, such as Flavors Band (Fry 1984), Canon (Dannenberg 1989), Common Music (Taube 1991), and the Lisp Kernel (Rahn 1990), all have much in common with the MODE. There are primary differences in the basic models, however, in that the MODE is the only one of these to present abstract models of music magnitudes for ensuring portability of scores, interoperability of applications, and a uniform model of event lists for the construction of densely interconnected hierarchies of parallel and sequential events. The notions of "phrase processors" (from Flavors Band) and "item streams" (from Common Music) have much in common with the MODE's EventGenerators and EventModifiers. The primary difference here is the intent of the EventGenerator and EventModifier hierarchies to model the structure of the musical vocabulary and to be an easily extensible system in which much of the work of composition takes place in terms of the development of new classes of generators or modifiers.

Carla Scaletti's Kyma system (Scaletti 1989) is another powerful Smalltalk-80-based composition environment that takes a radically different approach to many of the basic questions of the design of software tools for composition, but somehow the MODE and Kyma ended up being rather similar in many respects. The notions related to "composition by refinement," as mentioned above, are present as the main mode of interaction in Kyma as well, and the MODE is gradually breaking down the event list/event/timbre differentiations in much the same way as Kyma does.

With respect to much of the rest of the literature in "music input languages" or composers tools (e.g., the various Forth-based or C-based systems), it is important to stress again that the MODE is an open and flexible system, written in a very simple object-oriented programming language, which is embedded in a large, powerful, and extremely uniform programming system with a highly integrated software development environment. The issues of uniformity of programming languages, power of the object-oriented class libraries, and integration of the programming environment are discussed further in Goldberg and Pope 1989.

## Conclusions and Future Directions

The first-level goal of designing the MODE was to design a flexible and extensible set of basic tools in the Smalltalk-80 system as a framework for music software and user interface experimentation. The capability of the system to support comprehensive applications, such as interactive algorithmic performers and intelligent composer's assistants, has been demonstrated. Among the areas not addressed by the present article are the processing of sampled sounds, the construction of sound compilers, graphical music programming languages, high-quality music printing, and end-user applications.

As with several of its predecessors, MODE's main drawbacks are its size, both in terms of the complexity of its idiosyncratic vocabulary and in terms of lines of code, and the fact that it is embedded in (constructed upon) the Objectworks for Smalltalk-80 programming environment (which is both a blessing and a curse). New users can skirt the complexity issue by learning single subsystems one at a time; the environment issue is one that I am very reticent to confront, as I feel much the same way about the Objectworks for Smalltalk-80 programming system as Churchill felt about democracy (i.e., it's the worst possible system, aside from all the other systems that have been tried).

The current directions of MODE development involve enlarging the basic tool kit through addi-tional messages to the abstract classes, constructing more example front ends and task-language scripts, and embedding the entire system in a new view composition framework to allow for the use of graphical view layout tools. The intention in documenting and releasing the tool kit and its support classes is to offer a portable, high-level, integrated development environment for new computer music software and to facilitate experimental user interface design for event, score, and sound processing.

The system has been implemented to be portable among Smalltalk-80 interpreter implementations (version 2.0 or later) and has been tested on a variety of different microcomputers and engineering workstations. The newest version has been moved onto Objectworks for Smalltalk-80 release 4 from ParcPlace Systems, Inc., and makes use of many of the new release 4 language and library features, thus sacrificing backward compatibility altogether.

## Acknowledgments

It would be extremely unfair to present the design and/or the implementation of the MODE as my work alone. Over several years and versions of the HyperScore ToolKit, a number of users and programmers contributed design input, class implementations, and user interfaces to the system. Among those who were most present during the process are Mark Lentczner (whose scheduler is still the simplest Smalltalk-based one in use), Lee Boynton and Guy Garnett (who contributed the primitive scheduler used for MIDI performance), John Maloney (who sent in extensions to many parts of the system), Glen Diener and Danny Oppenheim (whose applications showed many of the weaknesses of the system), and Hitoshi Katta and John Tangney (both of whom contributed new implementations of important system components). Designs and ideas for parts of the system were also taken from the writings of, and numerous delightful discussions with, Roger Dannenberg, Lounette Dyer, D. Gareth Loy, and Bill Schottstaedt.

I would also like to specifically thank Jan Witt of PCS/Cadmus Computers GmbH in Munich and Adele Goldberg and Glenn Krasner of ParcPlace

Systems, Inc., in Mountain View, California, for their support (well, toleration at least) for the ongoing development of otherwise quite useless tools for composition, even within the framework of the software development teams of start-up companies.

## References

Baisnee, P.-F., et al. 1988. "Esquisse: A Compositional Environment." In *Proceedings of the 1988 International Computer Music Conference.* San Francisco: Computer Music Association.

Boynton, L., et al. 1986a. "MIDI-Lisp: A LISP-Based Music Programming Environment for the Macintosh." In *Proceedings of the 1986 International Computer Music Conference.* San Francisco: Computer Music Association.

Boynton, L., et al. 1986b. "Adding a Graphical Interface to FORMES." In *Proceedings of the 1986 International Computer Music Conference.* San Francisco: Computer Music Association.

Buxton, W., et al. 1978. *The Structured Sound Synthesis Project (SSSP): An Introduction.* Technical Report CSRG-92, University of Toronto.

Computer Audio Research Laboratory. 1983. *CARL Software Startup Kit.* San Diego: CARL, Center for Music Experiment, University of California.

Dannenberg, R. 1986. "The CMU MIDI Toolkit." In *Proceedings of the 1986 International Computer Music Conference.* San Francisco: Computer Music Association.

Dannenberg, R. 1986. "The Canon Score Language." *Computer Music Journal* 13(1): 47–56.

Fry, C. 1984. "Flavors Band: A language for Specifying Musical Style." *Computer Music Journal* 8(4): 20–34. Also in this volume.

Goldberg, A., and D. Robson. 1989. *Smalltalk-80: The Language.* Menlo Park: Addison-Wesley.

Goldberg, A. 1983. *Smalltalk 80: The Interactive Programming Environment.* Menlo Park: Addison-Wesley.

Goldberg, A., and S. T. Pope. 1989. "Object-Oriented Programming is Not Enough!" *American Programmer: Ed Yourdon's Software Journal* 2(7): 46–59.

Krasner, G., and S. T. Pope. 1988. "A Cookbook for Using the Model-View-Controller User Interface Paradigm in Smalltalk-80." *Journal of Object-Oriented Programming* 1(3): 26–49.

Lentczner, M. 1985. "SoundKit: A Smalltalk Sound Manipulator." In *Proceedings of the 1985 International Computer Music Conference.* San Francisco: Computer Music Association.

Lerdahl, F., and R. Jackendoff. 1983. *A Generative Theory of Tonal Music.* Cambridge: MIT Press.

Pope, S. T. 1984. *Composing with Expert Systems.* Unpublished manuscript, PCS GmbH, Munich.

Pope, S. T. 1986. "Music Notation and the Representation of Musical Structure and Knowledge." *Perspectives of New Music* 24(2): 156–189.

Pope, S. T. 1987. "A Smalltalk-80-based Music Toolkit." In *Proceedings of the 1987 International Computer Music Conference.* San Francisco: Computer Music Association. Also in *Journal of Object-Oriented Programming* 1(1): 6–14.

Pope, S. T. 1988. "Machine Tongues XI: Object-Oriented Software Design." *Computer Music Journal* 13(3): 14–29. Also in this volume.

Pope, S. T. 1989a. "Composition by Refinement." In *Proceedings of the 8th AIMI Colloquio di Informatica Musicale,* Cagliari, Sardinia.

Pope, S. T. 1989b. "EGens." In *Proceedings of the 1989 International Computer Music Conference.* San Francisco: Computer Music Association.

Pope, S. T. 1991a. "Object-Oriented Design Elements in the MODE System." Submitted to *Journal of Object-Oriented Programming.*

Pope, S. T. 1991b. "Producing *Kombination XI:* Using Modern Computer Music and Digital Audio Signal Processing Hardware and Software for Composition." Submitted to *Leonardo Music Journal.*

Pope, S. T., A. Goldberg, and D. Leibs. 1988. *The ParcPlace Systems Navigator Applications and Frameworks.* Presentation at the ACM SIGCHI User Interface Software Technology Symposium, Banff.

Pope, S. T., N. Harter, and K. Pier. 1989. *A Navigator for Unix.* Video presented at the 1989 ACM SIGCHI Conference. Available from Association for Computing Machinery.

Rahn, J. 1990. "The Lisp Kernel." *Computer Music Journal* 14(4): 42–58.

Rodet, X., and P. Cointe. 1984. "FORMES: Composition and Scheduling of Processes." *Computer Music Journal* 8(3): 32–50. Also in this volume.

Scaletti, C. 1989. "The Kyma/Platypus Computer Music Workstation." *Computer Music Journal* 13(2): 23–38. Also in this volume.

Taube, H. 1990. "Common Music." *Computer Music Journal* 15(1).

Vogt, H. 1972. *Neue Musik Seit 1945.* Stuttgart: Reclam Verlag.

**David Jaffe and Lee Boynton**
NeXT Inc.
3475 Deer Creek Road
Palo Alto, California 94304 USA

David_Jaffe@NeXT.com, Lee_Boynton@NeXT.com

# An Overview of the Sound and Music Kits for the NeXT Computer

## Introduction

The NeXT computer provides a powerful system for creating and manipulating sound and music. The software for this system is divided into two object-oriented class libraries known as kits. The Sound Kit provides object-oriented access to the basic sound capabilities of the NeXT computer, allowing sound recording, playback, display, and editing. The Music Kit provides classes for composing, storing, performing, and synthesizing music. It lets you communicate with external synthesizers or create your own software instruments. Both kits are implemented in the Objective-C object-oriented programming language. Although they are largely independent of each other, they can also be used to a unified end. The Sound Kit, for instance, can record sound data that can be used in a Music Kit performance.

This paper gives an overview of the NeXT sound and music software. A brief description of the NeXT sound hardware is also included.

## Sound Hardware

### Voice-Quality Input

At the back of the NeXT computer's monitor is a high-impedance microphone jack that is connected to an analog-to-digital converter known as the CODEC. The CODEC converter uses 8-bit mu-law encoded quantization at a sampling rate of 8012.8 Hz. This is generally considered to be fast and accurate enough for telephone-quality speech input.

The CODEC's mu-law encoding allows a 12-bit dynamic range to be stored in 8-bit samples. In other words, an 8-bit sound with mu-law encoding will yield the same dynamic range as an unencoded 12-bit sound.

### High-Quality Sound Output

The high-quality stereo digital-to-analog converters operate at 44,100 samples per second per channel with 16-bit linear quantization, the same as in commercial compact disc (CD) players. The converters include full deglitching and anti-aliasing filters, so no external hardware is necessary for basic operation.

For sound output, the NeXT computer contains a speaker built into the monitor. Stereo line-level output jacks are also provided at the back of the monitor, allowing you to connect the computer to your stereo for greater playback fidelity. Sounds are sent to both the built-in speaker and the line-out jacks during playback. The volume of the internal speaker can be controlled from the keyboard.

### The DSP56001

The Sound Kit and the Music Kit both use the Motorola DSP56001 microprocessor (the DSP) to create and process sounds. This state-of-the-art microprocessor can execute 10 million instructions per second and, with a single instruction, can perform a 24-by-24-bit multiply, a 48-plus-56-bit addition, and two parallel data transfers. The DSP communicates with the NeXT computer's host processor (a Motorola MC68030) through a direct memory access interface. Data can be transferred between the two microprocessors at rates of up to 5 Mbytes per second.

### The Sound Kit

The Sound Kit (designed and implemented by Lee Boynton), is used to record, play, display, and edit sounds. It is designed to accommodate both casual use of sound effects as well as detailed examination and manipulation of sound data.

To store a sound, the Sound Kit can write its data as a sound file in a file format provided by NeXT. This extensible, language-independent sound-file format is also used by NeXT's pasteboard, a data structure that lets applications share data.

The Sound Kit makes extensive use of the virtual memory and interprocess message passing provided by Mach, the operating system used by the NeXT computer. This allows efficient manipulation of large sounds by minimizing data relocation.

### The Sound Class

The most important class in the Sound Kit is the *Sound* class. It defines an Objective-C object that is a wrapper around the data structure that contains raw sound data and supports the basic recording, playback, and editing operations. This class also manages the binding of names to Sound objects, allowing a simple, symbolic way to locate and share sounds within an application.

Sound objects can be instantiated from a sound file, or from the pasteboard, or can be created empty (ready for recording). Reading from a sound file is instantaneous; the file's pages are simply mapped. The data are not actually brought in from disk until they are required by the application.

### Basic Sound Operations

To record into or play a Sound object, you simply send it *record* or *play* messages. Recording takes data from the CODEC microphone input; playback sends the data to the internal speaker and to the line-level output jacks. Digital sound samples can also be directed to (and from) the DSP port to allow external conversion.

Playback and recording operations are performed asynchronously by background threads. A thread is a lightweight Mach subprocess that shares address space with its parent process. When you invoke the *play* or *record* methods, a playback or recording thread is instantiated and the method returns immediately. When the thread finishes, the Sound object sends a notification message to a user-settable object called a delegate. For example, the *sound-*

*DidPlay:* message is sent to the delegate when a Sound has finished playing.

At any time, Sounds can be written to a sound file or copied onto the pasteboard. With the basic editing methods you can delete, erase, and copy a section of a Sound, and you can insert one Sound into another. For more advanced operations, the Sound object also knows how to find and execute a sound editor application (given that the editor has been properly registered with the operating system). NeXT provides a sound editor program that you can call from within an application, or you can build your own.

### Sound Data Management

The Sound Kit rarely moves sound data; rather, the data are remapped in virtual memory. Copying operations employ "copy on write" protocol; a copied section of sound is physically shared in memory until one copy is written, requiring the physical memory for that copy to be allocated. This memory management is transparent to the programmer and user. For example, even though the sampled data in an edited Sound can become fragmented in memory, the Sound can be immediately played back at any time.

### Sound Formats

A number of formats for representing sampled sounds are supported, from compressed, low-bandwidth sounds to high-fidelity, CD-quality data. To accommodate the DAC, which only accepts 16-bit data at either 22.05 or 44.1 KHz, the Sound object can use the DSP for run-time format conversion. Instantaneous playback of most of the available formats is thus made possible.

In addition to sampled sounds, the Sound class supports DSP-synthesized sounds. Instead of samples, the Sound object then contains loadable DSP code images and data streams. In either case, playback of a Sound is transparent. You never need to know whether a Sound contains samples or DSP code in order to play it. However, the basic editing

*Jaffe and Boynton*

operations apply only to sampled sounds; they cannot be used to manipulated DSP code.

While Sound objects are multichannel, the system throughput imposes a limit on the number of channels at a given sampling rate that can be played in real time. The standard sound output format (44.1 KHz stereo, 16-bit linear data) is a good match for the throughput abilities of both the optical and the magnetic hard disk drives.

### The SoundView Class

The SoundView class provides a mechanism for displaying the sampled data in a single Sound object (it cannot display a Sound that contains DSP code). A SoundView object can draw itself on the screen, and can scale, translate, and rotate its coordinates. Several viewing modes are available, including simple oscilloscope-style waveforms, envelope outlines, and spectrogram plots.

A SoundView maintains a selection in time, generally defined by the user with the mouse, and it can perform basic edit operations such as cut and paste on the selection. Like a Sound object, a SoundView maintains a user-settable delegate to which it sends notification messages when the selection changes. Figures 1 through 4 show four SoundView displays. Figure 1 illustrates a SoundView displaying sound data as a waveform; Fig. 2 shows the same sound displayed in outline mode. In Fig. 3 the sound has been magnified to reveal individual periods; Fig. 4 presents a SoundView with an area selected and shown in gray.

The SoundView class is well integrated with the NeXT Application Kit (the tool kit that provides user interface objects, such as Buttons and Windows) and with the NeXT Interface Builder (the application that lets you graphically design a user interface). By using these tools, you can make your own graphic sound editor without writing any code.

## The Music Kit

The Music Kit (designed and implemented by David Jaffe) provides tools for designing music applications. These tools address three topics: music

representation, performance, and synthesis (digital sound generation and processing). The Objective-C classes defined in the Music Kit fall neatly into these three areas and are presented as such in this section.

The design goal of the Music Kit is to combine the interactive gestural control of MIDI with the precise timbral control of MUSIC V–type systems in an extensible, object-oriented environment. To this end, the Music Kit fully recognizes MIDI; the Music Kit accepts MIDI in, and can send MIDI out through, the two serial ports at the back of the computer. The Music Kit is not limited by the MIDI specification, however; for example, its resolution of frequency and amplitude is much finer than MIDI's.

The Music Kit generates sounds by sending synthesis instructions to the DSP. The generality of the synthesis software surpasses that of commercial synthesizers. While most synthesizers employ only one synthesis algorithm—the Yamaha DX-7 uses only frequency modulation, for example—the Music Kit can implement virtually any sound synthesis strategy. Since the synthesis engine (the DSP) and the control stream are brought together in a single high-performance computer, the Music Kit makes possible an unprecedented level of expressive control.

### Music Representation

Music is represented in a three-level hierarchy of *Score*, *Part*, and *Note* objects. Scores and Parts are analogous to orchestral scores and the instrumental parts that they contain; a Score represents a musical composition while each Part corresponds to a particular means of realization. Parts consists of a time-sorted collection of Notes, each of which contains data that describe a musical event. If you read MIDI into a Music Kit application, the various MIDI channels become separate Part objects and the MIDI commands are turned into Notes.

A Score can contain any number of Parts, and a Part can contain any number of Notes. Methods are provided for rapid insertion, deletion, and lookup of Notes within a Part and Parts within a Score. You

*Fig. 1. SoundView display-ing sound data as a waveform.*

*Fig. 2. The same sound as in Fig. 1 displayed in out-line mode.*

*Fig. 3. The sound in Fig. 1 magnified to reveal indi-vidual periods.*

*Fig. 4. A SoundView with a selected area (shown in gray).*

Fig. 1

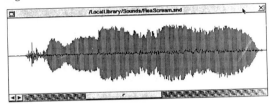

Fig. 3

Fig. 2

Fig. 4

can manipulate more than one Score at a time, as well as move a Part from one Score to another and move Notes between Parts.

## The Note Class

The Note is the basic package of musical informa-tion. The information in a Note object falls into four categories: a list of attribute-value pairs called *parameters* that describe the characteristics of a musical event; a *noteType* that determines the gen-eral character of the Note; an identifying integer called a *noteTag* used to associate different Notes with one another; and a *timeTag*, or the onset time of the Note.

## Parameters

A parameter supplies a value for a particular at-tribute of a musical sound—its frequency or ampli-tude, for example. A parameter's value can be simple (e.g., an integer, real number, or character string), or it can be another object. The Note object provides methods for setting the value of a parame-ter as an *Envelope* object or a *WaveTable* object. With the Envelope object you can create a value

that varies over time. The WaveTable object con-tains sound sample data that are used in wavetable synthesis.

The manner in which a parameter is interpreted depends on the *Instrument* that realizes the Note (the Instrument class defines the protocol for all ob-jects that realize Notes). For example, one Instru-ment could interpret a heightened brightness parameter by increasing the amplitude of the sound, while another Instrument, given the same Note, might increase the sound's spectral content. In this way, parameters are similar to Objective-C messages; the precise meaning of either depends on how they are implemented by the object that re-ceives them.

## NoteTypes and NoteTags

A Note's noteType and noteTag are used together to help interpret a Note's parameters. There are five noteTypes: *NoteDur* represents an entire musical note (a note with a duration); *NoteOn* establishes the beginning of a note; *NoteOff* establishes the end of a note; *NoteUpdate* represents the middle of a note; and *Mute* is general-purpose—its use is de-fined by the application.

**110**

*Jaffe and Boynton*

NoteDur and noteOn both establish the beginning of a musical note. The difference between them is that noteDur also has information that tells when the note should end. A note created by a noteOn simply keeps sounding until a noteOff stops it. In either case, a noteUpdate can change the attributes of a musical note while it is playing. The mute noteType is used to represent any additional information. For example, you can represent structural breakpoints such as barlines and rehearsal numbers in Notes of type mute.

A noteTag is an arbitrary integer that is used to identify different Notes as part of the same musical note or phrase. For example, a noteOff is paired with a noteOn by matching noteTag values. You can create a legato passage with a series of noteOns, all with the same noteTag, concluded by a single noteOff.

The Music Kit's noteTag system solves many of the problems inherent in MIDI, which uses a combination of key number and channel to identify events that are part of the same musical phrase. The Music Kit can, for example, create and manage an unlimited number of simultaneous legato phrases, while MIDI can only manage 16 (in MIDI mono mode). With MIDI's tagging system, mixing streams of notes is also difficult; notes can easily be clobbered or hyperextended. The Music Kit avoids this problem by reassigning unique noteTag values.

## TimeTags

A Note's timeTag specifies when the Note is to be performed. TimeTag values are measured in beats from the beginning of the performance, where the value of a beat can be set by the user. If the Note is a noteDur, its duration is also computed in beats.

## Storing Music

An entire Score can be stored in a score file. The score-file format is designed to represent any information that can be put in a Note object, including the Part to which the Note belongs. Score files are in ASCII format and can easily be created and mod-

ified with a text editor. In addition, the Music Kit provides a language called ScoreFile that lets you add simple programming constructs such as variables, assignments, and arithmetic expressions to your score file.

You can also store music as a time-stamped MIDI byte stream in a midifile. Utilities for converting to and from the standard MIDI file format are provided. Midifiles can be sent directly to an external MIDI instrument attached to one of the serial ports.

## Music Kit Performance

During a Music Kit performance, Note objects are dispatched in time-sorted order to objects that realize them in some manner, usually by making a sound on the DSP or on an external MIDI synthesizer. This process involves, primarily, instances of the classes *Performer*, *Instrument*, and *Conductor*. A Performer acquires Notes, by either opening a file, looking in a Part or Score, or generating them itself, and sends them to one or more Instruments. An Instrument receives Notes sent to it by one or more Performers and realizes them in some distinct manner. The Conductor—there is usually only one Conductor object per performance—acts as a scheduler, ensuring that Notes are transmitted from Performers to Instruments in time-sorted order and at the right time.

Before a Performer can send a Note to an Instrument, the two objects must be connected. A single Performer has a collection of outputs, each of which can be connected to any number of Instrument inputs. Performance connections are dynamic; you can connect and disconnect Instruments and Performers during a performance.

The Conductor provides control over the timing of a performance by letting you set the tempo dynamically as well as pause and resume an entire performance. You can also pause and resume individual Performers.

This system is useful for designing a wide variety of applications that process Notes sequentially. For example, a Music Kit performance can be configured to perform MIDI or DSP sequencing, graphic animation, MIDI real-time processing (such as echo, channel mapping, or doubling), sequential editing on a file, mixing and filtering of Note streams under interactive control, and so on.

## Performer and Instrument Subclasses

Both Performer and Instrument are abstract superclasses. This means that you never create and use instances of these classes directly in an application. Rather, they define common protocol (for sending and receiving Notes) that is used and refined by their subclasses. The subclasses build on this protocol to generate or realize Notes in some application-specific manner. In all cases, the actions of the user can easily be incorporated to create an interactive application.

The Music Kit provides a number of Performer and Instrument subclasses. The principal Performer subclasses are described next. *ScorePerformer* and *PartPerformer* read Notes from a designated Score and Part, respectively. ScorePerformer is actually a collection of PartPerformers, one for each Part in the Score. *ScorefilePerformer* and *MidifilePerformer* read score files and midifiles, respectively, forming Note objects from the contents of the file. *MidiIn* creates Note objects from the byte stream generated by an external MIDI synthesizer attached to a serial port.

The Instrument subclasses provided by the Music Kit also constitute a powerful and rich class hierarchy. *SynthInstrument* objects realize Notes by synthesizing them on the DSP. *MidiOut* turns Note objects into MIDI commands and sends the resulting byte stream out to an external MIDI synthesizer connected to a serial port. *ScoreRecorder* and *PartRecorder* receive Notes and add them to a Score and Part, respectively. *ScorefileWriter* and *MidifileWriter* write score files and midifiles. *NoteFilter* is a subclass of Instrument that also implements Performer's Note-sending protocol; thus, it can both receive and send Notes. Any number of NoteFilter objects can be interposed between a Performer and an Instrument. NoteFilter is itself an abstract class. The action a NoteFilter object takes in response to receiving a Note is defined by the subclass. One can, for example, create a NoteFilter subclass that creates and starts a new Performer for every Note it receives.

## Music Synthesis

By using the DSP for music synthesis, the Music Kit can generate sound with an attention to detail that equals MUSIC V–type systems; and it can do so in real time, without first writing the results out to some secondary storage medium as sample data.

The principal synthesis classes are *SynthElement*, *SynthPatch*, and *SynthInstrument*. SynthElements are the basic building blocks of DSP synthesis; they correspond directly to code or data on the DSP. A SynthPatch object is a configuration of SynthElements that defines a particular synthesis strategy. A SynthPatch is analogous to a voice or instrument setting on a commercial synthesizer. SynthInstrument is a subclass of Instrument that realizes Notes by assigning them to particular SynthPatches. It performs what in MIDI synthesizers is called "voice allocation."

Another class, called *Orchestra*, is provided to manage the DSP. For instance, allocation of all SynthElement objects is handled by the Orchestra. Each DSP is represented by a single Orchestra object. The basic NeXT configuration has one DSP; thus, there is ordinarily only one instance of Orchestra. The state of an Orchestra can be saved as DSP code in a sound file.

## The SynthElement Class

SynthElement is an abstract class with two subclasses: *UnitGenerator* and *SynthData*. Each subclass of UnitGenerator (which is an abstract class) implements a particular synthesis function. The Music Kit supplies classes that implement oscillators, envelope handlers, filters, mixers, and so on. In addition, tools are provided to help you create your own UnitGenerator subclasses.

SynthData objects correspond to DSP data memory. An important use of SynthData is to provide patchpoints or locations that can be written to by one UnitGenerator and read by another. For example, simple frequency modulation can be implemented by setting the output of an oscillator to write to a patchpoint that is read by the frequency input of another oscillator. SynthData objects can also be used to hold wavetables, delay memory, constants, and so on.

### The SynthPatch Class

SynthPatch is also an abstract class; each subclass represents a configuration of SynthElement objects. The SynthPatch class defines a standard set of methods that are implemented by each subclass to define the manner in which a Note's parameters are applied. In general, the manner in which parameters are interpreted depends on the Note's noteType.

A noteOn heralds a new Note stream or rearticulation of an existing stream; it is always the first noteType that a newly allocated SynthPatch sees. When a noteUpdate is received, the SynthPatch makes a transition in its SynthElements to accommodate the new parameter values. A noteOff causes the SynthPatch to wind down. It does not stop short, but rather begins the release portion of its envelopes. The SynthPatch can continue to receive noteUpdates after it receives a noteOff. The SynthPatch is never sent a noteDur; they are turned into noteOn/noteOff pairs by the SynthInstrument that owns the SynthPatch.

### The SynthInstrument Class

Each SynthInstrument object knows how to create and manage instances of a particular SynthPatch class. When it receives a Note, the SynthInstrument decides whether to create a new SynthPatch instance or to apply the Note to a SynthPatch that is already running. It makes this decision by looking at the Note's noteTag.

Each SynthPatch instance that a SynthInstrument manages corresponds to a particular noteTag. When a Note is received, the SynthInstrument checks to see if a SynthPatch with that noteTag is running, passing the Note along to the SynthPatch

if it exists, creating a new SynthPatch if it does not. The total number of SynthPatches that a SynthInstrument can create is limited by the memory restrictions of the DSP. If a SynthInstrument cannot find the resources to play a new Note, it normally preempts its oldest running SynthPatch. However, you can subclass SynthInstrument to provide a different preemption strategy, such as one based on amplitude.

### Real-Time Issues

When a computer generates music, it is often a race against the clock. The DSP can only do so much computing within a given period; in cases where the DSP cannot keep up with real time, music can be precomputed, possibly in multiple passes, and stored in a sound file for later playback. By using the Music Kit and the Sound Kit together in a single application, you can capture DSP output in a Sound object and easily mix it with other Sounds.

Any interactive music application requires that the latency between a user's action and its musical result be kept to a minimum. MIDI synthesizers, for example, operate in this realm, the lag between pushing down a key and the instantiation of the note must be imperceptible. This is referred to as critical real time. It is worth noting that critical-real-time performance has been proved to be possible without sacrificing the generality, extensibility, or clarity of design of the Music Kit.

### Conclusion

The Sound and Music Kits make it easy to design and use sound and music applications on the NeXT computer. Nevertheless, the Kits are simply tool boxes, they are not applications themselves. Their vitality will be determined by the imagination of the software developers who build on their foundation. We feel that the power of the concepts on which the Sound and Music Kits are based provides a framework capable of meeting the needs of a wide variety of application developers. Figure 5 shows the components for creating, playing, and storing

*Fig. 5. Music Kit and
Sound Kit components.*

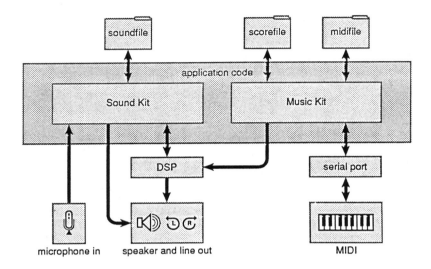

music and sound with the hardware and software of the NeXT computer.

## Acknowledgments

Julius Smith is the author of the DSP unit generator macro system, many of the unit generators themselves, the DSP system, and the DSP library functions. He has also made large contributions to the Music Kit design. Douglas Fulton documented the NeXT sound and music system and has made substantial design improvements in clarifying general protocol and the identity and mechanisms of the classes. He also helped us with this article. Gregg Kellogg is the author of the DSP, MIDI, and Sound device drivers. Michael McNabb brought wavetable synthesis to the Music Kit and designed and built a number of UnitGenerator and SynthPatch subclasses. Roger Dannenberg influenced both the Music Kit noteTag design and the design of the performance mechanism (using a data-flow discrete simulation model). Andy Moorer shaped the Envelope strategy and provided expert consultation in many areas. Dana Massie wrote the sound-reader unit generator and various Sound Kit modules. Doug Keislar helped with testing and developer support. The software of William Schottstaedt and others at CCRMA (at Stanford University) served as a model for some of the mechanisms in the Music Kit. John Chowning, Max Mathews, and others in the computer music community have lent moral and technical support. Finally, Steve Jobs and Bud Tribble made a place for music at NeXT.

## Addendum: Sound and Music Kits Version 1.0

The article "An Overview of the Sound and Music Kits for the NeXT Computer" describes the state of the version 0.9 release of the music and sound software. This update describes the version 1.0 release of the software. Additionally, an upcoming version 2.0 release (not described here) will have significant new features, improved performance, and more complete documentation.

The version 1.0 release of the Sound Kit is optimized significantly from the 0.9 version and provides additional functionality. In version 0.9, the Sound class provided efficient *insert* and *delete* operations on sampled sounds. In version 1.0, the SoundView makes use of this ability. The reading and writing the pasteboard is now "lazy," providing rapid *cut* and *paste* of sound samples. The Sound-Meter class is new and provides a simple bar-graph meter of a sampled sound's activity while playing or recording. It displays a moving average of the sound amplitude with "peak hold."

The version 1.0 release of the system software includes a Mach MIDI driver that provides time-stamped parsed input and scheduled output and communicates with the serial ports on the NeXT machine. With the addition of an inexpensive adapter, each of the two serial ports can be connected to a MIDI cable. Programming examples to direct play and record standard MIDI files are provided. Higher-level access to the Mach MIDI driver is provided by the version 1.0 Music Kit via the Midi class. Programming examples are included that illustrate using the Music Kit to do MIDI *echo*, MIDI *record* to and *playback* from a scorefile, etc. In addition, the Score object can now read and write standard MIDI files.

The version 1.0 Music Kit UnitGenerator library includes processing modules such as filters and oscillators. The Music Kit SynthPatch library includes general-purpose instruments to support a wide range of synthesis techniques, including simple frequency modulation with complex waveforms, cascade and parallel modulation FM, FM with noise modulation, wave-table synthesis with interpolation between wave tables, and plucked string synthesis. The FM and wave-table synthesis have the option of periodic vibrato, random vibrato, and amplitude and frequency envelopes with an arbitrary number of breakpoints. A library of wave tables for various timbres in various ranges is supplied.

There was a change in the Music Kit class hierarchy since the article was published. The SynthElement class, which was the superclass of UnitGenerator and SynthData, was eliminated. UnitGenerator and SynthData now inherit directly from Object.

Finally, we'd like to acknowledge the contributions to the project made by Mike Minnick and John Strawn.

# III

# Composition Systems

**Carla Scaletti**
CERL Music Project
University of Illinois
Urbana, Illinois 61801-2977 USA

hebel@cerl.uiuc.edu

# The Kyma/Platypus Computer Music Workstation

## Introduction

The Kyma/Platypus workstation is a graphic environment integrating sound synthesis, computer-aided composition, and digital audio signal processing. All sound generation and processing is done in software, and each copy of the system can be modified and extended by the composer using it.

Kyma is a language based on Sound objects; it is written in Smalltalk-80, running on an Apple Macintosh II. Real-time software synthesis is provided by the Platypus, a digital signal processor designed and built at the University of Illinois.

The Kyma/Platypus framework is flexible enough to support such application areas as composition, systematic musicology, digital audio post-processing, sound track production, psychoacoustics, digital signal processing, the design of test signals, communications research, the sonic representation of scientific data—in short, any application requiring the interactive design of high-quality digital audio signals.

Three factors contribute to the flexibility of this system: (1) the choice of Sound objects rather than standard music notation as the representation for musical signals, (2) the choice of Smalltalk-80 rather than a compiled procedural language as the programming environment, and (3) the choice of a *programmable* digital signal processor (rather than a *hardwired* synthesizer) for the production of sound.

## Kyma

Kyma is a language of Sound objects; it is not a single program supporting a particular technique or philosophy of composition. If Kyma reflects any

Computer Music Journal, Vol. 13, No. 2, Summer 1989
© 1989 Massachusetts Institute of Technology.

philosophy of composition, it is that composers make use of many different techniques and approaches—often within the same composition. Composers in their private workshops should be able to use the appropriate tool for each subtask, and they should be able to augment their tool collection with new implements of their own design. In Kyma, a composer can use methods of musique concrète, the instrument/score paradigm, the cut-and-splice techniques of the tape studio, context-free grammars, stochastic devices, and any number of individually designed techniques—all within the same composition, all within the same graphic environment, all with real-time feedback by means of software sound synthesis.

Many people are attracted to the field of computer music precisely because it straddles art and science. Kyma is a language for computer music in that it can be used in musical applications and in such applications as digital signal processing research, the sonic representation of dynamical systems, the design of test signals for psychoacoustic research, or generating the sonic component of a symbolic algebra program.

## Sound Objects

### Definition

The revolutionary idea that accompanied the first electroacoustic music was that the entire continuum of sound can be used in music composition. A language for composing electroacoustic music must be capable of representing and organizing any sound. The key to the generality and expressive power of Kyma lies in its representation for audio signals. The Sound object is like the *objet sonore* of Pierre Schaeffer—a collection of discrete objects functioning as unitary entity. A Sound object can be a collection of samples or an assembly of other

*Fig. 1. A directed acyclic graph (DAG). There can be more than one incoming and outgoing edge, but no loops are allowed.*

*Fig. 2. A DAG representing the expressions, (5 + 2) * 2.*

Sound objects. Every Sound object represents a stream of samples; it is this stream of samples that can be converted by a digital-to-analog convertor (DAC) into actual sound. More formally, a Sound object is (1) an Atom, (2) a UnaryTransform $T(s)$, where $s$ is a Sound object, or (3) an $N$-aryTransform $T(s_1, s_2, \ldots, s_m)$, where $m$ is any integer and $s_1, s_2, \ldots, s_m$ are Sound objects. A UnaryTransform, $T(s)$, is a Sound object that is the result of applying a function $T$ to a single Sound object. An $N$-ary-Transform is a Sound object that is the result of applying a function to one *or* more Sound objects.

## Structure

From the definition it follows that a Sound object can be represented as a directed acyclic graph (DAG) with a single root node. Each edge of the graph represents the relation "is-a-function-of." In Figure 1, the value of $A$ is a function of the values of $B$, $D$, and $H$, and the value of $D$ is a function of the values of $E$ and $G$. Notice that a node can have more than one input and more than one output, but that no cycles are allowed.

A Sound object DAG represents a function. The DAG in Fig. 1, for example, represents the function A(B(C), D(E(F), G), H(G)). The DAG in Fig. 2 represents the function Product (Sum (5, 2), 2), which could also be written as: (5 + 2) * 2.

## Evaluation

A Sound object represents a stream of samples. In order to hear a Sound object, it is necessary to "evaluate" it, that is, convert it to a sample stream. Every Sound object knows how to compute its next sample. For an atomic Sound object, the next sample algorithm is a sound synthesis technique such as a table-lookup algorithm. For a nonatomic Sound object, the next sample is a function of the subsounds' next samples. For instance, the next sample of a Kyma Mixer is defined to be the sum of its subsounds' next samples.

Functions like the one represented in Fig. 2 can

Fig. 1

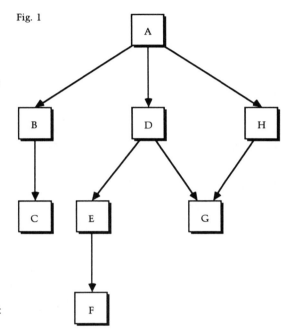

Fig. 2

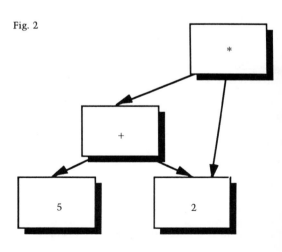

Fig. 3. Mixer (Multiplier
(S1, S2), S2).

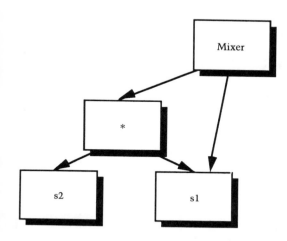

Similarly, a PotentialSound is expanded once, and the expansion is cached so it can be reused in other contexts. In Fig. 6a, the Pluck node expands to the subgraph: KSFilter (Concatenation (Noise, Silence)), which is shown in Fig. 6b. When the node is visited a second time, the cached subgraph is used.

### Substitution

Sound objects are uniform; therefore a given Sound object can be substituted for any other Sound object. In terms of the DAG, a given graph can be substituted for any subgraph of another graph. A substitution is, itself, a Sound object; in Kyma, the ReplacementSound is defined to be its subsound with every occurrence of an oldSound replaced by a newSound.

### Variables

A VariableSound represents a Sound object of a given class or its subclasses. The value of a VariableSound may be completely unrestricted, restricted to represent only atomic Sound objects, or even restricted to instances of a specific class such as Lookup. VariableSounds can be used in constraint satisfaction, in the incomplete specification of Sound objects, or in reasoning about Sound objects using sorted logic.

### Interface

Kyma's user interface is a direct manipulation system; that is, the composer manipulates the internal representation of Sound objects by manipulating graphic representations of those objects. A Kyma view, shown in Fig. 7, is a window on the display for creating and manipulating Sound objects. The graphic representation of a Sound object is called a SoundPoint, and it appears within a region of the Kyma view called a SoundPlane (the largest pane of the Kyma view). In the previous section the internal structure of a Sound was represented as an ab-

be evaluated by evaluating each node of the DAG in post-order; that is, evaluate 5, then 2, then Sum (5, 2), then 2 again, and finally the product at the top. Similarly, the next sample in a Sound object's stream of samples is obtained by traversing its DAG in post-order, computing the next sample of each of the nodes. The DAG in Fig. 3, for example, represents the Sound object, Mixer (Multiplier(s1, s2), s2). In order to compute the next sample of this Sound object, one must compute the next sample of s1, compute the next sample of s2, then compute the next sample of the Multiplier, compute the next sample of s2, and finally compute the next sample of the Mixer. To compute a Sound object's entire stream of samples, one repeatedly obtains the Sound object's next sample until the end of the stream has been reached.

When a Sound object DAG includes Delay nodes, the DAG is first expanded into a sequence of time-tagged DAGs, which are then evaluated. The Mixer shown in Fig. 4a would first be expanded into the three DAGs shown in Fig. 4b.

A PotentialSound node is one that expands into a subgraph during evaluation. Consider the expression tree represented in Fig. 5. When the f(2) node is evaluated the first time, its value can be cached and reused when the node is traversed a second time.

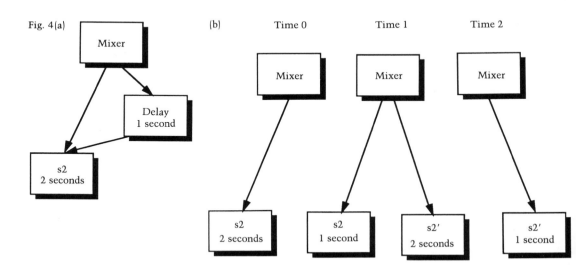

Fig. 4(a)     (b)     Time 0     Time 1     Time 2

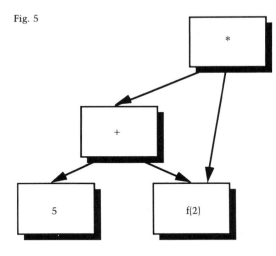

Fig. 5

stract graph in which the value of a node depended upon the values of the nodes *below* it. In the Kyma user interface, a Sound is represented as a Sound-Point whose value depends upon the SoundPoints *within* it. The relations *above* and *below* have been replaced by the relations *enclosing* and *within*. Each SoundPoint can be "opened up" to reveal its immediate subsounds.

The icons on the scrollable strip along the left edge of the Kyma view represent all the different kinds of Sound objects that are currently defined. To create an instance of one of the classes, the composer presses the button labelled *create*, which opens a creation view like the ones shown in Figs. 8 and 9.

Each parameter of a Sound instance is supplied by typing a value in the appropriate field or by dragging another SoundPoint into the field as shown in Fig. 10. When a SoundPoint is dropped into a parameter field, it responds by filling in *its* value for that parameter into the field. Once all parameters have been set, the new Sound object can be tested by pressing the *play* button in the creation view. Pressing the *save* button saves this new instance as a SoundPoint on the main SoundPlane.

*Fig. 6. The Pluck node in (a) expands to the subgraph in (b).*

*Fig. 7. A Kyma View. This is the main view for creating and manipulating Sound objects.*

Fig. 6(a)

(b)

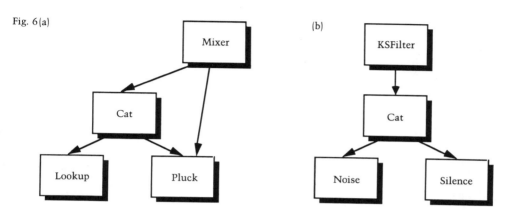

Fig. 7

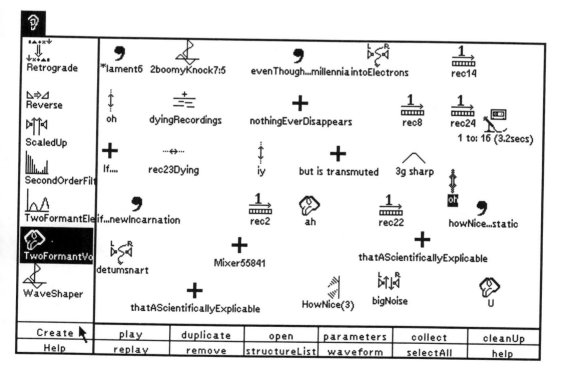

*Fig. 8. Creation View for a Pluck.*

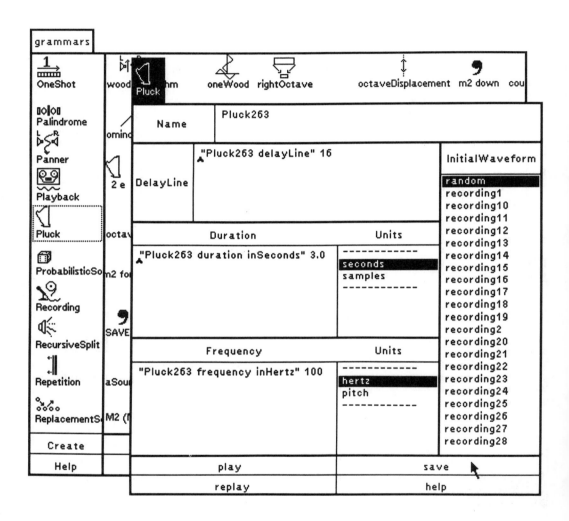

*Fig. 9. Creation View for an Echo.*

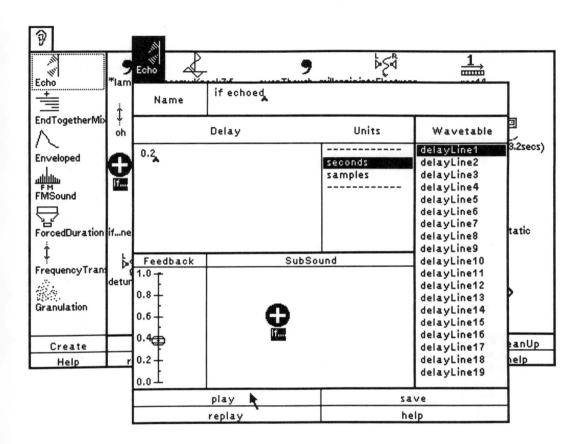

## Applications

Each Sound object is its own world with its own rules and its own elements, but these worlds co-exist in the same system. Once a Sound object has been created, it is opaque. It no longer matters how it was created or how it is implemented internally; it is a Sound object like any other Sound object. Thus, a Sound object that was generated algorithmically can be combined with a Sound object that was pieced together by hand or with a Sound object representing a processed live sound; the same transforms can be applied to a Sound object representing an entire composition as can be applied to a Sound object representing a single timbre.

### Composition

Kyma is a Greek word (pronounced kyuma) meaning wave; Kyma is a language for specifying sound pressure waves. The same word comes to us, by way of Latin, as "accumulate"—to amass or collect—and it is by amassing existing Sound objects that new Sound objects are created.

Various synthesis techniques are available in

*Fig. 10. Select a Sound-Point (a); Drag it into another view (b); Drop it in the parameter pane where it sets the parameter (c).*

(a)

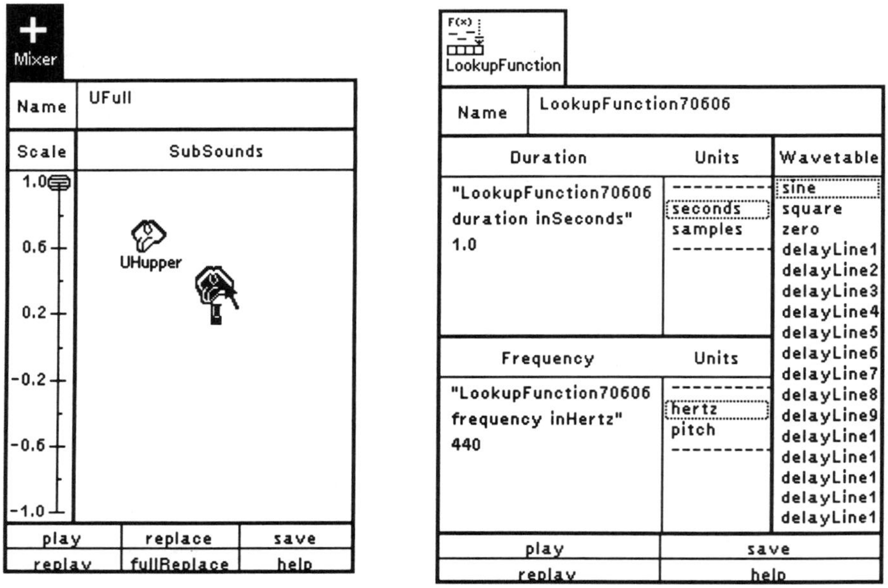

**Mixer**

| Name | UFull |
|---|---|
| Scale | SubSounds |

1.0
0.6    UHupper
0.2
-0.2
-0.6
-1.0

| play | replace | save |
|---|---|---|
| replay | fullReplace | help |

**LookupFunction**

| Name | LookupFunction70606 |
|---|---|

| Duration | Units | Wavetable |
|---|---|---|
| "LookupFunction70606 duration inSeconds" 1.0 | seconds samples | sine square zero delayLine1 delayLine2 delayLine3 delayLine4 delayLine5 delayLine6 delayLine7 delayLine8 delayLine9 delayLine1 delayLine1 delayLine1 delayLine1 delayLine1 |
| **Frequency** | **Units** | |
| "LookupFunction70606 frequency inHertz" 440 | hertz pitch | |

| play | save |
|---|---|
| replay | help |

(b)

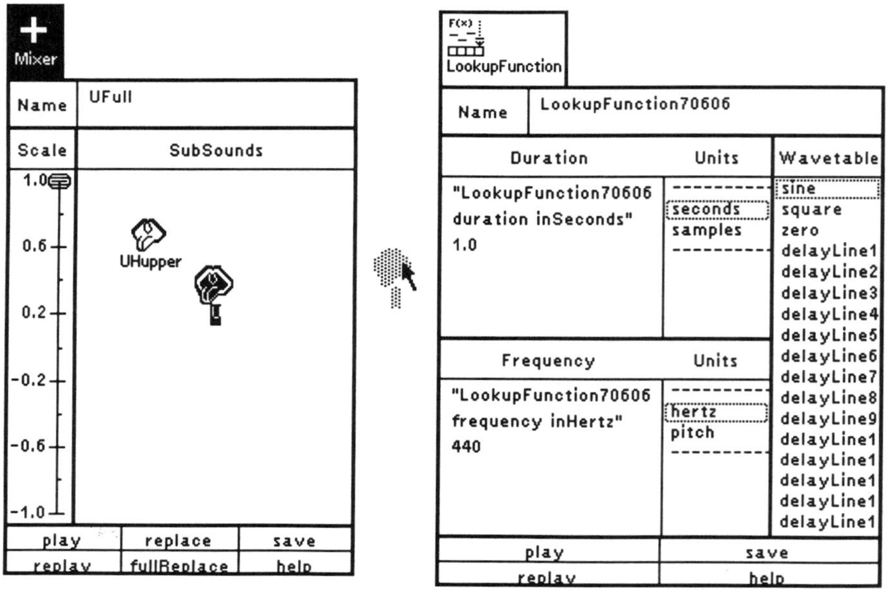

**Mixer**

| Name | UFull |
|---|---|
| Scale | SubSounds |

1.0
0.6    UHupper
0.2
-0.2
-0.6
-1.0

| play | replace | save |
|---|---|---|
| replay | fullReplace | help |

**LookupFunction**

| Name | LookupFunction70606 |
|---|---|

| Duration | Units | Wavetable |
|---|---|---|
| "LookupFunction70606 duration inSeconds" 1.0 | seconds samples | sine square zero delayLine1 delayLine2 delayLine3 delayLine4 delayLine5 delayLine6 delayLine7 delayLine8 delayLine9 delayLine1 delayLine1 delayLine1 delayLine1 delayLine1 |
| **Frequency** | **Units** | |
| "LookupFunction70606 frequency inHertz" 440 | hertz pitch | |

| play | save |
|---|---|
| replay | help |

(c)

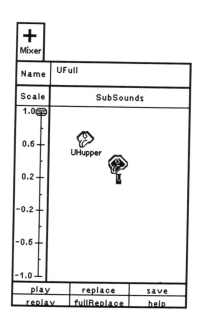

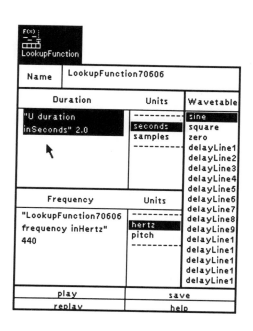

Kyma: Karplus-Strong filters, FOF (Formant wave synthesis), frequency modulation, amplitude modulation, granular synthesis. More importantly, new synthesis techniques can be incorporated into the framework of Kyma as they are developed (which is one of the advantages of implementing the sound synthesis algorithms in software rather than in hardware).

An IMSSound (so named because it emulates the IMS digital synthesizer developed at CERL (Haken 1984; Scaletti 1984)) is a Sound object based on the traditional instrument/score paradigm. In an IMSSound, the subsounds serve as instrument definitions, and an event list provides a sequence of pitch/duration/amplitude triples to each instrument. This is the place where a standard notation editor would fit in the Kyma framework—as the creation view editor for an IMSSound. A simple musical phrase is illustrated in Fig. 11 in common-practice music notation and as a DAG.

True to its name, the digital signal processor can *process* as well as synthesize sound. There are

Sound objects that record to or play back from the Platypus memory and a LiveSound object that represents the ADC input signal. These serve as tools for live or delayed musique concrète and the typical effects achieved using sampling keyboards.

Sound objects are not limited to representing synthesis techniques. There is a ContextFreeGrammar Sound object, a ProbabilisticSound, and a Cellular-Automaton Sound object, each of which creates a new sound from its subsounds according to a compositional algorithm. New computer-aided-composition algorithms, like new sound synthesis methods, can be added to the Kyma framework as desired.

### Digital Audio Signal Processing

Some of the Sound objects in Kyma represent post-processing techniques such as mixing, reverberation, equalization, or other filtering. New Sound objects could be added to do compression (for re-

Fig. 11. A Sound object (a) and its equivalent in standard music notation (b).

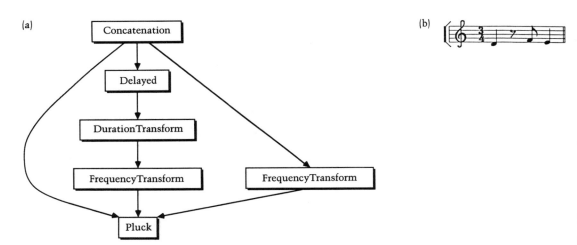

Fig. 11. A Sound object (a) and its equivalent in standard music notation (b).

cording onto cassette tapes) or other kinds of post-processing.

Javelina is a Smalltalk system for the design and evaluation of state variable systems (Hebel 1987, 1989). At some point, Javelina and Kyma will be merged, providing Kyma with some classical signal processing techniques as well as rule-based algebraic manipulation.

### Performance

The Kyma/Platypus system is a workstation—not a performance instrument, at least in the traditional sense. Nevertheless, the use of a Platypus/Kyma system in a live performance is possible and may define a new kind of performance instrument. The Platypus can do real-time processing of the input from the analog-to-digital converter. The live input can be recorded for modified playback, it can supply parameters to a synthesis algorithm, it can be reverberated or filtered—in short, a sort of live musique concrète composition can be created.

### Test Signals

Psychoacousticians and audio engineers both need to design audio test signals. Signals can be put together quickly and fine-tuned by ear when there is

real-time feedback. Using a stereo Z-plane editor (Hebel 1989), for instance, a researcher can design a signal in which each channel is filtered differently.

### Sonic Representations of Scientific Data

Computer graphics has been widely used as a tool for representing information in all of the sciences; the "audio imagining" of data is sometimes overlooked as an aid for interpreting data. Data that would be well represented in sound include systems that evolve over time, systems in which several parameters evolve in parallel, and systems in which small differences are important.

One example of such a sonic realization is the CellularAutomaton Sound object. This object represents the evolution of a one-dimensional cellular automaton over any number of generations, given any initial state and rule.

## Implementation

### Smalltalk's Influences on Kyma

What is it about Smalltalk that makes it the language of choice for the computer music researchers represented in this issue? A well-developed set of programming tools; the principles of encapsulation, polymorphism, inheritance; and even the history behind its development all contribute to the appropriateness of Smalltalk for musical applications.

### The Environment

Smalltalk is both a language and an environment. The environment is graphical and interactive; it provides, among other tools, a debugger, a file system, text and picture editing, process scheduling, a compiler, a decompiler, and a logging mechanism that makes it virtually impossible to lose work even in the event of a system crash. This environment and the paradigm of communicating objects make Smalltalk an ideal environment for designing and managing complex, evolving systems.

### A Philosophy of Open-Endedness

Smalltalk was developed by a team at the System Concepts Laboratory of the Xerox Palo Alto Research Center. In the early 1970s this group's mandate was to explore ways in which various people might effectively and joyfully use the computer. This original goal later expanded into the creation of a powerful information system that could be extended and modified to fit each person's use of the system (Goldberg and Robson 1983). Anyone who has worked with a black-box system knows what it is like to coerce that system into doing things it was never intended to do. Composers of experimental music know what it is like to work with a system based on someone else's idea of what composers ought to do. The designers of Smalltalk did not presume to specify one universal set of classes for all applications for all time. Rather, they provide a kernel set of classes that can be extended and modified by the user. Unlike the user-defined data types of Pascal, user-defined classes in Smalltalk are indistinguishable from the kernel classes. A user can redesign the language itself.

Similarly, Kyma does not pretend to provide all possible algorithms for sound synthesis and composition. Rather, it provides a framework on which to hang new techniques as they are developed. The framework provides a basic protocol for all Sound objects; for example, every Sound object can be played, every Sound object has a graphic representation on the display, and every Sound object has a name. In order to plug a new kind of Sound object into this framework, the user has only to specify how this new Sound object differs from other Sound objects. The use of this technique, called *programming by refinement*, allows new kinds of Sound objects to be plugged into the Kyma framework with a minimum of programming.

### The Object Paradigm

The object-oriented approach to computation is to define the computation in terms of an object that has a certain behavior in response to a message. Where the syntax of a procedure call in a procedural programming language is a verb followed by nouns (e.g., *play (aSound)*), the syntax of a function call (a message-send) in an object-oriented language is a noun (the object) followed by a verb (the message sent to the object), (e.g., *aSound play*).

### Encapsulation

In Smalltalk, an *object* is an *encapsulated* abstraction, that is, a package of properties and behavior (Krasner 1980). The properties (data) are called its *instance variables*; they can only be accessed through a sort of software "interface." This set of interface routines is called the object's *protocol*, and each routine within a protocol is called a *method*. A method is invoked by sending a message having the same name as the method; in the example above, sending the message, *play*, invokes the method, **play.** An object's set of messages and methods defines its behavior.

### Inheritance

Each object is an instance of a class of objects. A class description includes the specification of the instance variables and protocol shared by all of its instances. Classes are defined in order from the most general to the most specific, where the more specific classes inherit the protocols of the more general. A new class can be defined by making it a subclass of an existing class and then defining only those methods by which it differs from its superclass. Inheritance is what makes programming by refinement possible.

All classes of Sound objects in Kyma, for example, are subclasses of class Sound. There is a method in class Sound called **play** which describes how to play a Sound object on the Platypus. Because this method is defined in class Sound, every subclass of Sound inherits the method; thus, every Sound object knows how to play. More importantly, any new type of Sound object defined by someone using the system will automatically inherit the ability to play.

### Polymorphism

Polymorphism refers to using the same name for methods that accomplish the same goal by different means. For example, suppose that all classes of Sound objects were to implement a method called *nextSample*. Obviously the code for generating the next sample of a Lookup is different from the code used to generate the next sample of a Mixer. In C or Pascal, each different implementation of *nextSample* would have to have a different name (e.g., lookup_next_sample, and mixer_next_sample). In Kyma, however, the user can ask for a Sound object's next sample without knowing what kind of Sound object it is; thus, the principle of polymorphism contributes to the uniformity of all Sound objects.

As another example, consider the case of a FrequencyTransform. A FrequencyTransform transforms its subsound's frequency by some function of time. Rather than treating its subsound as a signal whose source is unknown, a FrequencyTransform relies on the subsound knowing how to transform its own frequency. Different kinds of Sound objects have different ways of changing their frequencies. A Lookup, for example, simply changes its sample increment. A Pluck (a simple Karplus-Strong imple-

mentation) changes the distance between its read and write pointers. A LiveSound must implement a frequency detection and time-scale modification algorithm in order to change the frequency of an input in real time. If a subsound does not know how to change its frequency, or it does not really have a frequency, then the FrequencyTransform has no effect. When a FrequencyTransform is told to play, it tells its subsound to make a copy of itself using a transformation. It then tells that copy to play. Every Sound object must implement the *copyWithTransformation:* method, even though each Sound object implements the method differently.

### The Framework

The Kyma/Platypus system provides a framework on which to construct new kinds of Sound objects. In Kyma, all Sound objects are instances of one of the subclasses of class Sound. The subclasses of Sound share a common protocol; that is, there is a set of messages that are understood by all subclasses of Sound. This set includes *play; download; storeOnDisk; name; duration; parameters; waveform;* and *size.*

A new kind of Sound object is created by defining a subclass of an existing class of Sound objects. The new subclass inherits many of the essential messages, such as *play.* Some of the messages are polymorphic and must be implemented in each class; for example, the duration of a Concatenation is the sum of its subsounds' durations, whereas the duration of a Mixer is the duration of its longest subsound.

### The Platypus

#### Object-Oriented Sample Generation

In object-oriented sample generation, all Sound objects respond to the message *nextSample.* The *nextSample* method is polymorphic in that every Sound object must respond to the message *nextSample,* but the actual implementation of the method differs from class to class. In general, an atomic Sound

Fig. 12. A block diagram of
the Platypus digital signal
processor.

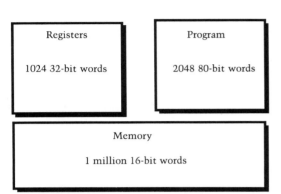

| Registers | Program |
|---|---|
| 1024 32-bit words | 2048 80-bit words |

| Memory |
|---|
| 1 million 16-bit words |

**Table 1. Platypus digital signal processor specifications**

A RISC machine designed for efficient computation of audio samples
Harvard architecture (i.e., separate data and program memories)

Three 16-by-16-bit multipliers with 35-bit accumulate
1024 32-bit registers
2 Megabyte main memory
2048 80-bit microcode program memory
512 Byte FIFO queues on input and output

Stereo 16-bit digital-to-analog and analog-to-digital converters
Variable-cutoff input and output filters
200 Hz to 50 KHz range of possible sample rates

Executes an 80-bit instruction every 50 nsec
As many as six operations can occur in parallel on each instruction
1000 instructions can be used for each sample at 20 kHz sample rate

object's *nextSample* method is an implementation of a sound synthesis algorithm, and the *nextSample* method of a nonatomic Sound object is an implementation of some function of the subsounds' next samples. In the case of a Mixer, for example, the Smalltalk version of the *nextSample* method would be something like:

```
↑subsounds inject: 0 into:
  [:sample:sub|
  sample+sub nextSample].
```

This method returns the sum of the subsounds' next samples.

### Real-Time Object-Oriented Sample Generation

Since it is essential to test sounds quickly in a computer music workstation, a specially designed co-processor is used to speed up the object-oriented sample generation. The Platypus is a RISC machine designed specifically for generating audio samples. It was designed and built in 1984 by Lippold Haken and Kurt Hebel working at the CERL Music Project of the University of Illinois (Haken and Hebel 1987). Figure 12 shows a simple block diagram of the machine, and Table 1 gives a more detailed list of its specifications.

The Platypus can execute 20 million instructions per second (MIPS). Since each instruction can contain as many as 6 parallel operations, an upper bound on the number of *operations* per second is 120 million. To put that in some perspective, consider that the Motorola 68020 processor in the Apple Macintosh II has a 3 MIPS peak and averages around 1.5 MIPS. However, while the streamlined architecture of the Platypus gives it speed, it also makes it difficult to program the Platypus to run a complex program like Smalltalk (not impossible, just difficult). In the Kyma/Platypus system, each machine is assigned the task for which it is best suited. The abstract structure and graphic representation of the Sound objects is handled by Smalltalk on the Macintosh, and the object-oriented sample generation is handled by the Platypus.

### Sound Objects on the Platypus

A Sound object in Smalltalk-80 is a record of values in *instance variables* and a pointer to its set of methods as shown in Fig. 13. This same Sound is represented on the Platypus as a MicroSound. A MicroSound is a record of values in *registers* with a

Fig. 13. Sound objects versus MicroSounds.

Fig. 14. A block diagram of the Platypus running the Kyma Microcode.

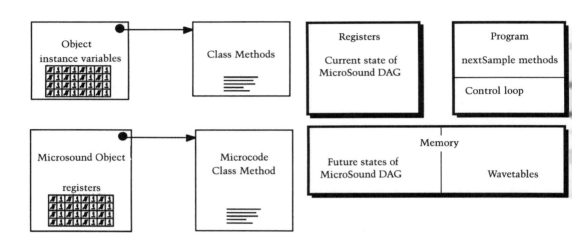

Fig. 13. Sound objects versus MicroSounds.

Fig. 14. A block diagram of the Platypus running the Kyma Microcode.

pointer to its *nextSample* method in microcode. When a Sound object is told to play in Kyma, it is translated to a MicroSound, and downloaded to the Platypus memory.

Figure 14 is a block diagram of the Platypus running the Kyma microcode. Once, at the beginning of each editing session, Kyma downloads a set of precomputed wavetables to the large memory of the Platypus. It then assembles the *nextSample* methods and the control loop into a Platypus microcode program and downloads this program to the microcode memory of the Platypus. Every time a different Sound object is told to play, it is converted to a MicroSound and downloaded to the registers of the Platypus. The microcode program and the wavetables are changed only rarely, so they remain in the Platypus for the duration of an editing session. However, a new MicroSound is downloaded each time a different Sound object is told to play. Recall that when a DAG with Delay nodes is evaluated, it expands into a *sequence* of time-tagged DAGs. On a given sample, only the current state of the Micro-Sound is stored in the registers, and all future states of the MicroSound are stored in the large memory, along with the wavetables (Scaletti 1987, 1989; Scaletti and Johnson 1988).

**A Sound Object Is a Program**

The *nextSample* algorithms in the microcode of the Platypus are like the primitive instructions of a language, and the Sound object is like a specific program in that language. Telling a Sound object to play is like compiling it for execution on the Platypus. Thus, by manipulating SoundPoints on the display, the composer is actually writing a program.

**Plans for the Future**

An ongoing enhancement to Kyma will be the addition of new classes with specialized editors to the Sound framework. The most obvious additions would be editors that emulate specialized programs such as notation editors, block diagram editors, or waveform editors.

The most important development planned is one that will further increase Kyma's flexibility. Kurt Hebel's Javelina, a Smalltalk environment for the development of digital signal processing software, includes a facility for automatically generating signal processing microcode (Hebel 1989). Javelina takes a function and translates it into a register transfer language (RTL) for an abstract machine having an infinite number of registers. The RTL was developed by Ralph Johnson to serve as the first step of an optimizing compiler for Typed-Smalltalk (Johnson, Graver, and Zurawski 1988). In Javelina this abstract language, along with a machine model, is used to generate code for the target processor. This scheme can be used to generate assembly language programs for machines such as the Platypus, the MC56001 signal processing chip, the TI series of digital signal processors, and the MC68000. It can also be used to generate programs in high-level languages such as C or Smalltalk. Incorporating automatic code generation into Kyma will allow it to be used with signal processors other than the Platypus, and it will keep the Kyma software from becoming obsolete when the Platypus is upgraded.

## Conclusion

The Kyma/Platypus workstation was created to address the needs of artists and researchers in musical computation. Its primary design goal—flexibility—is reflected in the choice of the language Smalltalk-80 over other, less malleable languages; the choice of a digital signal processor over a hardwired digital synthesizer; and the goal of specifying synthesis algorithms as mathematical functions rather than in the assembly language of a particular machine.

The Sound object serves as a uniform, abstract structure for organizing all levels of a composition—from the composition of timbre to the composition of an entire piece. The composer creates Sound objects by manipulating graphic representations of those objects on the display. Sound objects form a basis that is general enough to bring multisynthesis techniques and multiple compositional philosophies together within a single environment.

The Kyma/Platypus workstation offers hardware and software programmability; access to the general-purpose computing environment of Smalltalk; multiple synthesis techniques; and computer-aided

composition. The Kyma software was designed to be flexible enough and general enough to survive and adapt to changing hardware environments.

## Acknowledgments

In 1988, this work was supported by a fellowship from Apple Computer and the InterUniversity Consortium on Educational Computing. A research assistantship from the CERL Music Project enabled me to complete a master's degree in computer science at the University of Illinois while doing research in computer music.

I'd like to acknowledge the many discussions I've had and continue to have with Kurt Hebel regarding both the philosophy and details of Kyma. My thanks to Ralph Johnson for his insights and suggestions and to Stephen Pope for his enthusiastic support of musical applications of Smalltalk; also thanks to Lippold Haken, Kurt Hebel, and Charlie Robinson for their efforts in designing and debugging the Platypus.

## References

Goldberg, A., and D. Robson. 1983. *Smalltalk-80: The Language and Its Implementation.* Reading, Massachusetts: Addison-Wesley.

Haken, L. 1984. "A Digital Music Synthesizer." M.S. thesis. Urbana: University of Illinois, Department of Electric Engineering.

Haken, L., and K. Hebel. 1987. "The Platypus Programmers' Reference Manual." Technical Report. Urbana: University of Illinois Computer-based Education Research Laboratory.

Hebel, K. 1987. "Javelina: An Environment for the Development of Software for Digital Signal Processing." In J. Beauchamp, ed. *Proceedings of the 1987 International Computer Music Conference.* San Francisco: Computer Music Association, pp. 104–107.

Hebel, K. 1989. "Javelina: An Environment for Digital Signal Processing Software Development." *Computer Music Journal,* this issue.

Johnson, R. E., J. O. Graver, and L. W. Zurawski. 1988. "TS: An Optimizing Compiler for Smalltalk." In N. Meyrowitz, ed. *Proceedings of the 1988 Conference* on *Object-Oriented Programming Languages and Systems.* New York: ACM Press, pp. 222–233.

Krasner, G. 1980. "Machine Tongues VIII: The Design of a Smalltalk Music System." *Computer Music Journal* 4(4):4–14.

Scaletti, C. 1984. "The CERL Music Project at the University of Illinois." *Computer Music Journal* 9(1):45–58.

Scaletti, C. 1987. "Kyma: an Object-Oriented Language for Music Composition." In J. Beauchamp, ed. *Proceedings of the 1987 International Computer Music Conference.* San Francisco: Computer Music Association, pp. 49–56.

Scaletti, C., and R. E. Johnson. 1988. "An Interactive Graphic Environment for Object-Oriented Music Composition and Sound Synthesis." In N. Meyrowitz, ed. *Proceedings of the 1988 Conference on Object-Oriented Programming Languages and Systems.* New York: ACM Press, pp. 18–26.

Scaletti, C. 1989. "Composing Sound Objects in Kyma." *Perspectives of New Music* (27)1. In press.

Fig. 1. By typing expres-
sions into parameter
fields, you can specify
constraints between pa-
rameters. In this simple
example, the amplitude
scale factor on the right
channel will always be
constrained to be one mi-
nus the left scale factor.

## Addendum: A Kyma Update

In the time since the article was written, Kyma has
been expanded and slightly modified in the interests
of greater flexibility, consistency, and ease of use.
The introduction of variables brings Kyma closer to
being a full-fledged visual language. Among other
things, variables have made it possible to implement an extended Music-N-type score language and
a graphic editor for defining new classes of Sound objects. In the original version, a Sound object that was
too complex to be realized in real time had to be
simplified or realized at a lower sampling rate. Now
there is a third option: a Sound object's samples can
be recorded to disk for later playback. Experience
with the user interface suggested changes that make
it easier to keep track of the links between Sound
objects and that make it possible to create new Sound
objects in fewer steps. Kyma will continue to evolve
as more and more people use it and offer their reac-
tions and suggestions.

### Lifted Sounds

In Kyma, one can generalize from a specific Sound
object to a class of Sound objects by introducing
variables for some of the parameter values. A Sound
object with variables is called a "lifted" Sound object—lifted in the sense that it is described at a
"higher" level of abstraction than a Sound object
with no variables. A single lifted Sound object represents an infinite number of specific Sound objects. By typing expressions into parameter fields,
as in Fig. 1, one can specify relationships between
the parameters of a Sound object.

### Music-N

A lifted Sound object can function as an "instrument" that is instantiated and scheduled from a
"score," as in the Music-N-style languages. In Kyma,
a MusicN is a Sound object whose parameters include a score and a collection of subsounds to be
used as instruments. Any variable parameters of a
subsound can be set from the score.

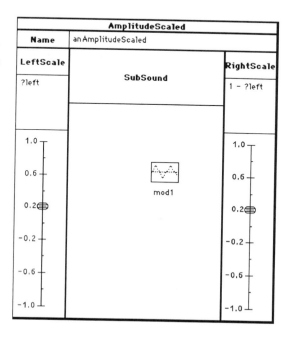

In the score language an event is specified as the
subsound name, a start time, and any number of
<parameter:value> pairs. The <parameter:value>
pairs can occur in any order, and any unspecified
parameters default to their (lexically) previous set-
tings. Parameter values are not limited to typed expressions; a subsound can take one of the other subsounds as an argument. Variables embedded within
a MusicN score are declared as external variables so
they can be set from outside the Sound object. A
score can include any Smalltalk-80 expression, thus
allowing for algorithmically generated event lists.
Figure 2 shows an editor for a simple MusicN object. Figures 3 and 4 illustrate the score language
which can be used with MusicN objects.

### Parameter Transformer

Where a MusicN object instantiates and sets the
variable parameters of a lifted Sound object, a

Fig. 2. *An extended Music-*
*N-style score language can*
*be used to instantiate and*
*schedule its subsounds.*
*Any variable parameters*

*in the subsound can be set*
*from the score. In the case*
*shown here, the subsound*
aSine *has two variables:*
?freq *and* ?dur.

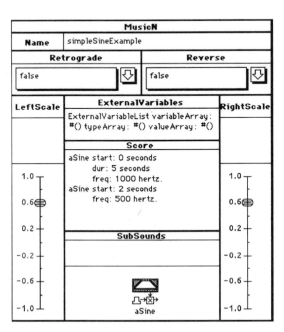

ParameterTransformer takes a specific Sound object and modifies or resets the values of its parameters. In the previous version of Kyma there were two different transformers—a FrequencyTransformer and a DurationTransformer. Now only one kind of transformer is needed; the ParameterTransformer can transform any parameter of its subsound. An example of the use of ParameterTransformer can be seen in Fig. 5.

### Defining Classes By Example

Once a Sound object has been designed, it is sometimes useful to generalize it for use in several contexts, i.e., to design a kind of "Sound macro" in order to reuse the Sound object and to hide some of its implementation details. The Sound class editor, shown in Fig. 6, lets you define a new class of Sound objects based upon a particular lifted Sound object.

In the example in Fig. 6, the new Sound class is based on a lifted Sound object. The variables in the basis Sound object become the parameters of the new Sound class. The name for the new class goes in the upper left. Just below that is an icon editor for designing an icon for the new class. The upper right is reserved for a class description that will appear whenever a user asks for a description of this class in the future. Below that is a small diagram showing the arrangement of the parameter fields in an editor for this class of Sound objects. The list on the far lower left is a list of this Sound object's parameters; next to that is a list of parameter types; next to that is a list of different types of editing views. On the right is a specification of a rectangle for that parameter field (above) and a place to type in a help string for this parameter (below).

### Triggered Sound Objects

Time-varying Sound objects are triggered by, and receive their parameters from, other Sound objects. Time-varying Sound objects can act as "patches" controlled in real time, either by a MIDI device or (using pitch and amplitude-tracking Sound objects) by input from the A/D converters. Triggered Sound objects differ from other Sound objects in that a triggered Sound object is scheduled for the entire period during which it might be triggered. When it is inactive, a triggered Sound object is still scheduled, but its output is zero. Sound objects whose start times and durations are known *a priori* can be swapped in and out of memory as they are needed, thus saving program memory space and computation time.

### Graceful Ways to Fall Out of Real Time

Because it takes a finite amount of time to compute a sample, it is inevitable that the signal processor will not be able to realize all Sound objects in real time. Two methods have been devised for attacking this problem in Kyma.

*Fig. 3. Since any Small-talk-80 expression can be used in the score, events can be specified algorithmically. In this example, 400*

*wavelets are specified, each having a random start time, duration, and number of cycles.*

*Fig. 4. Parameter values set by the score are not limited to numbers; they can be any Smalltalk object—including other Sound objects. In this example, the Sound object inst takes another Sound*

*object,* **Pluck,** *as its argument. Pluck is not given its own start time, so it will derive its start time from the context of* inst; *the parameters,* left *and* right, *are set from the score.*

```
| r t d c |

r ← Random new.
t ← 0.
400 timesRepeat: [
    t ← t + (0.05 * r next) seconds.
    d ←
        (r next * 0.05) seconds
            max: 2 samples.
    c ← (r next * 40 * t inSeconds // 4) truncated.
    Wavelet
        start: t
        duration: d
        cycles: c].
```

```
| p0 prevStart |
MM ← 480.
p0 ← #(0 1 11 5 2 4 3 9 10 6 8 7).
prevStart ← 0.

"p0"
1 to: 12 do: [:i |
    inst start: (prevStart ← prevStart + (p0 at: i)) beats
        offset: (p0 at: i)
        sound: (Pluck left: 1 right: 1)].
"r5"
prevStart ← 6.
12 to: 1 by: -1 do: [:i |
    inst start: (prevStart ← prevStart + (p0 at: i)) beats
        offset: (p0 at: i) + 5
        sound: (Pluck left: 0 right: 1)].

"i0"
prevStart ← 6.
12 to: 1 by: -1 do: [:i |
    inst start: (prevStart ← prevStart + (p0 at: i)) beats
        offset: (p0 at: i) negated - 24
        sound: (Pluck left: 0.6 right: 0)].

low start: 9 seconds carFreq: 100 hertz cmRatio: 2.0 dur: 0.5 seconds.
```

Fig. 5. *ParameterTransformers are used to modify or reset the parameter values of an existing Sound object. In this example,* *any parameters named frequency will be multiplied by 1.5, parameters named duration will be multiplied by 0.5, and any* *parameters named modulation index will be set to the current time divided by the total duration of the subsound.*

| **Name** | aParameterTransformer |
|---|---|

| **Retrograde** |
|---|
| false |

| **Reverse** |
|---|
| false |

| **ExternalVariables** |
|---|
| ExternalVariableList variableArray: #() typeArray: #() valueArray: #() |

| **Transformation** |
|---|
| snd frequency: snd frequency * 1.5<br>   duration: snd duration * 0.5.<br>   modulationIndex: time/totalDuration |

| **SubSound** |
|---|
| ▱<br>⇓<br>▱▱...<br>fiveReps |

### Variable Sample Rate

If a Sound object cannot be realized in real time, one option is to lower the sample rate and try again. In many cases, the degradation in signal is a reasonable tradeoff for being able to test the Sound object in real time.

### Samples To Disk

By allowing the output samples to be stored on disk, the new version of Kyma can accommodate Sound objects of arbitrary complexity. The sample file on the disk can be treated just like any other Sound object; thus, previously recorded sounds can be mixed with and altered by sounds being generated in real time.

## Improvements to the User Interface

On the basis of my experiences using Kyma to compose and my observations of others as they use Kyma, the user interface has been redesigned in order to make the links between Sound objects clearer and to shorten the number of steps required for some commonly used operations.

### Structure View

Originally, the structure of Sound objects was represented as "boxes within boxes." In other words, a Sound object $f(g(x))$ would be represented as an $x$ within a $g$ within an $f$. In practice, it was found that the box representation could become confusing and awkward for navigating through more complicated structures. It was time-consuming to get to a deeply nested Sound object, and, once opened, the links between Sound objects were no longer represented on the display.

In the new user interface, the Sound object's structure is represented directly as a graph. The subsounds of each node can be either hidden or revealed by double-clicking on that node. Links between Sound objects are always apparent, and one can jump to arbitrarily deeply nested Sounds. An exemplary Structure view is shown in Fig. 7.

### Prototypes

In practice, it was observed that most Sound objects are created by modifying existing Sound objects, and that it was often frustrating to have to go through the create-save-place method of creating Sound objects. The new interface provides a collection of prototype Sound objects that can be dragged directly to the SoundPlane or to any part of an edited Sound object's structure. Once in position, the prototypical Sound object can be modified as desired. Composers can also define their own prototype collections as they accumulate useful Sound objects.

*Fig. 6. The Sound class
editor.*

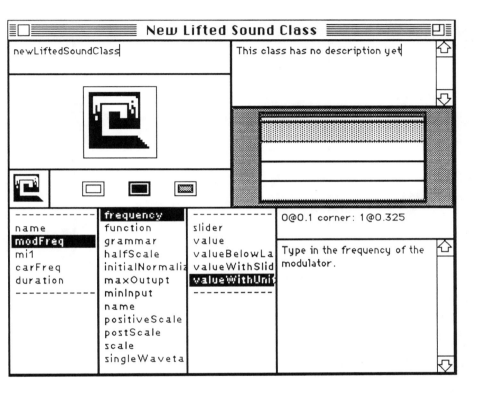

**Summary**

Kyma continues to evolve to reflect the desires and
practices of those who use it. The modularity and
polymorphism encouraged by object-oriented programming have made it practical to add logical extensions to the basic language without having to
rewrite the entire system.

*Fig. 7. The structure of a Sound object is shown on the left. When a node is selected, its parameters can be changed by using the editor on the right.*

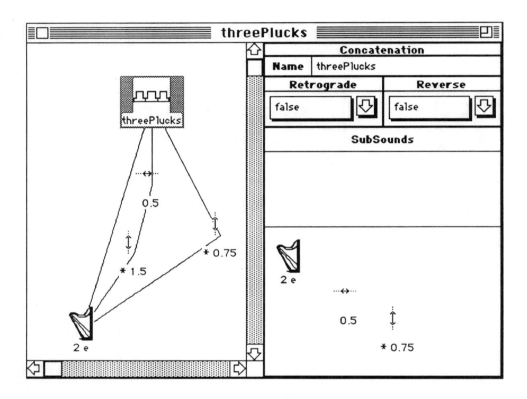

*Scaletti*

**Henry S. Flurry**
Center for Performing Arts and Technology
School of Music
University of Michigan
1100 Baits Drive
Ann Arbor, Michigan 48109 USA

# An Introduction to the Creation Station

## Introduction

The Center for Performing Arts and Technology (CPAT) is located in the School of Music at the University of Michigan in Ann Arbor. Partially funded by a five year grant administered by the Regents of the University, CPAT is preparing to enter its third year. CPAT's goal is to provide "personnel, equipment, and facilities to support research and development of technological applications in the performing arts" (Gregory 1987). We provide support for art creation and performances, and we explore and develop software for small computers, but it is the Creation Station that promises to be the most exciting venture of CPAT.

The Creation Station, codeveloped by CPAT director David Gregory and associate directors Hal Brokaw and Henry Flurry, is a NeXT workstation-based software package that will provide an artist with the tools necessary to create multimedia works. It utilizes the advanced sound synthesis and graphics capabilities of the NeXT workstation, creating a unified environment for the artist wishing to integrate multiple media without sacrificing flexible and sophisticated storage, editing, and performance capabilities. While the initial version of the Creation Station is strictly a composition and performance tool, we aim to provide a software foundation that will support different and perhaps yet undeveloped aspects of computer-aided art, including computer-based art research.

This paper introduces the Creation Station and describes the actual implementation of the software in some detail. Because the Creation Station software is written in the Objective-C programming language, a brief introduction to object-oriented programming languages is included. Other

Computer Music Journal, Vol. 13, No. 2, Summer 1989
© 1989 Massachusetts Institute of Technology.

object-oriented programming tutorials are also recommended (Krasner 1980; Lieberman 1982; Pascoe 1986).

## Overview of the Creation Station

One of the current problems in multimedia productions is that the artist must deal with a wide range of equipment. There are countless manuals to read and cables to connect, and, more often than not, the difficulties of synchronizing the different media distract from the creative process. By seamlessly integrating multiple media within one box, the Creation Station attempts to eliminate many of these distractions (Flurry 1988).

The first step toward unification is establishing a single user interface. We utilize traditional music metaphors to present an interface that will allow control of multiple art forms. For instance, one window of the Creation Station user interface will contain the master recorder panel (with PLAY, STOP, and RECORD buttons), which will govern the performance and recording of all events. From this window, the button labeled PLAY will perform any Creation Station–based piece consisting of musical elements, graphic elements, or both.

We borrow another notion from traditional tape players: that of "tracks." Like many existing music sequencing programs, the Creation Station allows the artist to break up a composition into various tracks containing fragments of the whole. There are, however, two major differences in the Creation Station. The first is that tracks can be designated to hold a variety of media, including, but not limited to, MIDI data, sampled sound, algorithmically-generated sound, animation, and video. Multiple tracks containing different media can be performed simultaneously. The second is that the user is allowed to organize the tracks hierarchically. Typically, an artist does not think of his or her creation as a single indivisible unit. A hierarchical track system allows the artist to organize any creation into progressively smaller and more manageable units. For example, a composer writing a traditional sonata might hierarchically organize the tracks in the following manner: one track defines the whole sonata; three subordinate tracks define the three main sections of the sonata (exposition, development, and recapitulation); and further subordinate tracks represent, as tradition would dictate, the thematic areas. In another example, a choreographer might create a track that specifies the movement of a dancer across the floor. This track might also have subordinate tracks that define the more detailed movements of the limbs, torso, and head. Here the hierarchy reflects the various degrees of the dancer's motions. In these examples, it is likely that the track hierarchies would roughly parallel the performance order of the tracks. However, tracks may be sequenced in whatever order and with whatever timing the artist desires. Our mechanism of sequencing the various tracks allows artists to organize their pieces into hierarchies that reflect their individual creative process.

Working with different media frequently requires that the user work within multiple timing bases. The Creation Station allows the user to display the passage of time in any timing base desired, including minutes and seconds, measures and beats, SMPTE time code, and user-defined timing bases. This last option allows the support of new standards as well as the creation of unusual ones. For example, a colleague once suggested that, "If you were writing a piece of music based upon the ups and downs of the New York Stock Exchange averages, you would likely want to be able to index your music in a timing base of weeks and days."

The Creation Station is designed to work with an undefined and potentially unlimited set of event classes, each with associated device drivers and event editing environments. In the initial version of the Creation Station, we provide tools to work within two different media: sound and three-dimensional animation. The sound tools support a variety of output devices (including support for MIDI command output and the NeXT workstation's internal 56001 digital signal processor),

and a number of ways to enter and edit musical events. With animation, choreographers and directors will be able to define three-dimensional motion paths for dancers and actors, and view the resulting movement in three-dimensional perspective. Furthermore, choreographers will be able to add musical accompaniment, and actors will be able to record, edit, and play back spoken lines. These initial tools are designed to help performing artists in the creative process through software simulation.

As the hardware evolves and the software base grows, the Creation Station will better fulfill the needs of more artists. We hope to provide other artistic tools (such as theater set and lighting design simulation, interactive performance tools, and interactive video editing), direct creative output (such as video art), educational tools (such as musicianship lessons), and research tools (such as large sound and video databases, and applications supporting interactive testing of theories) in later versions of the Creation Station. In addition, the Creation Station will support third party development of new media and editing tools. This capability will allow programmers outside of CPAT to develop software for new types of peripherals and to meet the specific needs of other artists.

**Programming the Creation Station**

By now, the reader can probably envision many potential programming obstacles within the Creation Station project. One task that seemed insurmountable was how to create a software package where an undefined and potentially large set of media must cooperate. Although the Creation Station could be implemented in many different programming languages, most programmers would agree that the complexity of the necessary code would be almost too great to manage within languages such as C or Pascal. However, the Creation Station is being developed in Objective-C (Cox 1986; NeXT 1988). In an object-oriented programming language, programming tasks are conceptually simplified so that even the largest problems become manageable.

## Object-Oriented Programming Languages

### Message Passing

In procedural programming languages, data are passed as arguments to procedures to be processed. For example, the calculation of the square root of some numerical value $x$ might be executed by the procedure call **sqrt(x)**. There is, somewhere inside the program code, a unique function accessed by the **sqrt()** call. This function accepts an argument, evaluates the square root of the argument, and returns the resulting value. However, the **sqrt()** procedure expects a particular type of value, typically a double-precision floating-point number. It is the responsibility of the programmer to make sure that the **sqrt()** function is not passed a character, integer, or a user-defined structure. The user must also make sure that the function's return value is assigned to a variable of the proper type.

Because so much of the burden of data typing and procedure management is placed upon the programmer, there is a "complexity barrier" that prevents economical coding and maintenance of complicated systems (Winograd 1979). We believe the complexity of the Creation Station would have approached this barrier.

### Objects and Classes

Object-oriented programming languages encourage a different approach by blurring the distinction between data and procedural code. To explain the concepts behind object-oriented programming languages and the terms used in them, I will start by discussing the *object*, the basic construct of an object-oriented programming language. You may think of an object as analogous to any entity within the "real" world. Like anything else around us, an object can be described as a combination of various properties and behaviors.

To command an object to do something, one sends it a *message*. As in the real world, the same message sent to different objects may mean completely different things. For example, sending the message *run* to the objects "boy," "computer pro-

gram," and "stocking" would generate three very different actions. In object-oriented programming languages, this is called *polymorphism*, the use of a single message to evoke different actions from different objects.

Objects may be of the same *class* or of different classes. A class is simply a definition of the properties and behaviors of a group of objects. Objects of the same class exhibit similar properties and behaviors, whereas objects of different classes will likely display different properties and behaviors. "Fred," "Kevin," and "Nancy" may all be elements of the class "People," and they will all exhibit certain similarities. However, these three people are unique, even if they are of the same class. In object-oriented programming languages, an *instance* of a class is an object that belongs to that class but has a unique identity.

At this point, it becomes necessary to discuss the structure of an object. Within a class definition, the programmer defines an object's *instance variables* and its *methods*. Methods are the "procedures" associated with an object. A message sent to an object invokes a method of the same name, executing the program code of that method and returning a value to the caller. Instance variables are variables that are accessible only by the methods associated with an instance. One may liken the instance variables to the "properties" of an object, and the messages and methods to the "behavior" of an object. Thus, objects of the same class all respond to the same messages, execute the same methods, and have the same data format for their instance variables. Different instances of the same class each contain their own copy of the instance variables, however, and the instance variable values associated with one instance may be changed without affecting the values of any other instances.

### Encapsulation and Inheritance

There are several other valuable characteristics of object-oriented programming languages, most notably encapsulation, inheritance, and dynamic binding. The instance variables of an object can only be accessed and changed by the methods associated with that object. This process of information hiding, called *encapsulation*, has some obvious benefits to software design. Because the data of an object can only be accessed by that object's methods, there is less chance of accidental data corruption by outside routines.

*Inheritance* is a natural by-product of the hierarchy of classes in which all objects reside. In creating a class, the programmer defines only the differences between the desired class and its *superclass*. Instance variables and methods that are not redefined are inherited by the *subclass*, causing this new class to exhibit properties and behaviors similar to those of its superclass. Inheritance is a powerful capability of object-oriented programming languages. Valuable programming time is saved by writing only the code that is necessary to differentiate a new class from its superclass. Inheritance also extends the life cycle of a class definition by allowing it to be tailored to the unique needs of other applications.

A third aspect of object-oriented programming languages that is often overlooked is *dynamic binding*, the postponement of deciding what method to invoke for a particular message until run time. Without dynamic binding, the ability to assign any object to a variable would not exist, for the variable would have to be statically defined in order for the compiler to determine successfully which methods are bound to the messages that are being sent. Dynamic binding also allows the creation of new classes that will work with existing precompiled code. Dynamic binding is key to enabling third party extensions to the Creation Station software.

### Programming in Object-Oriented Programming Languages

Many programmers accustomed to traditional programming languages find it difficult at first to program with object-oriented programming languages. Two basic concepts that are useful in designing object-oriented software are also useful for understanding many programming decisions presented in this paper. The first is that the methods of an object should closely relate to the data held within the instance variables of that object. The second is that objects with conceptual similarities should be acted upon with a common protocol (set of messages).

The first concept is fundamental to programming within an object-oriented programming language. It might make sense, for example, to have an object representing a musical note be responsible for playing itself as staccato, but it would not make sense to have this same note object be responsible for deleting a file on the computer disk. This would be counterintuitive and would make management of the programming project difficult.

The second concept is not as clear as the first. It does not dictate how to program in an object-oriented programming language as much as it displays the power of dynamic binding combined with polymorphism (dynamic polymorphism). Consider the hypothetical generic class Event, which might contain any type of performable event. When we look at a group of proposed event classes (Musical Events, Animation Events, Video Events, etc.), we can begin to formulate a list of several conceptually common methods: for example, perform the next event; return the real time of following event to occur; or compare the event attack-point timings of two individual events within the same class.

Each event class would be more than likely to execute each method differently; the performance of a musical event might produce sound, and the realization of a dance event might generate visual images. However, the methods applied to the event classes share the same general concepts. Thus, if these methods carry a common protocol (i.e., respond to the same set of messages), it would be possible to write code that would carry out many of the desired functions for an object of any event class.

To perform an event—be it musical or graphic—we could write the single line of code:

```
[anEvent performNextEvent];
```

which, in Objective-C, sends the message *performNextEvent* to the event object stored in the variable referred to by the identifier *anEvent*. By changing the value of the variable *anEvent*, we could per-

Fig. 1. Polymorphism: different objects may respond
in different ways to the
same message.

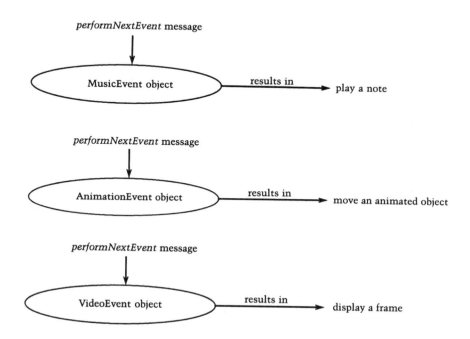

*performNextEvent* message

MusicEvent object — results in → play a note

*performNextEvent* message

AnimationEvent object — results in → move an animated object

*performNextEvent* message

VideoEvent object — results in → display a frame

form any event defined within this hypothetical program.

This is how we handle many objects of similar function within the Creation Station. Dynamic polymorphism allows us to define different "genres" of objects, where each object of a single genre implements a set of messages in conceptually similar but physically different ways. We can then use the same messages to control different objects of one genre producing varying results. Figure 1 demonstrates this dynamic polymorphism for the example of sending the message *performNextEvent* to instances of three different Event classes.

### The Modules of the Creation Station

The Creation Station may be divided into two sections: the kernel, which is its "engine," and the installable modules, which actually make it functional. The modules define the media available on the Creation Station, how a medium's event data are created and stored, and how the user edits and interacts with the media. Our goal is to provide a mature and stable kernel, allowing us, and third party programmers, to focus the majority of the Creation Station's evolution on the development of new modules.

In actuality, a module does not need to be anything more than a single object of a predefined genre. To be more precise, we define a module by the following criteria:

A module is an object following the protocol defined by one of a predefined set of object genres.
Multiple different modules of the same genre may simultaneously reside within the Creation Station.
The user may choose which modules to activate in order to vary the characteristics of the Creation Station.

The protocols of the various types of modules define the functionality of the Creation Station, and the actual implementations of the protocols within each individual module define the diversity of the Creation Station.

We can briefly examine the module termed "Performer" as an example. For any single module to be of type Performer, it must follow a strictly defined set of protocols, meaning that it must understand and properly implement a given number of messages. One such protocol or message that a Performer-type module must understand is *perform anEvent*. A module not responding to this message will not function properly as a Performer. One can immediately begin to see the functionality of any Performer-type module; its duty is to *perform anEvent*. This entails translating at a specified time the computer representation of an event into a perceptible realization of the event. The potential diversity of the modules becomes apparent when one examines how each individual Performer module interprets the message *perform anEvent*. The MIDI Performer of the Creation Station responds to the message *perform anEvent* by sending MIDI commands out over the MIDI data lines to connected synthesizers. On the other hand, the Dance Performer interprets the same command by updating the three-dimensional position of a dancer on the simulated stage. Both of these Performer modules have, in effect, the same functionality, but each module's unique interpretation of the message adds to the diversity of the Creation Station.

In addition to the Performer module, there are several different types of modules defined for the Creation Station, including the three modules discussed next: the Recorder, the Event, and the Conductor.

The Recorder module accepts external input and translates this input into a time-stamped internal representation of the event. The Creation Station currently includes Recorder modules that record music from the MIDI data lines, dance choreography from the user's mouse movements, and voice from a microphone. Two of the messages that Recorder modules must implement are *recordEvents* and *stopRecording*.

The Event module is probably the most interesting of all the modules defined within the Creation

Station. An Event module is responsible for storing and retrieving internal representations of one or more events that are recorded and performed. Like other modules, Event modules must recognize a predefined set of messages, such as *getNextEvent* (during performance) and *storeNewEvent* (during recording). These two messages make the Event module unique in that the Event becomes the link between input and output. However, the module is not interesting because of what is defined in the protocol, but because of what is not defined, that is, how the protocol is to be interpreted.

A Music Event module that accepts input from a MIDI Recorder and sends output to a MIDI Performer is not much more complex than an object which stores and retrieves MIDI data. A Dance Event module, on the other hand, does not simply give the Dancer Performer the same points received from the Dance Recorder. Instead, the three-dimensional positions handed to the Performer are points interpolated from a three-dimensional spline constructed from the original points passed by the Recorder. It is even possible to create a "hybrid" Event module that takes as input the three-dimensional points recorded by the Dance Recorder and creates as its output music events performable by the MIDI Performer. Event modules can also be purely algorithmic. One could create an Event module that is actually a music programming language interpreter which stores a user-defined program. During or prior to the performance, the user's program is executed, and the music events to be performed are calculated.

The Conductor module is responsible for converting virtual time to real time and vice versa. A conductor should, for example, be able to tell at what time during a performance measure 32, beat 3 would occur if the tempo was a constant 90 beats per minute. Likewise, a conductor should be able to tell at what measure and beat the performance was at when 52 seconds had passed with a tempo varying according to user specifications. A conductor should properly respond to *conduct aTime* (translate virtual-time to real-time) and *unconduct aTime* (translate real-time to virtual-time). A Conductor module may be likened to an object containing a function (for *conduct aTime*) and its inverse function (for *unconduct aTime*), whereby the function has the additional restriction of now allowing time to go backwards.

The Conductor is designed as a module of the Creation Station instead of as a hard-coded feature so that the user will have the ability to choose how the tempo will be altered. Currently, the Creation Station supplies a Conductor module whose tempo map is formulated from line segments the user defines with the mouse. Other Conductors could be created based on exponential tempo maps, splines, or even algorithms. One or more of these Conductor modules could be used to control the tempo of Creation Station–based performances.

## The Node

Each of the modules described above has very specific functions. To coordinate all of these functions, we have created the *Node* object. Although it is directly analogous to a "track," it is called "Node" to emphasize its ability to fit within a hierarchy. For every track created by the user within the Creation Station, there is an instance of a Node object. The track hierarchy created by the user directly corresponds to the hierarchical graph defined by the Node object instances.

A Node is not distinct from any other Node object unless it is associated with individual instances of each of the four modules discussed above. The modules that define the Node are what type of event is stored, be it music, dance, or another type; how events are performed; how events are recorded; and the tempo (tempi) of the event sequence.

Modules are nothing more than object classes which are instantiated for use at run time. An association between a Node instance and an instance of a module is simply a mutual reference to each other. It is useful to think of an "association" somewhat more abstractly, as a communication channel. Whenever an Event, Recorder, Performer, or Conductor module "plugs into" a Node instance, it forms a communication channel with that Node. Each of these modules may communicate with the Node object, but never with one another. While it may seem inefficient for the Recorder to pass infor-

mation indirectly to the Event through the Node, the design follows good object-oriented encapsulation practice. Modules are isolated from other modules, facilitating kernel control of modules and software maintenance.

In addition to managing the communication channels of many modules, the Node has the ability to maintain an ordered list of multiple instances of the same type of Event module. In essence, this creates a kind of "event list" whose performance is determined by the actual Event modules and the Performer modules attached to the Node. In discussing the interaction between the Event and other modules, however, it is easiest to speak as if the Node only referred to a single Event object. Figure 2 illustrates the connection of a Node to the objects that use it within the Creation Station software.

By now, the extensibility of the Creation Station should be clear to the reader. For example, if the NeXT computer were to be hooked up to a Pixar computer, a new Dance Performer module could be written to create images of the dancers upon the Pixar machine. The user could then enter and edit the choreography on the NeXT computer, and use it together with the Pixar machine to create high-quality imaging of the finished choreography. All that is necessary for this is for the new Pixar Performer module to follow the required Performer protocol, and to accept the choreographic event construct.

## The Recording Cycle

To clarify the structure of the Creation Station modules, I will outline two processes involved in the creation of art on the Creation Station: the recording process and the performing process. The descriptions that follow are not detailed, but they should give the reader an idea of how the modules relate to each other and how the communication channels are used.

It is assumed that, in some way, the Recorder module is notified when events from the real world occur. The event might be a MIDI *Note On* command coming in over the NeXT computer's serial

*Fig. 2. Communication
channels during a
performance.*

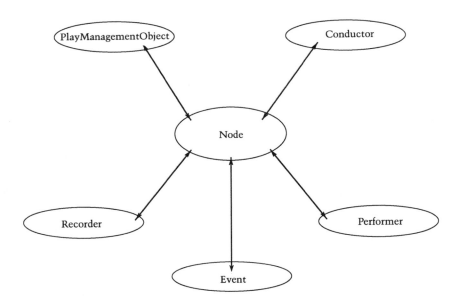

ports or a mouse position update coming from the display postscript server. When an event is received, the Recorder module buffers it for later processing. This prevents the Recorder module from stealing precious CPU cycles during a period when performance timing is critical. After the performance, the Recorder processes the events and begins a cycle of repeatedly generating an event construct and its associated time-stamp, sending this information to the Node. Note that the value of the time-stamp indicates in real time (minutes and seconds) where an event occurred relative to the start of the performance.

Upon receiving an event construct and time-stamp, the Node requests that the Conductor *unconduct* the real-time time-stamp into the timing base expected by the associated Event module. This unconduct stage is what ensures that events recorded with a predefined tempo graph (possibly involving accelerandi and other tempo changes), are mapped onto the correct internal timings. The Conductor calculates from the real time a virtual

time to return to the Node. For example, the real time 54.2 seconds might unconduct into the virtual time of measure 35, beat 3.

Having accepted the data, the Node passes the event construct and its virtual-time time-stamp to the Event module. The Event module stores the event for possible playback or editing, converting the event construct into a more useful data format if necessary. The cycle begins again and is repeated for every event construct the Recorder module generates.

### The PlayManagementObject

The performance cycle involves correctly juggling the many Node instances that make up a Creation Station piece. In order to manage all of these different Nodes, there is one object that controls the performance of all Nodes: the *PlayManagementObject*.

There is only one instance of the PlayManagementObject, and during a performance, the Play-ManagementObject can only communicate with one Node instance at a time. When the Play-ManagementObject is communicating with a Node, it is again useful to visualize it as temporarily attaching itself to that Node instance and forming a new communication channel. As in the other objects attached to the Node, the scope of the PlayManagementObject's communication channel extends only to the Node instance and never to any of the modules.

It is probably clear by now that the Creation Station is an "event-based" system. It works under the assumption that all applicable art forms can be broken down into discrete events. For example, a composition can typically be broken down into individual notes, and these individual notes can be further broken down into attack and release points. MIDI is, in fact, an international standard defining how music can be broken down into these and other discrete events. The Creation Station simultaneously performs many Nodes on potentially different media by repeatedly having each of the Nodes take a turn at sending out one discrete event. Ideally, the user then perceives all of these discrete events as a multimedia performance.

The PlayManagementObject determines which Node will send out an event next. During a performance, each Node requests the PlayManagement-Object to allow it to send a single discrete event. Each of these requests includes a real-time time-stamp denoting when the discrete event is to occur. These requests are sorted according to several criteria, and when the PlayManagementObject responds to the request with the highest priority, many things can happen.

## The Performance Cycle

First, the PlayManagementObject sends a message to the chosen Node instance to "perform its next event" at a given time. This time is the same as the time-stamp that was attached to the Node instance's original request. The event to be played might be a musical pitch attack or release, or it might be a position change by an actor in three-dimensional space. In any case, the PlayManagementObject does not know what type of event is being performed, so it is up to the Node to respond properly.

Once the Node receives the request, it needs to retrieve the actual discrete event to be performed from the attached Event module. The Node issues a *getNextEvent* request to the Event module. In order to respond to this request the Event object must calculate what event is to happen next. The calculations may be as simple as retrieving an event from a sequential list of discrete events, or as complicated as evaluating an expression within a user-defined algorithm. In either case, the discrete event to be performed is stored within an event construct. The Event object then calculates the virtual time at which a following event should occur. This virtual time will be used by the Node to calculate a real-time time-stamp to be used in the next performance request to the PlayManagementObject. The event construct and the virtual time are returned to the Node.

The Node now asks the Performer to *performAn-Event*, passing along with the message the Event module's event construct and the real-time time-stamp originally received from the PlayManagementObject. A MIDI performer might realize the event by sending MIDI commands to some external synthesizers; a Dance Performer might realize the event by changing the position of a dancer on the stage. Once the event has been performed, the Node turns its attention to preparing for the next discrete event. However, the Node is not allowed to perform a second event just yet; rather, it must issue a real-time time-stamped message to the PlayManagementObject to permit the performance of this new event. The Node takes the virtual time returned from the Event object and asks the Conductor to *conduct aTime*, using the user-defined tempo map. The real time returned specifies in seconds at what time, relative to the start of the performance, the Node's next discrete event should occur.

The Node then passes this real-time time-stamp to the PlayManagementObject, where it is associated with a new event performance request from this Node. Remember that this real-time stamp will be the same real-time stamp that is passed to the Node when the performance request is acknowledged. The PlayManagementObject quickly resorts the performance request list and decides which Node should perform its event next. The performance cycle is repeated until all events of the performance are played or until the user intervenes.

## Editing Nodes

So far, I have discussed the parts of the Creation Station necessary for performance and recording. However, equally important to the success of the Creation Station are its editing capabilities. As with the other aspects of our software, we have approached editing with the assumption that we ourselves will not be able to develop all of the tools desired by users of the package. To achieve our goals of extensibility, we have designed two other modules, the *Editor* and the *EditorUI* (short for Editor User Interface).

These modules divide the tasks of editing into two groups. The first group, covered by the Editor modules, does the actual "brain work" of editing. Ideally, code contained within the Editor modules implements the actual algorithms that realize the given tasks. For example, Editor modules might contain code that inverts a given sequence of musical notes, augments the time taken to traverse a path, or deletes a word from recorded speech. The second group of functionality, that involving the user interface, is delegated to the EditorUI modules. These modules are responsible for representing the events stored within a Node in some form, allowing the user to select and deselect a number of events, and invoking the necessary code for the actions chosen by the user. Figure 3 shows several of the user interface components of the Creation Station. A spline path control panel and editor are shown in the two windows in the upper region of Fig. 3, the views of a text editor and its menu for editing a ScoreFile are shown in the lower region,

and a global control panel for management of multiple media within the integrated environment are in the leftmost window.

In theory, different EditorUI modules can be created to present the same information to the user in different formats. Likewise, different Editor modules can be created that will allow the user to apply different sets of functions to the same set of events. The artist will be able to mix and match these different modules to tailor the editing environment to his or her specific needs. To illustrate the possibilities, we can examine various ways of approaching music editing. For example, there are many ways of displaying music information: common-practice music notation, piano-roll notation, ScoreFile text format, or MIDI data format. EditorUI modules could be created to present music information to the user in any of these formats. In fact, it is quite possible that a scholar of medieval music would want an EditorUI module that displayed plainsong notation. Once an artist has chosen a particular EditorUI module, he or she can then optionally load up a number of Editor modules to provide various editing functions. For instance, there would likely be an Editor module that contained the "old favorite" score editor functions: insert, delete, invert, transpose, quantize, and swing. There could be other Editor modules more geared toward compositional methods, including modules for manipulating tone rows and modules for generating rhythmic patterns. Our medieval scholar, who is also a composer, might use the plainsong notation editorUI in conjunction with the old favorites editor, the tone row editor, and the rhythm editor. Figure 4 illustrates the use of multiple editors on the same structure. In this case, one can see two cameras presenting different views of a simulated stage where animated dancers are visible. The control panels can be used to move, pan, or zoom the cameras.

While the above design provides for much versatility, it is also potentially limiting. Sometimes an EditorUI module must be tightly coupled with a specific Editor module, meaning that the "mix-and-match" design is not easily implemented. To accommodate this, we allow Editor and EditorUI modules to work as paired objects.

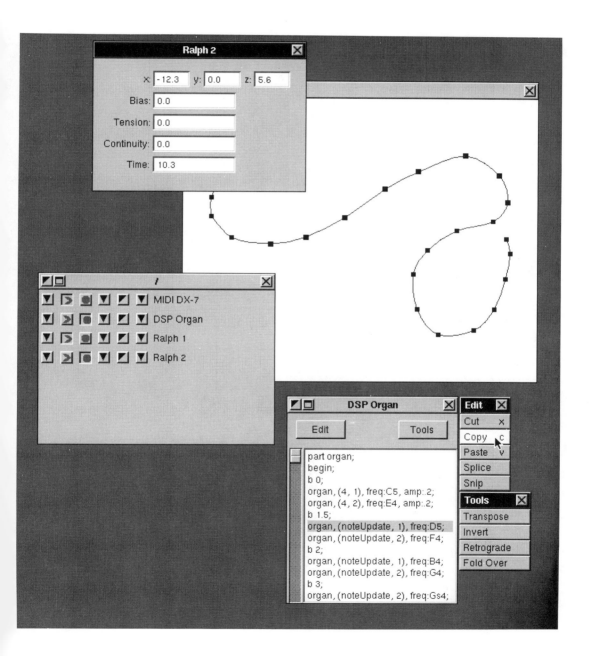

*Fig. 4. Multiple perspec-
tives on an animated
choreography.*

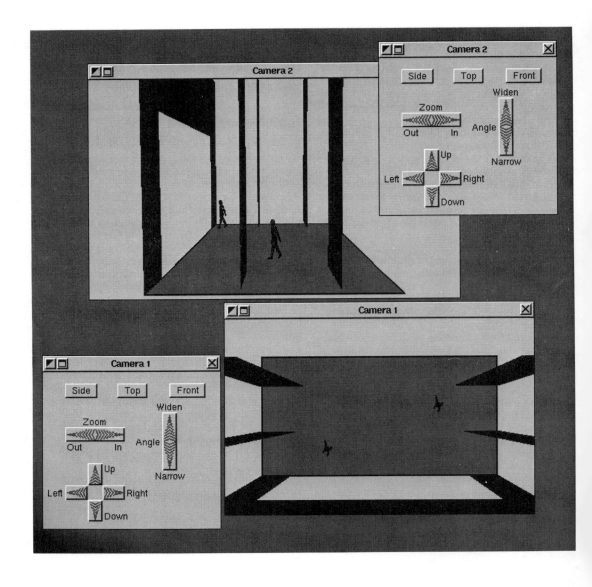

## Problems of the Creation Station

When developing a large and complex package, one encounters situations where the advantages and disadvantages of a design decision must be weighed. In many cases, a design is implemented because of its strong points, and the developer must cope with the negative side effects. The Creation Station is no exception to this tendency in that it has presented its fair share of challenges to us.

One of the problems of the Creation Station is that it is an event-based system which tries to accomplish much in real time or close to real time. This means that there is a coarseness to the timing of discrete events that is not present in non-real-time systems. For example, when performing Creation Station–controlled digital signal processing sounds, it is difficult to transmit continuous parameter changes as the sound is created in real time. In a non-real-time system, the computer could leisurely calculate the sound to be performed, ensuring that parameter changes of the calculated material could appear smooth and continuous to the listener. To help alleviate this problem, new Performer and Event modules can be created that will precalculate certain types of events for later performance. Complex three-dimensional and real-time animation, for example, must be rendered with crude approximations of the desired results. We plan to provide the ability to precalculate segments of the animation, so that during a performance, the user will be presented with a reasonable rendering of the scene with an adequate refresh rate.

The realization of any event takes a certain amount of time, but certain events take so much time that it is conceivable for the realization of one event to delay the realization of a following event noticeably. It is imperative that computation-intensive events, such as graphics, not be allowed to delay timing-sensitive events such as music. To minimize the likelihood of this, we employ the use of an "intelligent buffer." Performer modules precalculate the realization of an event before it is actually time to realize the event. The results of this precalculation are stored within a buffer. When it

is time for the event to occur, the buffer requests the Performer module to realize the precalculated event. Theoretically, the actual realization should take little time, and delays during dense passages should be minimal. The buffer is enhanced by the fact that it can optionally discard queued events of the same type if the performance is running behind. For example, if five animation frames are queued, and it is time for the last frame, then the first four frames will be discarded. This discard technique will only work for media where successive events supersede old events; it will not work for music.

Regardless of the nonlinearity of the track structure within the Creation Station, the performance of a piece is perceived as a progression from beginning to end. This perception encourages the user to wish for functions such as rewind, fast forward, and random access to some point within the piece. Because the user can define the track structure to be any form, these "taken-for-granted" functions are difficult to implement. The easiest solution we can devise is to keep track of Node launches and Node stops during a performance. If these data are sorted according to time, then it is simple to recreate a performance context for a time close to the desired position. Then, each individual Node active during this context can be asked to "fast forward" to the exact time desired. This process will work, but it is slower than the quick indexing of linear tracks, and it can potentially require a large amount of memory.

Finally, the Creation Station is designed to allow third party extensions. We are hoping for the ability to perform dynamic linking of Objective-C programs, but it is unclear when we will be able to do this. Without dynamic linking, it is difficult to distribute a single package into which other people can add modules. At this point, it seems probable that the Creation Station will be distributed not only as a ready-to-run program, but also as a set of libraries with which the user can run a "Creation Station–builder." With this builder, the user would specify what modules he or she wants linked into a particular version of the Creation Station. The builder would then run the appropriate linking routines to build a completely new Creation Station application. The user would be able to create as

*Fig. 5. A sample Creation
Station screen.*

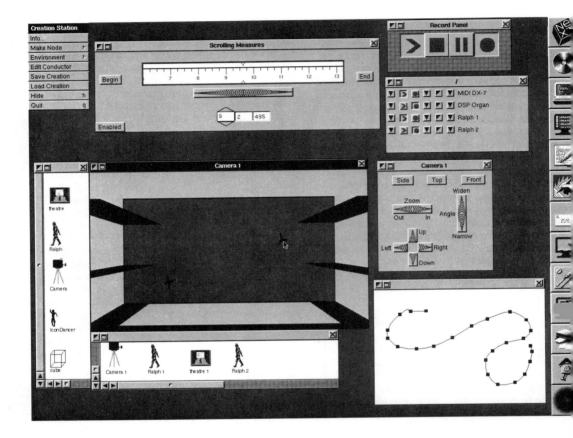

many different versions of the Creation Station as
he or she would like, with each version tailored to
meet certain artistic requirements.

## Conclusion

The Creation Station is still in its infancy, but we
are excited about its future. We have recognized
that both hardware and software will continue to
evolve, and we have tried to design the Creation
Station with this evolution in mind. In addition, the
NeXT workstation platform, along with the benefits
of object-oriented programming in Objective-C,
have immensely facilitated the development of our
software.

During the EDUCOM 1988 conference in Wash-
ington, D.C., the Creation Station was publicly
demonstrated for the first time. The enthusiastic
and imaginative responses to this early "alpha" version demonstrated the potential of our software. In
addition to expressing excitement about the multimedia capabilities, people envisioned innovative
uses for the Creation Station. A band director, for
example, could choreograph acts for a marching
band. A criminologist could use the Creation Sta-

tion to recreate scenes of a crime, complete with sound effects, for use in the courtoorm. A laryngologist could use the package to animate the vocal tracts with the appropriate sounds. From these and other ideas, it appears that the Creation Station may well influence not only the way educators produce and teach the arts, but also the way educators teach science and the humanities.

In closing, Fig. 5 shows the Creation Station software user interface in action, with the system's main menu visible in the upper-left corner of the display, a performance time window next to it, a record panel and track window in the upper-right region, and the icons for several other applications of the NeXT workstation along the right side. The camera control panel, spline editor, and stage animation are linked to the choreography sequence that is being edited.

## References

Cox, B. J. 1986. *Object-Oriented Programming: An Evolutionary Approach.* Reading, Massachusetts: Addison-Wesley.

Flurry, H. S. 1988. "The Creation Station: An Approach to a Multimedia Workstation." *Leonardo,* Special FISEA Issue 1988, pp. 31–37.

Gregory, D. 1987. *A Proposal for a Center for Performing Arts and Technology.* Ann Arbor: University of Michigan.

Krasner, G. 1980. "Machine Tongues VIII: The Design of a Smalltalk Music System." *Computer Music Journal* 4(4):4–14.

Lieberman, H. 1982. "Machine Tongues IX: Object-Oriented Programming." *Computer Music Journal* 6(3):8–21.

NeXT, Inc. 1988. *Programming Guide.* Palto Alto, California: NeXT, Inc.

Pascoe, G. A. 1986. "Elements of Object-Oriented Programming." *BYTE: The Small Systems Journal.* August 1986, pp. 139–44.

Winograd, T. 1979. "Beyond Programming Languages." *Communications of the Associated for Computing Machinery* 22(7):391–401.

## Addendum: An Update on the Creation Station

The programming for the Creation Station project started on a Sun 3 workstation running the NeWS windowing system. During the development process, Creation Station was ported from NeWS to version 0.3 and then to version 0.6 of the NeXT operating systems on the Sun workstations. Its development peaked in the version that ran on top of the version 0.8 NeXT operating system on the NeXT machine, and was crippled in the ports to the version 0.9 and version 1.0 NeXT operating system. The evolution of NeXT's application programmer's interface and Objective-C libraries seriously hindered any further Creation Station development short of a complete rewrite. Faced with the necessity of such, we now have the luxury of critically examining the problems of the original Creation Station and applying what we have learned to a new Creation Station.

The architecture of the Creation Station described in the article does not take advantage of many features now offered in the NeXT OS and software library. In the original architecture, graphic calculations often interfered with the high timing accuracy required by MIDI and sound performance. Creation Station's newer design is multi-threaded,[1] preventing lengthy graphic calculations from delaying time-critical MIDI and sound calculations. In addition, instead of directly calling a procedure to perform an event, a Mach message may be sent, allowing the computations of an event to be executed in a task separate from the Creation Station core and possibly running on a secondary, networked machine (Dannenberg 1988). It is easy to imagine a Creation Station setup involving two different NeXT cubes—one handling all of the sound processing and a second cube, conceivably "turbo-charged," handling all of the graphics.

Despite these design changes, much of the architecture of the original Creation Station remains solid. The hierarchical Node structure, the inheritance of performance parameters, and the generalized treatment of different mediums' events will continue to distinguish future Creation Stations from other architectures. In a few cases, the design has been expanded. The requirement that Nodes contain only one type of event is relaxed, and the PlayManagementObject no longer needs to receive scheduled events in strict performance order.

Currently, much of the development effort that will contribute to the new Creation Station is being worked out in a MIDI and a sound sequencer we are developing. Although the project is much smaller in scope than the Creation Station, the basic architecture is very similar. Early results show promise not only for the sequencer but also for the generations of Creation Stations that will follow.

### Note

1. A "thread" (frequently called in other operating systems a "lightweight process") is a line of execution that may operate simultaneously with the primary thread of a "task" (i.e., process) (NeXT 1989).

### References

Dannenberg, R. 1988. "A Better Real-Time Scheduler/ Dispatcher." In *Proceedings of the International Computer Music Conference.* San Francisco: Computer Music Association.

NeXT. 1989. *NeXT Version 1.0 Preliminary Programming Reference Documentation.* Redwood City: NeXT Inc.

**Glendon Diener**

Center for Computer Research in Music and
Acoustics (CCRMA)
Department of Music
Stanford University
Stanford, California 94305 USA

# TTrees: A Tool for the Compositional Environment

## Introduction

Over the past several years, Smalltalk-80 has become the favorite research language of a growing
number of musicians and engineers in the computer music community. Smalltalk-80 provides a
highly interactive, visually stimulating environment that lends itself to rapid prototyping and an
adventurous, exploratory programming style. At
Stanford's Center for Computer Research in Music
and Acoustics, several of my colleagues and I have
been using the system to try out new ideas for the
design of compositional environments. This paper
describes my own creation, code-named Forest, an
interactive, real-time MIDI composition system
based on the TTree concept.

## TTrees: The Theory

This research grew out of a desire to manipulate
high-level formal aspects of a developing composition with a precision normally reserved for the
work's foreground detail. The TTree, pronounced
tee-tree (Diener 1985, 1988), is a strictly binary
branching structure whose interior nodes function
both as the work's formal sections, and as mechanisms controlling the temporal behavior of each
section.

The interior nodes of a TTree are called TEvents
(time events), while its leaves are called SEvents
(sound events). TEvents are data structures that
consist of four state variables: name, a name; wait,
a wait time value; is, a pointer to an SEvent or
another TEvent; and then, a pointer to another
TEvent.

In their graphical representation, the first of the

Computer Music Journal, Vol. 13, No. 2, Summer 1989
© 1989 Massachusetts Institute of Technology.

TEvent's two pointers is conventionally drawn ver-
tically downward and called "is," while the second
pointer, drawn horizontally to the right, is called
"then." This unusual terminology furnishes a
simple natural language tool for understanding the
TTree. Reading from Fig. 1, we have "fugue is exposition wait 20 then development wait 10 then
stretto," or "stretto is tenorEntry wait 5 then
altoEntry."

TTrees are performed by traversing them from
their root, with "wait" values specifying time delays between TEvents connected by horizontal
"then" branches. The stretto of Figure 1, for example, starts 20 + 10 = 30 time units after the exposition begins. By contrast, downward "is" branches
are traversed without delay. Thus, the alto entry
starts 20 + 10 + 5 = 35 time units after the fugue
begins.

TEvents say nothing about the duration of the
events below them. In Figure 1, the subject could
last anywhere from microseconds to millennia; its
duration has nothing whatsoever to do with the
tenor entry's wait value, which is solely concerned
with when the alto entry should begin. If the subject lasts more than five time units, then it will
overlap with the alto entry, and this stretto in name
will be a stretto in fact.

Though all the TEvents of Figure 1 are simple delays, their wait values can be as abstract as imagination permits. Processes like "wait until my 'is'
branch has finished playing" and "wait until the
ballerina assumes her arabesque downstage right"
exemplify some of the possibilities. Anything that
defines wait behavior, regardless of the nature of
that behavior, can serve as a TEvent's wait value.

TTrees without SEvents are mute entities.
TEvents model only the temporal relationships
of the composition's background structure, delegating audible surface details to the SEvents. Shown
in bold italics in Figure 1, these SEvents symbol-
ize audible sound units which "make sense" for a

*Fig. 1. A TTree represent-
ing a partially completed
school-fugue form.*

*Fig. 2. A TTree compared
to its multibranching
equivalent: time representation in TTrees (a); time
representation in a multibranching tree (b).*

Fig. 1

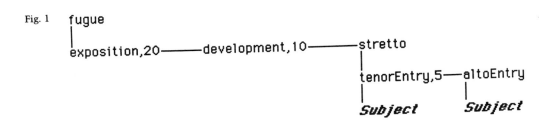

Fig. 2(a)

Fig. 2(b)

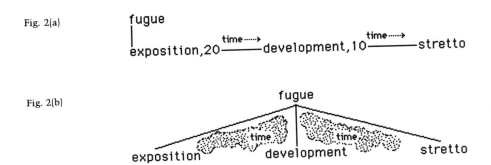

particular compositional objective and synthesis technology. Note lists, prerecorded sound files, wavetables, arbitrary blocks of computer code: all these are possible SEvents. In fact, SEvents really do not need to be audible at all: "Stage Manager: dim the house lights, raise the curtain, press return" or "R2D2 ← cueIn(violins[1])" will do just fine. TEvents provide the temporal structure, SEvents fill in the content.

So why use TTrees? TEvents define the start-times of their offspring SEvents by a multilevel delay structure. At the same time, they perform a conceptual task; they group the subtrees below them into formal compositional units. Seen in this light, they incorporate much of the hierarchical thinking so pervasive in contemporary music theory. Deutsch (1982, pp. 287–291) discusses hier-

archies in both music theory and psychoacoustics. TTrees are different from other tree structures proposed for music representation in several important ways. First, there is an overall gain in efficiency whenever we use binary-branching instead of multibranching representations (Knuth 1973, p. 315 ff. With the TTree, moreover, time flows "along" the horizontal branches (as shown in Fig. 2a), rather than somehow "between" them, as it must in the corresponding multibranching representation (as shown in Fig. 2b). This provides a more straightforward implementation strategy for the programmer. At the same time, it offers a simpler conceptual model for the composer, and it preserves the relationships of vertical simultaneity and horizontal succession so deeply ingrained in musicians accustomed to common music notation.

## Forest: The Implementation

The TTree lends itself to implementation in many ways. A Music Automaton (Diener 1985) is a compositional environment for the Synclavier II in which TTrees are built using a formal language, *rewrite rule* style of interaction. More recently, TTrees have been used as the principal component of a Smalltalk-80 MIDI compositional environment dubbed *Forest*.

Forest provides, in addition to its TTree component, four completely independent compositional modules: ASCII note lists; recorded sequences; common music notation; and a purely algorithmic, "code" compositional system. Though entire works can be built using any single module, the presence of a TTree component lets these diverse systems coexist within the same compositional entity. To the TTree, each module is merely another SEvent.

TTree theory is deeply linked to the concepts of hierarchy and abstract data types, two issues addressed directly by object-oriented programming technology. The use of a language that is expressly designed to support the object-oriented style has accelerated the implementation process enormously. Smalltalk-80 (Goldberg and Robson 1983) is a class-based language, and both SEvents and TEvents naturally translate into subclasses of a common event class. Smalltalk-80's subclassing model then makes it easy to define new event classes from these existing ones. Moreover, the wealth of programming tools provided by the Smalltalk-80 programming environment has inspired the design of a highly graphical, mouse-based interactive user interface. The following scenario attempts to communicate an impression of this interface. It is a walk-through demonstrating the use of the Forest user interface, written in an informal, narrative style.

### Using the Forest User Interface

After invoking Smalltalk, type *TTreeEditor name: 'sonata'* in any workspace view and choose *doIt* from the workspace's pop-up menu to execute the expression. The Forest system is now launched. A single TEvent named *sonata* appears at the top of an otherwise empty graphics editing window. Pop-up menus are available around the edges of this view; if you drag the cursor near the lower-left corner, it turns into a menu offering a variety of events. If you choose the menu item *aTimer*, the menu becomes an icon. After moving the icon underneath *sonata*, a mouse click forges an "is" link from *sonata* to *aTimer*, as shown in Figure 3a. To make this more meaningful, move the cursor to the top of the window, choose *rename* from this menu, and rename *aTimer* to *exposition*. Looping through these steps several more times, the entire structure of the sonata is quickly built up, as shown in Fig. 3b.

The *edit* message can be sent to any object in the tree. When you choose *edit*, then click near *exposition*, a pop-up, slider-type input box offers the event's delay value for adjustment. This is demonstrated in Fig. 3c. SEvents respond to *edit* in diverse ways. A MIDI staff SEvent, for example, provides a graphics window mapping the entire MIDI pitch space onto a grand staff. This simple score editor is shown in Fig. 3d. Equipped with a proportional notation scheme, this staff permits specifying MIDI channel and program information down to the level of the individual note. When you click on a note, then choose one of the squares on the program matrix switch shown in Fig. 3d, a one- or two-digit program number is selected.

Forest offers a legion of additional features. The TTree itself may be altered by a form of cut-and-paste-style editing called, by extension of the *arboreous* metaphor, prune-and-graft. If you choose the *close* menu item and click on a TEvent, you can hide its subtree from view. This suppression of detail is handy when the TTree becomes excessively bushy. The *spawn* message isolates sections of the composition. It causes a TEvent to display itself and its subtree in their own private window. Every Forest menu presents a *play* option. Selecting the *play* menu item and clicking on any event causes it, as well as its offspring, to be performed. The mechanism is so quick that the TTree can be used as a bank of motives whose final performance order is determined, in real time, by mouse selection.

*Fig. 3. The Forest user interface: adding elements to a TTree using the interactive user interface (a); renaming a TTree element* (b); editing the wait time of a TEvent (c); a Music Notation Editor and MIDI program matrix selection box (d).

(a)
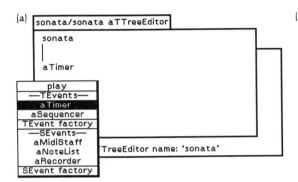

(c)
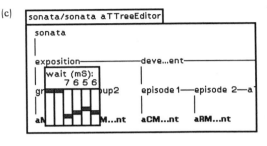

(b)
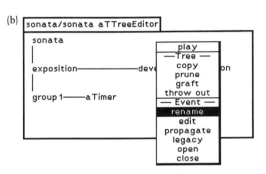

(d)
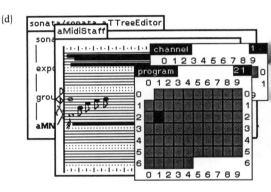

## Inner Issues

### Minimal Message Sets

The ability of Forest to effortlessly unite completely independent music representation schemes in the same score is due to its underlying object-oriented architecture. In Smalltalk-80, interaction among objects is accomplished entirely by message passing. Hence, for an object to function as an SEvent, all that is required is that it understand a certain minimal set of messages. For Forest's SEvents, the most important messages are *reset*, *tick*, and *edit*.

The *reset* message, when sent to an SEvent, is simply a warning that it is about to be performed. Should the event require preliminary setup before playing, then this is a signal to perform that setup. Normally, a *reset* message precedes a series of *tick*

messages. These messages are the heartbeat of the TTree's performance algorithm.

As we have seen, events respond to the *edit* message in diverse ways. Forest's *MIDI staff* SEvents offer the composer a unique common-practice music notation representation for editing. A *Recorder* SEvent responds by recording the arrival time and value of all incoming bytes from its MIDI input port until a mouse button is clicked. It is the responsibility of each SEvent class to define its own response to the *edit* message. Figure 4 shows how three of Forest's SEvents editors—a MIDI Staff, a note list, and a purely algorithmic "code" event—effect that response.

Any compositional environment as comprehensive as Forest will surely use more messages than these examples suggest. Fortunately, Smalltalk-80's inheritance mechanism makes it unnecessary to explicitly write code for all such messages with

*Diener*

Fig. 4. Three of Forest's
SEvent editors.

Fig. 5. TEvents A, B, and D
have not yet timed out, so
the tick message reaches
only the SEvents num-
bered 1 and 2.

Fig. 4

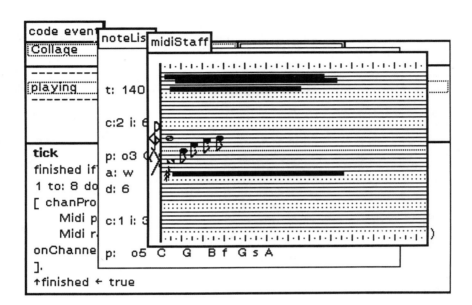

Fig. 5

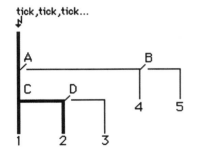

tick,tick,tick...

every new SEvent we define. If a particular event
does not understand a message, it forwards it up its
inheritance hierarchy until an object is found that
does understand the message. This makes it easy to
specify default behavior to be shared by all events,
reducing the process of creating a new SEvent type
to defining how that event differs from other
events.

## Performance

TTree performance is simple and elegant. Time is
quantized into discrete *tick* messages sent repeatedly to the root TEvent. Sparked by each such message, a chain reaction courses through the TTree as
shown in Figure 5. Every TEvent along the path of
reaction relays the message downward, then con-
sults its wait value to decide whether or not to relay it to the right. Eventually, the reaction bottoms
out in SEvents.

On receiving a *tick* message, each SEvent has the
opportunity to do whatever computation it wishes
before the next such message arrives. Compute a
sample, send out a byte over MIDI, read a keyboard;
a SEvent's reaction to *tick* is its own affair. Its only
obligation is that it respond to the message in a
timely fashion, allowing control to return back up
the tree for the next tick.

As successive *tick* messages arrive at a TEvent,
its wait value has the chance to evolve. To Forest's
timer TEvents, wait values are nothing more than
count-down timers which are decremented with

every incoming tick. When the counter has timed out (i.e., reached zero), the TEvent propagates the *tick* message to the right as well as downward. Thus, when a *tick* message next goes pulsing through the tree, a new subtree will have opened up, and another TEvent's wait value will begin its evolution.

Many other kinds of *wait* behavior are possible; Forest even provides a "TEvent factory" to facilitate their construction. The performance process always remains the same. Without recourse to preliminary sorting or complex parallel processing, it effortlessly handles the multitude of simultaneous, overlapped, and successive temporal relationships which can hold among a group of polyphonic events.

This one-sample-at-a-time, time-sliced synthesis approach can be very inefficient (see Rahn 1988 for an examination of efficiency in synthesis algorithms). Many of Forest's SEvents perform such simple tasks that the overhead of decoding incoming *tick* messages approaches the cost of performing the task. Here, we would prefer SEvents to compute not only their present time slice, but also some number of future slices. They can then simply ignore the next number of *tick* messages. If an event can compute all its future slices in one tick, so much the better. But if it is to compute actions that properly belong in the future, then we must provide some mechanism to buffer those actions until the appropriate time. In Forest's MIDI world, the solution is a background scheduler, a program (running concurrently with TTree performance), that is capable of buffering time-tagged bytes and delivering them to the MIDI port when their time arrives (see Dannenberg 1988 for a discussion of real-time scheduler/dispatcher algorithms).

Whenever a Forest SEvent has computed its entire evolution, it responds to the tick message with *done*. To the TEvent that originated the message, a *done* response from a subtree means that subtree can be ignored from then on. Moreover, when both a TEvent's branches have answered *done*, the TEvent itself responds *done* to whomever sent it the *tick* message. As this *done* response propagates up through the TTree, any branch whose evolution is complete effectively falls off. The next time around, the path of the *tick* message will reach only those

events who really need it. Performing a TTree, then, is accomplished entirely by repeatedly sending *tick* messages to its root TEvent until it answers *done*.

Even though a *tick*'s time-slice may represent, say, a millisecond, Forest's performance algorithm disregards the actual length of time between *ticks* as the tree is played. Instead, the tree is simply pulsed as quickly as Smalltalk-80 allows, with the low-level scheduler handling the job of ensuring that bytes are delivered to the MIDI port at the proper time. As a consequence, if a TTree grows to the point where it cannot be performed in real time, then an extra TEvent can be patched into the beginning of the tree, effectively delaying the start of the composition to allow the performance algorithm to precompute as much of the work as necessary.

### Copying

Every object-oriented programming system must define what it means to copy an object. To see what impact this issue has on the design of a compositional environment, imagine starting with some compositional event and making a copy of it. If we later modify the original in some way, do we wish the copy to be modified as a result? The answer is *maybe.* If the original event were intended as the opening unit of a ternary form, with the copy functioning as its *da capo* repetition, we would probably want changes we make in the original to show up in the copy. But suppose the copy was destined to become one of a set of variations on the original. In this case, we would probably want the copies to be completely independent entities so that we could edit them individually without these edits affecting each other.

In computer science terms, this issue is one of "deep" versus "shallow" copying. Most objects are complex structures containing references to other objects. A shallow copy creates a new object, but the new object refers to exactly the same instance variable objects as the original. Changes to these referenced objects will show up as changes in both the original and the copy. With a deep copy, all referenced objects (i.e., an object's instance variables) are copied as well, as are any objects referenced by these objects, and so on. Only with deep copies are truly independent entities created.

Clearly, both methods are musically useful. Forest, however, provides only deep copying, relying on a more flexible concept that might loosely be termed "identity propagation" to achieve the effect of shallow copying. More specifically, every Forest event responds to the message *propagate* by locating all events in the TTree that share its name, then replacing each such event with a clone of itself. By default, a clone is nothing more than a deep copy, and the *propagate* message merely mimics the effect of shallow copying; after a propagate operation, all events with the same name will be identical. But since each event may redefine its response to this *clone* message in its own way, the composer can arrange for every clone to be different from its model. In this way, copying becomes an interesting compositional dimension in its own right.

## Communication, Inheritance, and the Legacy Dictionary

The minimal message set that every Forest TEvent is expected to understand is somewhat different from that of an SEvent. In particular, a TEvent responds to *is* and *then* messages by answering its vertical and horizontal pointers respectively. In response to the *ancestor* message, the TEvent will return the unique event in the tree that is currently pointing to it (the root TEvent responds with a nil value). By simply specifying a chain of these *is*, *then*, and *ancestor* messages, any event in a tree has the ability to communicate with any other event.

One of the basic tenets of object-oriented programming is the concept of inheritance. In a class-based system such as Smalltalk-80, this takes the form of a hierarchy of classes, with instances of classes lower on the hierarchy inheriting the state and behavior of their ancestors (superclasses). This has proved to be an economical way to arrange

computing resources; it allows code required by many different classes to be pushed as far up the hierarchy as possible, where it can be shared by the classes lower down that need it.

There is an important similarity between such inheritance and a good deal of compositional practice, for in music we often find passages that are dissimilar on the surface yet clearly result from the application of some transformation applied to identical underlying material. The classic example is the second key area of a sonata-allegro movement's exposition; it typically returns in the recapitulation intact save for transpositional level. Representing this situation in a computer, we might choose to preserve the structural similarity between the two sections by maintaining exactly the same representation at the surface level of the score, while pushing the transformation—a simple transposition in this case—further up the tree. When the work is performed, we would arrange that the surface of the score "inherit" the transformation from its ancestors in the hierarchy, and alter itself accordingly.

Just such a sharing-via-inheritance scheme is a major feature of the SSSP's digital music system (Buxton et al. 1977), and is an integral part of many other compositional programs. The approach taken in Forest is to attach a dictionary, called the *legacy dictionary*, to every event of the TTree. This dictionary is nothing more than a collection of associations between keywords and arbitrary, user-supplied blocks of Smalltalk-80 code. An example is shown is Fig. 6. As part of its response to the *tick* message, any SEvent can send the message *inherit: keyword* to its ancestor, where *keyword* is the name of any desired trait that the composer wishes to define. The ancestor TEvent will respond to the message by looking up the keyword in its legacy dictionary. If found, the corresponding code is executed. Typically, this code will compute a value, which is passed on as an argument to the object's own ancestor. This whole process is then repeated there, eventually propagating all the way back to the root before returning the value of the final evaluation to the object that originally sent the *inherit* message.

This scheme easily handles the more obvious candidates for inheritance, such as transposition,

*Fig. 6. Forest's legacy dictionary.*

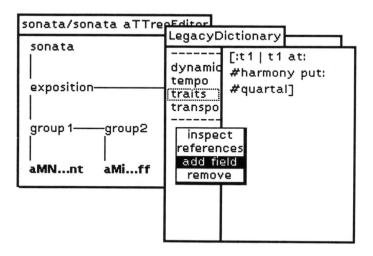

*Fig. 6. Forest's legacy dictionary.*

tempo, and dynamic control. But because it is completely extensible, the legacy dictionary gives the composer's imagination an added dimension to explore.

### Where to Next?

Just how flexible an environment is Forest? Smalltalk-80 is noted for the modularity of its code, so it should not be difficult to merge Forest with the compositional systems of other Smalltalk-80 projects. The user interface tools of Stephen Pope's HyperScore ToolKit (Pope 1987) would enrich the power and feel of the Forest environment enormously, as would the interactive compositional tools of Daniel Oppenheim's Dmix.

Forest is not simply a MIDI engine. I believe the TTree concept will prove an ideal framework for software synthesis. The Kyma project (Scaletti 1989) has proved Smalltalk-80 to be a formidable tool for organizing and controlling special-purpose synthesis hardware. At CCRMA, both Perry Cook (Cook 1988) and Guy Garnett (Garnett 1988) have been using Smalltalk-80 for research in physical modeling using digital waveguides. I hope that Forest will soon provide an environment in

which the fruits of such research can be explored compositionally.

### Conclusion

The TTree is a high-level, hierarchical score representation tool allowing diverse music representation schemes to coexist within the same work. Its strictly binary-branching architecture and embedded temporal control suggest a simple yet elegant performance algorithm, while providing well-defined pathways of communication and inheritance among its constituent events. The class-based, object-oriented language Smalltalk-80 has greatly facilitated the implementation process, and has inspired the creation of Forest, a highly interactive MIDI compositional system based on the TTree concept.

### Acknowledgments

The author wishes to thank both Stanford University and the Social Sciences and Humanities Research Council of Canada for their support of this research. Thanks to Lee Boynton of NeXT Inc. for his MIDI driver, to Guy Garnett of Yamaha Music Technologies, Inc. for interfacing it to Smalltalk-80, and to fellow CCRMA-ites for all their help.

## References

Buxton, W., et al. 1977. "The Use of Hierarchy and Instance in a Data Structure for Computer Music." *Computer Music Journal* 2(4): 10–20.

Cook, P. R. 1988. "Implementation of Single Reed Instruments with Arbitrary Bore Shapes Using Digital Waveguide Filters." Stanford Department of Music Report STAN-M-50.

Dannenberg, R. B. 1988. "A Real Time Scheduler/ Dispatcher." In *Proceedings of the 1988 International Computer Music Conference.* San Francisco: Computer Music Association, pp. 239–242.

Deutsch, D. 1982. "The Processing of Pitch Combinations." In D. Deutsch, ed. *The Psychology of Music.* New York: Academic Press, pp. 271–316.

Diener, G. 1985. "AMA User's Manual: Volume II of Formal Languages in Music Theory." Master's thesis, McGill University.

Diener, G. 1988. "TTrees: An Active Data Structure for Computer Music." In *Proceedings of the 1988 International Computer Music Conference.* San Francisco: Computer Music Association, pp. 184–188.

Garnett, G. E. 1988. "Designing Digital Instruments with Hierarchical Waveguide Networks." Stanford Department of Music Report STAN-M-49.

Goldberg, A., and D. Robson. 1983. *Smalltalk-80: The Language and Its Implementation.* Reading, Massachusetts: Addison-Wesley.

Knuth, D. 1973. *The Art of Computer Programming, Volume I: Fundamental Algorithms.* 2nd. ed. Reading, Massachusetts: Addison-Wesley.

Pope, S. T. 1987. "A Smalltalk-80-based Music Toolkit." In *Proceedings of the 1987 International Computer Music Conference.* San Francisco: Computer Music Association, pp. 166–173.

Rahn, J. 1988. "Computer Music: A View from Seattle." *Computer Music Journal* 12(3): 15–29.

Scaletti, C. 1989. "The Kyma/Platypus Computer Music Workstation." *Computer Music Journal*, this issue.

## Addendum: A Hierarchical Approach to Music Notation

There are many ways to depict tree structures. In *Forest,* TTrees were drawn as nodes connected by horizontal and vertical lines—a scheme closer to mathematical convention than to common music notation practice. This addendum—portions of which originally appeared in Diener 1989—describes research using the TTree as the fundamental structure of a general music notation system.

### Hierarchical Music Notation

The following discussion introduces a music notation system embedded in a visual programming environment. To the system, the images and conventions of particular notational styles takes the form of data encapsulated as object specifications in an object-oriented programming language. Objects in the system display a specifiable graphics image; they are characterized as much by this image as by their state and behavior.

The system provides a consistent visual metaphor: two-dimensional musical scores are seen as three-dimensional constructs made of piles of objects. Equivalent to tree structures, these piles specify hierarchical relationships defining temporal ordering among their component objects. Manipulation of these piles is equivalent to manipulation of their temporal ordering.

This system is an excellent basis for conveniently expressing a variety of notational styles. A software package, dubbed Nutation, has been developed as an existence proof of this claim. Nutation is capable of executing data sets defining a variety of notational styles, including a working subset of common music notation.

### The Visual Metaphor

In Nutation, visual elements of musical scores are represented as special objects called *glyphs.* Visually, these glyphs offer a two-dimensional rectangular surface displaying a specifiable image. Conceptually, glyphs are cubes of unit thickness, and may be piled on top of or alongside one another in a virtual three-dimensional space (more precisely, two-and-a-half-dimensional, or two continuous dimensions and one discrete one). The rectangular surface on which a glyph's image is drawn is completely transparent; only the image itself is visible, and thus complex images can be built up by creating piles of individual glyphs. Figure 1 shows a portion of a score in common music notation alongside a representation in which glyphs are made opaque and given thickness in order to emphasis their three-dimensional structure.

### Communicating Objects

Nutation is an object-oriented system, and glyphs communicate with one another by sending messages. The individual glyph, then, in addition to displaying its image, can respond to incoming messages by executing the corresponding methods. These methods may be used to modify the way the glyph displays itself, to change its location on the screen, to alter the way it is performed, and so on. Because methods are completely programmable, the glyph's behavior is limited only by the skill and imagination of the programmer. Nutation's three-dimensionality is responsible for more than just its imaging model.

When one or more glyphs are piled on top of another, those glyphs are installed as subglyphs of the glyph they are piled upon, which is in turn a subglyph of the glyph it is piled upon, and so on, to the depth of recursion. These piles of glyphs, then, are simply the visual analog of an underlying tree structure, maintained by Nutation in the form of a TTree. Nutation gains considerable power through this underlying hierarchical structure, for the hierarchy functions as a network for channeling messages among glyphs. Messages sent to an individual glyph have the potential of being relayed automatically to the entire glyph subtree rooted in that individual. The program's user-interface component, for example, gains a ready-made mechanism for specify-

*Fig. 1. Two views of a
score fragment.*

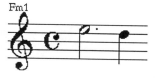

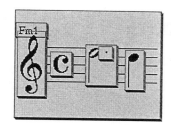

*Fig. 1. Two views of a score fragment.*

ing the scope of such operations as moving, copying,
and deletion—whenever one of these operations is
done to a single glyph, it is done to the entire pile
of glyphs resting upon it.

Another beneficiary of this hierarchical message-
channeling scheme is Nutation's performance mechanism. When the root of the hierarchy is sent a *play*
message, the message eventually trickles down
through the tree until it "bottoms out" at the leaves—
generally, some kind of *note* glyph. Along the way,
the flow of the message can be controlled by the
glyphs it passes through. A *page* glyph, for example,
might relay the message to its subglyphs (usually
*staff* glyphs) successively from the top of the page
to the bottom. Each *staff* subglyph, upon receipt of
the *play* message, responds in turn by relaying the
message from its leftmost subglyph to its right-
most. These subglyphs, generally *note* glyphs, respond by instructing the underlying hardware to
synthesize the note. The mechanism ensures that
the score is performed in the correct top-to-bottom,
left-to-right order, and allows for the accumulation
of such global state as current key and time signature, dynamic level, etc. in a manner analogous to
the way in which a human performer would read the
score. Note that the program's hierarchical scheme
is by no means fixed. The number of hierarchical
levels and their interrelationships constitute data
which can be crafted by the musician. The program's
role is to provide a convenient framework for building such structures and for associating them with
graphic representations. Owing to the openness of
this architecture, it is easy to extend the system to
embrace nonstandard notational schemes.

## Conclusion

The notation system described here uses the hierarchical TTree structure as the basis for a fully extensible and programmable system of music notation.
The system gives musicians the power to define
their own notational worlds—worlds which may
bear little or no resemblance to common practice
notation. In support of this claim, Fig. 2 shows a
screen image from Nutation containing a decidedly
non-Western notational style. The figure presents
an example of the Okinawan notation system for
samisen and voice, as described in La Rue 1951.
Essentially a tablature notation, Okinawan notation is read from top to bottom and from right to
left. Like Fig. 1, this figure is accompanied by a
"raised" view in order to emphasize the three-
dimensional hierarchy of glyphs underlying the
image.

## References

Diener, G. R. 1989. "Nutation: Structural Organization
    Versus Graphical Generality In a Common Music No-
    tation Program." In *Proceedings of the International
    Computer Music Conference.* San Francisco: Computer
    Music Association.
La Rue, J. 1951. "The Okinawan Notation System." *Jour-
    nal of the American Musicological Society.* 4(1):
    27–35.

Fig. 2. A screen image
from the Nutation system
showing two views of a
score using Okinawan
Notation.

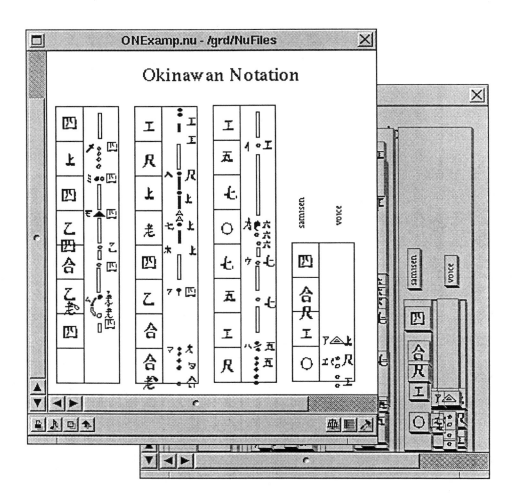

# IV

# Signal Processing Systems

**Kurt J. Hebel**

CERL Music Project
University of Illinois
Urbana, Illinois 61801-2977 USA

hebel@cerl.uiuc.edu

# Javelina: An Environment for Digital Signal Processing Software Development

## Introduction

Javelina is a software environment for the development of discrete-time signal processing systems. It is written in the Smalltalk-80 programming environment and includes notation editors and tools for digital filter design, mathematical optimization of state variable systems, and the generation of optimized machine language programs for a variety of digital signal processors.

Prior to the introduction of general-purpose digital signal processors (DSPs), the design of special hardware was required in order to get many signal processing algorithms to execute in real time. The new, general-purpose DSP hardware need only be designed once, but a new program must be written for each algorithm, typically in microcode or assembly language. The time spent in software design now exceeds the time spent in hardware design.

This paper describes Javelina, an environment for the development of software for digital signal processors. This environment translates discrete-time systems into the machine language of any of several digital signal processors. Javelina includes facilities for manipulating, evaluating, and measuring the discrete-time system throughout the development process.

## Overview of the System

Figure 1 shows a functional diagram of the major software elements within Javelina. At the highest level, discrete-time systems are designed graphically through the use of the Z Plane Editor or other mathematical function editors. The mathematical

Computer Music Journal, Vol. 13, No. 2, Summer 1989
© 1989 Massachusetts Institute of Technology.

description of the discrete-time system derived from one of these editors is manipulated in the middle level. Algebraic transformations are used here to improve characteristics of the implementation such as output roundoff noise, memory use, or processing time. The resulting mathematical function is compiled into an intermediate register transfer language (RTL) program. Finally, the RTL program is optimized and machine-level code is generated for a particular digital signal processor. The code generation and optimizations of the low level are more or less independent of the particular target digital signal processor due to the encapsulation of the machine-dependent information in a machine model object.

## The Z Plane Editor

The primary filter development tool is the Z Plane Editor. It is divided into several regions: the z plane, the "unrolled" z plane, and the filter scale slider, as seen from right to left in Fig. 2. The z plane is a coordinate system used to plot the locations of a digital filter's complex poles and zeroes (Moore 1978). The "unrolled" z plane serves a dual purpose: it describes the pole and zero locations and the normalized magnitude of the frequency response of the filter simultaneously. This "unrolled" plane helps the user develop an intuitive relationship between the pole and zero locations and the frequency response of the corresponding filter.

The filter scale slider is used together with the peak filter response (the number in the pane immediately above the slider) to set the overall attenuation or gain of the filter. The buttons on the bottom of the window are used to select various operations within the editor: toggle between linear and decibel frequency response plots; select poles or zeroes to

*Fig. 1. The major components of Javelina.*

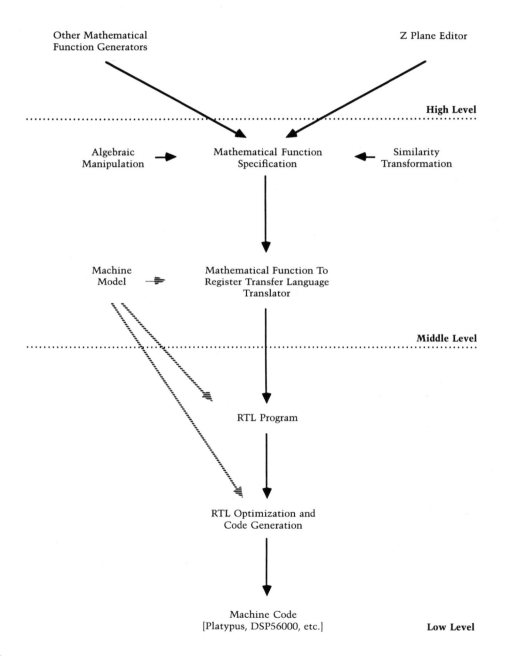

Other Mathematical
Function Generators

Z Plane Editor

**High Level**

Algebraic
Manipulation

Mathematical Function
Specification

Similarity
Transformation

Machine
Model

Mathematical Function To
Register Transfer Language
Translator

**Middle Level**

RTL Program

RTL Optimization and
Code Generation

Machine Code
[Platypus, DSP56000, etc.]

**Low Level**

Fig. 2. The Z Plane Editor.

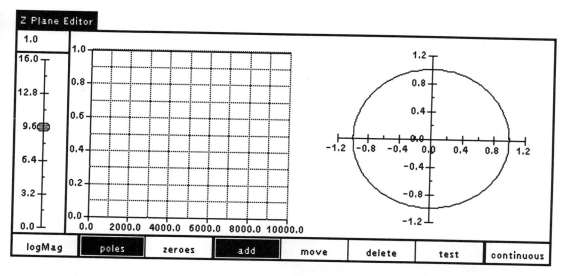

edit; select whether poles or zeroes should be added, moved, or deleted at the next mouse operation; or select one of two different ways to audition the filter. The frequency response and the pole and zero locations always reflect the current filter during editing operations; changes in the location of a pole or zero are animated on the display.

The Z Plane Editor can also simulate the digital filter under design to obtain its impulse response, and a complete magnitude and phase response of the filter can be displayed. When editing the filter, the Platypus Digital Signal Processor (Haken and Hebel 1987) and the Kyma language (Scaletti 1989) are used to implement the digital filter for auditioning in real time.

The Z Plane Editor can be used to design a filter completely by hand or through the use of filter prototypes and frequency transformations. In Fig. 3, a filter prototype for a third order Chebyshev lowpass filter (Roberts and Mullis 1987) with a cutoff frequency of 5000 Hz has been used to place the poles and zeroes onto the z plane. Applying a lowpass-to-lowpass filter transformation which maps 5000 Hz to 1000 Hz results in a new third order Chebyshev filter with a cutoff of 1000 Hz, as shown in Fig. 4.

## The State Variable System

The state variable form of a discrete-time system is a pair of matrix equations that describes the current system output and next system state in terms of the current input and the current state:

$$y_i = \mathbf{C}\mathbf{x}_i + d u_i$$

$$\mathbf{x}_{i+1} = \mathbf{A}\mathbf{x}_i + \mathbf{B}u_i$$

In the state variable form of a digital filter with $n$ poles, $y_i$ is the current output, $\mathbf{x}_i$ is the current state, $u_i$ is the current input, and $\mathbf{A}$, $\mathbf{B}$, $\mathbf{C}$ and $d$ are parameters which determine the input/output characteristics of the discrete-time system being modeled. Figure 5 shows a representation of the state variable system for an interesting digital filter; note that $\mathbf{A}$ is an $n * n$ matrix, and that $\mathbf{B}$ and $\mathbf{C}$ are $n$ element vectors.

The state variable form has several advantages over other mathematical descriptions: the matrix equations exactly describe the implementation of the discrete-time system; many performance measures can be obtained directly; and it is easy to find alternate implementations of the same system through the use of *similarity transformations*. A

Fig. 3. A third order
Chebyshev lowpass filter
with cutoff frequency of
5000 Hz.

Fig. 4. The filter of Fig. 3
after the application of a
frequency transformation
that maps 5000 Hz to
1000 Hz.

Fig. 3

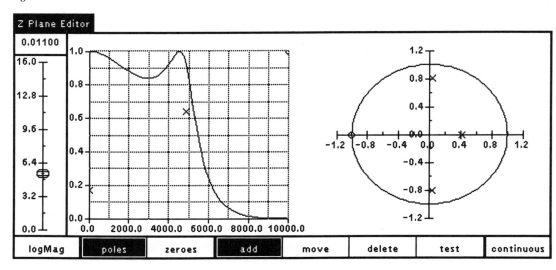

Fig. 4

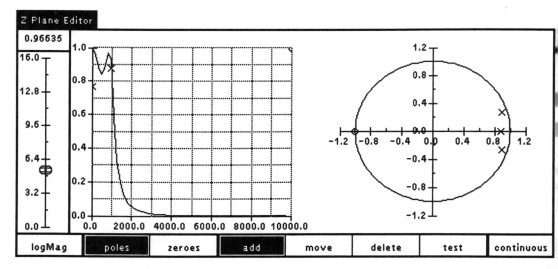

Fig. 5. The filter of Fig. 4 as
a state variable system in
the "direct form"
implementation.

Direct Form Filter

$$y \leftarrow \left(\left(\left[0.007275026482241181 \ 7.092183728865129e\text{-}4 \ 0.002270021618975493\right] * x\right) + \left(0.001283488003537059 * u\right)\right)$$

$$x \leftarrow \left(\left(\left[\begin{array}{ccc} 2.668168663978577 & -2.447428903946093 & 0.7686348549575282 \\ 1 & 0 & 0 \\ 0 & 1 & 0 \end{array}\right] * x\right) + \left(u * \left[\begin{array}{c} 1 \\ 0 \\ 0 \end{array}\right]\right)\right)$$

FunctionComputationCost assignments: 7 differences: 0 sums: 6 products: 7 references: 20 ratios: 0
The system is stable. The system can overflow oscillate, since the measure 3.83 is greater than one. The
quantization error intensity is 3.27. The normalized output error variance is 29.1. The best equal word length
variance is 0.055.
Storage efficiency = 0.0114. Quantization efficiency = 0.00582.

similarity transformation is a mapping between two state variable systems specified by an invertible transformation matrix **T**:

$$\mathbf{A} \rightarrow \mathbf{TAT}^{-1}$$

$$\mathbf{B} \rightarrow \mathbf{TB}$$

$$\mathbf{C} \rightarrow \mathbf{CT}^{-1}$$

$$\mathbf{d} \rightarrow \mathbf{d}$$

The new state variable system exhibits the same input/output characteristics as the original system; however, the two systems differ in their internal implementations.

Figure 5 shows the state variable system obtained from the lowpass filter of Fig. 4 implemented in the *direct form* (i.e., as a single recursive difference equation). The lower pane of the window displays some performance measurements of the filter. These measures include the cost of implementing this system, the likelihood of overflow oscillations, and several measures of filter output noise due to roundoff errors during computation.

Several algorithms exist for finding similarity transformations which can improve these mea-sures; Fig. 6 shows the result of applying a transformation that yields an "optimal" system in terms of overflow oscillations and output roundoff noise (Roberts and Mullis 1976). This new system has the disadvantage of being very expensive to implement due to the very large number of multiplies (related to the square of the number of filter poles).

Figure 7 shows the result of transforming the system of Fig. 6; this system has many fewer multiplies (now related linearly to the number of filter poles), is slightly more likely to overflow oscillate, and has about the same output roundoff noise characteristics (Hebel 1989).

## Code Generation and Optimization

Code generation and optimization is typically the last step in the compilation of computer programs, and has been the target of much research since the 1950s. However, optimizing machine language compilers for Smalltalk are just now being developed.

The Typed Smalltalk (TS) system (Johnson, Graver, and Zurawski 1988) contains a machine

*Fig. 6. Figure 5 after the application of a similarity transformation to put it into the "optimal" round-off noise form.*

*Fig. 7. The system of Fig. 6 transformed to a new system with many fewer multiplications.*

Fig. 6

**Many Multiply Filter**

$$y \leftarrow \left(\left(\begin{bmatrix} 0.1500901519491039 & 0.1916468517299919 & 0.1018817149100676 \end{bmatrix} * x\right) + \left(0.001283488003537059 * u\right)\right)$$

$$x \leftarrow \left(\left(\begin{bmatrix} 0.9237938498553692 & -0.2084765151852952 & 0.1678345075865835 \\ 0.2943901718224813 & 0.8609510912212127 & -0.04324968027562941 \\ -0.08136435058942705 & 0.008609953375146016 & 0.8834237229019948 \end{bmatrix} * x\right) + \left(u * \begin{bmatrix} -0.04775032393532851 \\ -0.208755518041492 \\ 0.5344356219297262 \end{bmatrix}\right)\right)$$

FunctionComputationCost assignments: 7 differences: 0 sums: 12 products: 16 references: 35 ratios: 0
The system is stable. No overflow oscillation is possible. The quantization error intensity is 5.73. The normalized output error variance is 0.0568. The best equal word length variance is 0.055.
Storage efficiency = 0.777. Quantization efficiency = 0.777.

Fig. 7

**Optimized Filter**

$$y \leftarrow \left(\left(\begin{bmatrix} 0.0 & 0.29815673828125 & 0.0 \end{bmatrix} * x\right) + \left(0.00128173828125 * u\right)\right)$$

$$x \leftarrow \left(\left(\begin{bmatrix} 1.0 & -0.238189697265625 & 0.26220703125 \\ 0.23162841796875 & 0.784942626953125 & 0.087249755859375 \\ -0.11749267578125 & 0.0 & 0.88323974609375 \end{bmatrix} * x\right) + \left(u * \begin{bmatrix} 0.0 \\ 0.024383544921875 \\ 0.55389404296875 \end{bmatrix}\right)\right)$$

FunctionComputationCost assignments: 7 differences: 0 sums: 8 products: 11 references: 26 ratios: 0
The system is stable. The system can overflow oscillate, since the measure 1.08 is greater than one. The quantization error intensity is 3.26. The normalized output error variance is 0.0616. The best equal word length variance is 0.0551.
Storage efficiency = 0.605. Quantization efficiency = 0.814.

language compiler for a typed variant of the Smalltalk-80 language. The compiler generates an intermediate register transfer language from the Smalltalk source code; this machine-independent intermediate language is then translated into the machine language of the host computer.

Javelina builds upon and extends the TS system compiler to generate code for discrete-time systems for digital signal processors. The code generation is performed in several phases: conversion of the state variable system into a set of scalar equations; translation of the mathematical specification into an RTL program; caching and combining these RTL instructions; and finally, the assignment of real machine instructions to correspond to the RTL instructions. Figure 8 demonstrates these phases in a schematic manner.

### Serializing

The state variable form of the digital system is a matrix equation that describes the simultaneous update of the output variable and all components of the state variables. In this form, the equations could be evaluated only on array or vector processors; however, if the matrix equation is transformed into an equivalent set of scalar equations, the scalar system can be evaluated on virtually all digital signal processors and computers.

### Translation to RTL

Each scalar equation is translated into an RTL program; this program is written for a hypothetical machine that has an infinite number of registers but can only execute simple, two-address instructions. No attempt is made to generate optimal code; in fact, simpler and less optimal code allows the later optimization steps more freedom in selecting better code sequences.

### Caching

The first optimization step is caching. The RTL program is scanned linearly; every evaluation is performed symbolically and saved in a table. During the scan, evaluations that are more expensive to compute are replaced with less expensive, equivalent forms. This is called common subexpression elimination. As an example:

$$x \leftarrow a * b - 4$$
$$y \leftarrow a * b + x$$

could be replaced by:

$$z \leftarrow a * b$$
$$x \leftarrow z - 4$$
$$y \leftarrow z + x$$

### Combining

The next step in optimization is called combining. During combining, a pair of RTL instructions are combined into a single new instruction if the new instruction represents a legal machine instruction on the target machine.

### Assigning

Assigning, the final phase of code generation and optimization, is the selection of a target machine instruction to implement each RTL statement in the program.

### Conclusion

Javelina is the first step toward automatic high-level programming of digital signal processors. Javelina can mathematically optimize digital filters in the state variable form and can generate machine language programs for several different DSPs.

Specifying a discrete-time system with a purely mathematic description, rather than as a microcode program, has several advantages:

The mathematical specification is machine independent.
It is nicer to work at a higher level.
Graphic editors can be designed for specifying the functions.

Fig. 8. Code generation for the state variable representation of a simple first order digital filter: a simple state variable system (a); steps of generating optimized code for this system (b). Column A shows the result of translating the equations into a simple, unoptimized RTL program. Column B shows the RTL program after simple caching has been allowed. Column C shows the result after the application of the combining optimizations. Column D shows the equivalent C programming language statements, and column E shows the mathematical expression that is being evaluated.

(a)

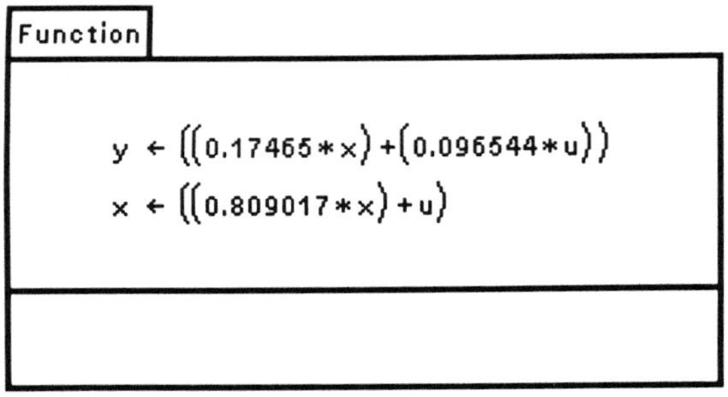

**Function**

$$y \leftarrow \big((0.17465 * x) + (0.096544 * u)\big)$$
$$x \leftarrow \big((0.809017 * x) + u\big)$$

(b)

| A | B | C | D | E |
|---|---|---|---|---|
| d04 ← 0.1747<br>d03 ← d04<br>a01 ← 1<br>d05 ← m[a01]<br>d03 ← d03 * d05 | d04 ← 0.1747<br>d03 ← d04<br>a01 ← 1<br>d05 ← m[a01]<br>d03 ← d03 * d05 | d01 ← m[1], d05 ← m[1]<br>d01 ← 0.1747 * d01 | d1 = d3 = m[1];<br>d1 *= 0.1747; | 0.1747 * x |
| d02 ← d03<br>d07 ← 0.09654<br>d06 ← d07<br>a02 ← 2<br>d08 ← m[a02]<br>d06 ← d06 * d08 | d02 ← d03<br>d07 ← 0.09654<br>d06 ← d07<br>a02 ← 2<br>d08 ← m[a02]<br>d06 ← d06 * d08 | d02 ← m[2]<br>d01 ← d01 + 0.09654 * d02 | d2 = m[2];<br>d1 + = 0.09654 * d2; | (0.1747 * x) + 0.09654 * u |
| d02 ← d02 + d06<br>d01 ← d02<br>a03 ← 3<br>m[a03] ← d01 | d02 ← d02 + d06<br><br>a03 ← 3<br>m[a03] ← d02 | m[3] ← d01 | m[3] = d1; | y ← (0.1747 * x) + 0.09654 * u |
| d12 ← 0.809<br>d11 ← d12<br>a04 ← 1<br>d13 ← m[a04]<br>d11 ← d11 * d13 | d12 ← 0.809<br>d11 ← d12<br><br>d13 ← d05<br>d11 ← d11 * d13 | d02 ← d02 + 0.809 * d05 | d2 + = 0.809 * d3; u + 0.80902 * x | |
| d10 ← d11<br>a05 ← 2<br>d14 ← m[a05]<br>d10 ← d10 + d14 | d10 ← d11<br>d10 ← d10 + d08 | | | |
| d09 ← d10<br>a06 ← 1<br>m[a06] ← d09 | m[a01] ← d10 | m[1] ← d02 | m[1] = d2; | x ← u + 0.80902 * x |

A large body of techniques exists for manipulating functions.

The system can be optimized for any of several machines.

All of these advantages can speed up the development time for both musicians and engineers.

## References

Haken, L., and K. Hebel. 1987. "The Platypus Programmers' Reference Manual." Technical Report. Urbana: University of Illinois at Urbana-Champaign, Computer-based Education Laboratory.

Hebel, K. 1989. "An Environment for the Development of Software for Digital Signal Processing." Ph.D. diss., University of Illinois at Urbana-Champaign.

Johnson, R. E., J. O. Graver, L. W. Zurawski. 1988. "TS: An Optimizing Compiler for Smalltalk." In N. Meyrowitz, ed. *1988 Object-Oriented Programming Systems, Languages, and Applications Conference Proceedings.* New York: ACM Press, pp. 18–26.

Moore, F. R. 1978. "An Introduction to the Mathematics of Digital Signal Processing. Part II: Sampling, Transforms, and Digital Filtering." *Computer Music Journal* 2(2):38–60.

Roberts, R. A., and C. T. Mullis. 1976. "Synthesis of Minimum Roundoff Noise Fixed Point Digital Filters." *IEEE Transactions on Circuits and Systems* CAS-23(9): 551–562.

Roberts, R. A., and C. T. Mullis. 1987. *Digital Signal Processing.* Reading, Massachusetts: Addison-Wesley.

Scaletti, C. 1989. "The Kyma/Platypus Computer Music Workstation." *Computer Music Journal*, this issue.

## Addendum: Filter Design and Optimization Examples

The examples presented below trace the entire process from filter design through code generation for two example digital filters designed using Javelina.

### A Fourth-Order Butterworth Band-Pass Filter

The first example is a fourth-order Butterworth band-pass digital filter, with cutoff frequencies of 300 and 3000 Hz, operating at a sample rate of 20,000 Hz.

Figures 1 and 2 illustrate the filter design steps. The initial low-pass prototype filter is selected from a menu, and the desired band-pass filter is obtained by applying a frequency transformation to the prototype. Figure 3 shows the state variable system in the direct form; Fig. 4 shows the Mullis-Roberts optimal roundoff noise form (Roberts and Mullis 1976) and Fig. 5 shows the IOSS-optimized form (Hebel 1989) of this digital filter. Below each state variable system is a list of some of that system's performance measures. The final implementation of this filter has about 250 times less output roundoff noise power than the direct form, and requires only four more multiplications. Figure 6 shows the Platypus source code (Haken and Hebel 1987) generated automatically by Javelina.

### A Third-Order Chebyshev High-Pass Filter

The second design example is a third-order Chebyshev low-pass digital filter with a cutoff frequency of 8000 Hz operating at a sample rate of 20,000 Hz.

Figure 7 shows the $z$ plane for the final filter, after an initial low-pass prototype filter has been transformed into the desired high-pass filter. Figures 8–10 show the direct form, the Mullis-Roberts optimal roundoff noise form, and the IOSS-optimized form of this digital filter. In this case, the final implementation of this filter has about 40 times less output roundoff noise power than the direct form, while requiring only three additional multiplications. Figure 11 shows the Platypus source code implementation of the IOSS form of the filter.

### References

Haken, L., and K. Hebel. 1987. The Platypus Programmers' Reference Manual. Technical Report, University of Illinois Computer-based Education Research Laboratory, Urbana.

Hebel, K. 1989. An Environment for the Development of Digital Signal Processing Software. Ph.D. dissertation, University of Illinois, Urbana-Champaign.

Roberts, R., and C. Mullis. 1976. "Synthesis of Minimum Roundoff Noise Fixed Point Digital Filters." *IEEE Transactions on Circuits and Systems* CAS-23(9): 551–562.

Fig. 1. The initial second-order Butterworth proto-type low-pass filter.

Fig. 2. The band-pass filter resulting from the low-pass to band-pass transformation of the low-pass prototype filter.

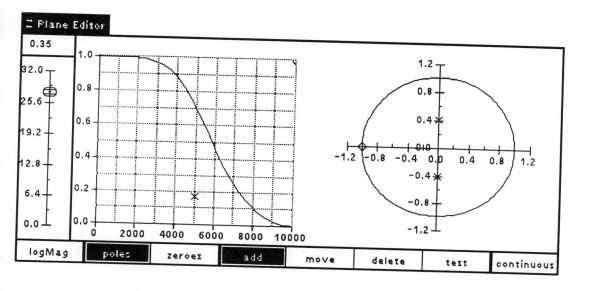

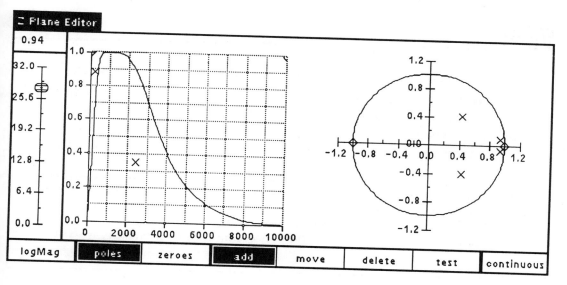

*Fig. 3. The state variable system for the band-pass filter implemented in the scaled direct form. The output roundoff noise*

*(quantization error) in this form is very large, but only ten multiplications are needed to implement the filter in this form.*

*Fig. 4. The scaled Mullis-Roberts optimal roundoff noise form of the band-pass filter. The output roundoff noise is now at*

*its theoretical minimum, but 25 multiplications are needed to implement the filter in this form.*

**Function**

$$y \leftarrow \left(\left(\begin{bmatrix} 12.0382087 & -21.32764153 & 6.211579587 & 3.056767184 \end{bmatrix} * x\right) + \left(0.1039047614 * u\right)\right)$$

$$x \leftarrow \left(\left(\begin{bmatrix} 2.729811847 & -2.836304967 & 1.408552051 & -0.306840454 \\ 1.0 & 0.0 & 0.0 & 0.0 \\ 0.0 & 1.0 & 0.0 & 0.0 \\ 0.0 & 0.0 & 1.0 & 0.0 \end{bmatrix} * x\right) + \left(u * \begin{bmatrix} 0.02356168228 \\ 0.0 \\ 0.0 \\ 0.0 \end{bmatrix}\right)\right)$$

FunctionComputationCost assignments: 9 differences: 0 sums: 8 products: 10 references: 27 ratios: 0. Coefficient word length will be 16 bits using double-length accumulators. The system is stable. No D exists since filter fails the Diagonal Entries Test.
The quantization error intensity is 433.0. The best quantization error intensity is ~1.66.

**Function**

$$y \leftarrow \left(\left(\begin{bmatrix} -0.200706826 & 0.268227278 & 0.0501420331 & -0.234482404 \end{bmatrix} * x\right) + \left(0.103912354 * u\right)\right)$$

$$x \leftarrow \left(\left(\begin{bmatrix} 0.917297363 & 0.220867483 & 0.173874761 & -0.0899920042 \\ -0.122691077 & 0.447631836 & 0.563691352 & -0.259683608 \\ 0.0100105945 & 0.0110168229 & 0.533294678 & 0.245980203 \\ -0.103276458 & 0.44355671 & 0.0235892705 & 0.831604004 \end{bmatrix} * x\right) + \left(u * \begin{bmatrix} -0.349874047 \\ 0.266959529 \\ 0.803257222 \\ -0.433015159 \end{bmatrix}\right)\right)$$

FunctionComputationCost assignments: 9 differences: 0 sums: 20 products: 25 references: 54 ratios: 0. Coefficient word length will be 16 bits using double-length accumulators. The system is stable. This filter cannot sustain overflow oscillations.
The quantization error intensity is 1.66. The best quantization error intensity is ~1.66.

*Fig. 5. The result of apply-*
*ing the IOSS to the Mullis-*
*Roberts form of Fig. 4. The*
*IOSS increased the round-*
*off noise by 20 percent,*
*and removed 11 multipli-*
*cations. The final system*
*has much less roundoff*
*noise than the direct form*
*of Fig. 4, and requires only*
*four more multiplications.*

**Function**

$$y \leftarrow \left(\left(\left[0.0 \quad 0.161468506 \quad 0.0 \quad -0.487304687\right] * x\right) + \left(0.103912354 * u\right)\right)$$

$$x \leftarrow \left(\left(\left(\begin{bmatrix} 0.936035156 & 0.0 & 0.117584229 & 0.0 \\ 0.0 & 0.235046387 & 0.766571045 & -0.464904785 \\ -0.0473327637 & 0.0 & 0.934204102 & 0.0 \\ 0.0 & 0.434234619 & 0.0 & 0.624542236 \end{bmatrix} * x\right) + \left(u * \begin{bmatrix} 0.0 \\ 0.0 \\ 0.411407471 \\ -0.582061768 \end{bmatrix}\right)\right)\right)$$

FunctionComputationCost assignments: 9 differences: 0 sums: 9 products: 14 references: 32 ratios: 0. Coefficient word length will be 16 bits using double-length accumulators. The system is stable. D may or may not exist.
The quantization error intensity is 1.97. The best quantization error intensity is ~1.66.

*Fig. 6. The memory map and assembly language program for a Platypus implementation of the state variable system in Fig. 5.*

| Location | | High | Low |
|---|---|---|---|
| 1 | → | u | 0.0519561768 |
| 2 | → | x{1} | -0.0236663818 |
| 3 | → | x{3} | 0.467102051 |
| 4 | → | x{2} | 0.0807342529 |
| 5 | → | x{4} | -0.243652344 |
| 6 | → | y | 0.205703735 |
| 7 | → | x'{3} | 0.21711731 |
| 8 | → | x'{4} | 0.312271118 |
| 9 | → | | -0.291030884 |
| 10 | → | | 0.468017578 |
| 11 | → | | 0.0587921143 |
| 12 | → | | 0.117523193 |
| 13 | → | | 0.383285522 |
| 14 | → | | -0.232452393 |

```
multx0H = r4H, multx2H = r4H, multy2L = r4L;
multx2H = r4H, product2, add;
multx2H = r5H, multy2L = r5L, product2, add;
multx1H = r2H, multy1L = r2L, product2;
product1, multx2H = r1H, multy2L = r1L, product2, add;
multx1H = r2H, product2, add;
multx1H = r3H, multy1L = r3L, product1, product2, add;
product1, r6H = multp2H;
multy1L = r6L, product1;
multx1H = r1H, add;
multy0L = r7L, product1;
multx0H = r4H, product0, product1, add;
product0, r7H = multp1H;
multy0L = r8L;
multx0H = r5H, add;
multy1L = r10L, product0;
multy0L = r9L, product0;
multx0H = r1H, add;
multx1H = r2H, product0;
multx1H = r2H, product1, product0, add;
product1, r8H = multp0H;
multy1L = r11L;
multx1H = r3H, add;
multy2L = r12L, product1;
multx2H = r4H, product1;
product2, r2H = multp1H;
multx2H = r4H, add;
multy2L = r13L, product2;
multx2H = r3H, add;
multp0H = r7H, product2;
multy2L = r14L, product2;
multx2H = r5H, add;
r3H = multp0H, product2;
multp0H = r8H, product2;
r4H = multp2H;
r5H = multp0H;
```

*Fig. 7. The high-pass filter resulting from the low-pass to high-pass transformation of a Chebyshev low-pass prototype filter.*

*Fig. 8. The state variable system for the high-pass filter implemented in the scaled direct form. The output roundoff noise in this form is large, but only eight multiplications are needed to implement the filter in this form.*

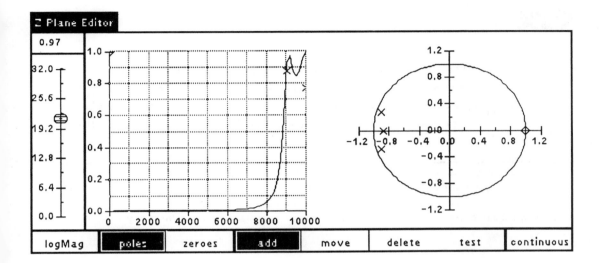

**Z Plane Editor**

| logMag | poles | zeroes | add | move | delete | test | continuous |

**Function**

$$y \leftarrow \left(\left(\begin{bmatrix} -0.216833782 & 0.0211384166 & -0.0676585 \end{bmatrix} * \mathbf{x}\right) + \left(0.00129475701 * u\right)\right)$$

$$\mathbf{x} \leftarrow \left(\left(\begin{bmatrix} -2.66816854 & -2.44742878 & -0.768634844 \\ 1.0 & 0.0 & 0.0 \\ 0.0 & 1.0 & 0.0 \end{bmatrix} * \mathbf{x}\right) + \left(u * \begin{bmatrix} 0.0338457453 \\ 0.0 \\ 0.0 \end{bmatrix}\right)\right)$$

FunctionComputationCost assignments: 7 differences: 0 sums: 6 products: 8 references: 21 ratios: 0. Coefficient word length will be 16 bits using double-length accumulators. The system is stable. No D exists since filter fails the Diagonal Entries Test.
The quantization error intensity is 80.0. The best quantization error intensity is ~1.67.

*Fig. 9. The scaled Mullis-Roberts optimal roundoff noise form of the high-pass filter. The output roundoff noise is now at its theo-* *retical minimum, but 16 multiplications are needed to implement the filter in this form.*

*Fig. 10. The result of applying the IOSS to the Mullis-Roberts form of Fig. 9. The IOSS increased the roundoff noise by 20 percent, and removed five* *multiplications. The final system has much less roundoff noise than the direct form of Fig. 9, and requires only three additional multiplications.*

---

**Function**

$$y \leftarrow \left(\left(\left[-0.0523588157 \;\; -0.299728281 \;\; 0.0918577568\right] * \mathbf{x}\right) + \left(0.00129475701 * u\right)\right)$$

$$\mathbf{x} \leftarrow \left(\left(\left[\begin{array}{ccc} -0.862801588 & 0.0473599062 & 0.118641801 \\ -0.0548839935 & -0.909940739 & -0.213944958 \\ -0.163778108 & 0.247448106 & -0.895426217 \end{array}\right] * \mathbf{x}\right) + \left(u * \left[\begin{array}{c} 0.610743024 \\ -0.00760428978 \\ 0.243416131 \end{array}\right]\right)\right)$$

FunctionComputationCost assignments: 7 differences: 0 sums: 12 products: 16 references: 35 ratios: 0. Coefficient word length will be 16 bits using double-length accumulators. The system is stable. This filter cannot sustain overflow oscillations.
The quantization error intensity is 1.72. The best quantization error intensity is ~1.67.

---

**Function**

$$y \leftarrow \left(\left(\left[-0.0151977539 \;\; -0.291168213 \;\; 0.0\right] * \mathbf{x}\right) + \left(0.00128173828 * u\right)\right)$$

$$\mathbf{x} \leftarrow \left(\left(\left[\begin{array}{ccc} -0.875396729 & 0.0 & 0.0 \\ -0.0985412598 & -0.976196289 & -0.19317627 \\ -0.263763428 & 0.418792725 & -0.816589355 \end{array}\right] * \mathbf{x}\right) + \left(u * \left[\begin{array}{c} 0.48348999 \\ 0.0 \\ 0.0 \end{array}\right]\right)\right)$$

FunctionComputationCost assignments: 7 differences: 0 sums: 7 products: 11 references: 25 ratios: 0. Coefficient word length will be 16 bits using double-length accumulators. The system is stable. D may or may not exist.
The quantization error intensity is 1.99. The best quantization error intensity is ~1.67.

Fig. 11. The memory map
and assembly language
program for a Platypus implementation of the sys-
tem in Fig. 10.

| Location | | High | Low |
|---|---|---|---|
| 1 | → | x{2} | -0.145584106 |
| 2 | → | x{1} | -0.00759887695 |
| 3 | → | x{3} | -0.408294678 |
| 4 | → | u | 6.40869141e-4 |
| 5 | → | y | -0.131881714 |
| 6 | → | x'{3} | 0.209396362 |
| 7 | → | | -0.0492706299 |
| 8 | → | | -0.488098145 |
| 9 | → | | -0.0965881348 |
| 10 | → | | -0.437698364 |
| 11 | → | | 0.241744995 |

```
multx0H = r2H, multx1H = r2H, multx2H = r2H, multy2L = r2L;
multx2H = r2H, product2, add;
multx2H = r1H, multy2L = r1L, product2, add;
multy1L = r5L, product2;
product1, multx2H = r4H, multy2L = r4L, product2, add;
multx1H = r2H, product2, add;
multy1L = r6L, product1, product2;
r5H = multp2H;
multx1H = r1H, add;
multy0L = r7L, product1;
product0, multx1H = r3H, multy1L = r3L, product1, add;
multx0H = r2H, product1, add;
multy0L = r8L, product0, product1;
r6H = multp1H;
multx0H = r1H, add;
multy1L = r10L, product0;
multy0L = r9L, product0;
multx0H = r3H, add;
multx1H = r2H, product0;
multx1H = r2H, product1, product0, add;
product1, r1H = multp0H;
multy1L = r11L;
multx1H = r4H, add;
multp2H = r6H, product1;
r3H = multp2H, product1;
r2H = multp1H;
```

**David K. Mellinger**
Center for Computer Research in Music
and Acoustics (CCRMA)
Department of Music
Stanford University
Stanford, California USA

davem@Polya.Stanford.edu

**G. E. Garnett**
Yamaha Music Technologies
Larkspur, California USA

pixar!ymt!guy@ucbvax.Berkeley.edu

**Bernard Mont-Reynaud**
Center for Computer Research in Music
and Acoustics (CCRMA)
Department of Music
Stanford University
Stanford, California USA

davem@Polya.Stanford.edu

# Virtual Digital Signal Processing in an Object-Oriented System

## Introduction

We describe in this paper a prototype environment for digital signal processing in terms of a *virtual processor* and its associated *virtual data*. The basic operations of the processor are designed for fast vector operations on a variety of different types of hardware. One finished implementation is presented and others are planned.

The modern digital signal processing environment is one of great flux. New chips are being developed and brought to market at ever faster rates. Those creating signal-processing software applications wish to take advantage of the speed of these hardware devices, but are faced with the problem of interfacing each application to each piece of hardware. The work required can be reduced immensely by using a signal-processing software environment that is common to all the low-level hardware devices, but such an environment must have hardware independence "designed in" from the very start.

It is with goal that we have implemented a prototype system for vectorized digital signal processing in the Smalltalk-80 programming system. The development discussed here is the high-level front end to this vector processor. Smalltalk-80 is itself highly machine-independent, due mainly to its being constructed on top of a *virtual machine* (Goldberg and Robson 1983). A primary design choice in the current system has been to abstract the notions of digital signal processors and data, and to provide a standard interface and a virtual machine to support these abstractions. The system is called the Virtual Digital Signal Processing system, or VDSP.

## Virtual Processors and Virtual Data

A *virtual processor* is an object that includes the following functionality: it provides a means for allocating and deallocating data objects; it provides a

Computer Music Journal, Vol. 13, No. 2, Summer 1989
© 1989 Massachusetts Institute of Technology.

standard set of vector, scalar, and vector-scalar operations; it provides input/output to external devices capable of handling data formats commonly used in signal processing; and it provides communication between real processors and the user's computing environment.

*Virtual data* are objects that encapsulate their data and have the following functionality: they provide a handle that is used by the virtual processor to refer to the actual data; they provide representations of useful data types, including floating-point and integer vectors and scalars; and they respond to messages requesting operations on their data by invoking the corresponding operation on a virtual processor.

The example of multiplying two Smalltalk arrays of integers using a virtual processor would be executed using the steps:

1. Send a message telling the virtual processor to allocate two vector objects whose contents are obtained from the two Arrays.
2. Tell one vector object to multiply itself by the other.
3. Tell the result vector to make a new Smalltalk Array whose contents are the data of the result vector.

In real applications, data normally live in virtual objects, so the overhead of transferring arrays of data from and to the user's interactive environment is rarely encountered. The allocation and state of virtual data are shown in Fig. 1.

## What VDSP Is Not

The VDSP system does not aim to be an optimizing compiler for the many signal-processing chips available. Rather, it is a portable high-level interface to common signal-processing functionality. The system is not a layered stream-computation system, as is the signal representation language SRL (Kopec 1985). At user request, it performs one operation on one block of data at a time.

## Using the Object-Oriented System

Using an object-oriented programming system with class-based inheritance allowed us to develop the VDSP system quickly. One class, *VdProcessor*, contains procedures and data common to all the types of processors available, including methods for transferring data, dispatching arithmetic primitives, error handling, and naming processors. Subclasses of *VdProcessor* represent different types of processors—for example, Motorola 56001 integrated circuits—and instances of these subclasses correspond to actual pieces of hardware. These processor classes have actual primitive calls and also handle memory allocation, which can vary in nature from one type of processor to another. It is possible in the system to be using more than one type of processor at a time. Figure 2 illustrates the class hierarchy of virtual processors.

A separate subclass hierarchy holds virtual data objects. Again, a fair amount of common functionality is placed in an abstract class, *VdDatum*, reducing the amount of code duplication needed to implement virtual data objects. This includes type information and coercion, part of the work of instance creation, use of handles, and delegation of arithmetic messages to the appropriate processor object. The subclasses of *VdDatum*, namely *VdVector* and *VdScalar*, have code that is specific to their types, such as size information and vector reduction operations. The class hierarchy of Vd-Datum and an example VdVector instance are shown in Fig. 3.

Another feature of the Smalltalk-80 programming environment was immensely helpful: rapid prototyping. Because of the interactive nature of the environment, we were able to write and test code very quickly, making the time needed for construction of the initial prototype system quite short.

## Primitive Operations

Smalltalk currently provides a simple capability to execute external code from within the interactive computing environment. The user writes a piece of

*Fig. 1. Allocation and state
of a virtual data object.*

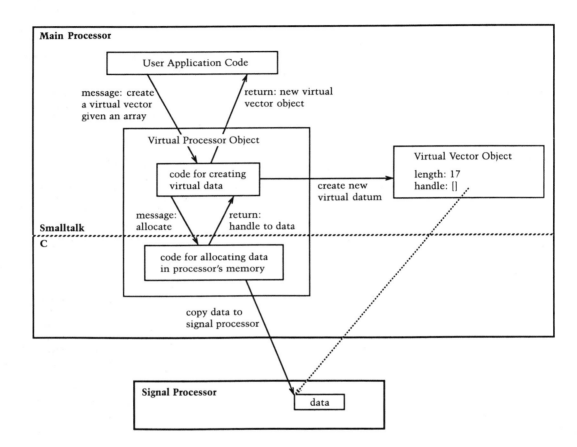

code in C (or some other low-level language) that will be linked to the Smalltalk virtual machine as a *user primitive*. This primitive can be invoked from within the interactive environment, passing data to and from the C data space and executing the C code of the primitive. This interface mechanism is useful for accessing hardware devices, which are otherwise inaccessible. The virtual processor described here is the high-level, object-based end of such an interface.

There are several types of operation that a virtual processor needs to perform. The primary ones are the vectorized computations that are the *raison d'etre* of the VDSP system. In addition to arithmetic, there are operations for creating (allocating) virtual data objects, for storing and reading objects in external files, and for communicating data objects to and from the user's interactive environment. The set of operations is kept as small as possible for several reasons: a small size makes implementation on a given hardware processor easier and more reliable; it keeps the Smalltalk virtual machine small; and we would rather write code in a high-level object language than in C. On the other

Fig. 2. Class hierarchy for
virtual processors showing
an instance of a concrete
class.

Fig. 3. Class hierarchy for
virtual data showing an
instance of a concrete
class.

Fig. 2

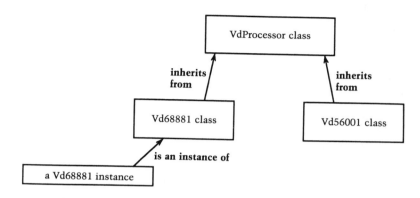

Fig. 3

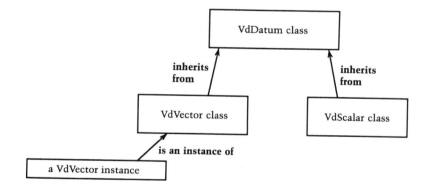

hand, we want to be able to do all common digital signal processing operations efficiently, so the kernel of operations that are implemented as user primitives must be reasonably complete.

## The Primitive Kernel

This kernel is based on arithmetic operations: add, subtract, multiply, divide, negate, reciprocal, and absolute value. Each of these operations is available for vectors and scalars, with the binary operations ($+$, $-$, $\times$, $/$) working pairwise on the elements of two vectors. Binary operations also have a vector-scalar form so that one can, for example, multiply each element of a vector by a given scalar. The kernel also includes vectorized exponential functions (log, exp, sqrt) and trigonometric functions (sin, cos, arctan). In addition, there are special operations that take a vector and reduce it to a scalar: sum or product of elements, minimum and maximum values, and dot-product. Table 1 summarizes these kernel operations.

## Table 1. VDSP kernel primitive operations

| | |
|---|---|
| Unary arithemtic: | $-\times$, $1/\times$, $|\times|$, log, exp, sqrt, sin, cos<br>(vector only) min, max |
| Binary arithmetic: | $+$, $-$, $\times$, $/$, arctan<br>(vector only) dot-product |
| Type conversion: | Floor, truncate, asInteger |
| Memory management: | allocate, free |
| File I/O: | open, close, read, write, seek, readStream, writeStream |

## Table 2. Benchmarks for VDSP speed enchancement (operation times, in microseconds)

| | Floating point | | Integer | |
|---|---|---|---|---|
| Operation | Smalltalk | VDSP | Smalltalk | VDSP |
| $+$ | 200 | 18 | 120 | 3 |
| $\times$ | 200 | 20 | 120 | 6 |
| $/$ | 200 | 22 | 560 | 9 |
| Sine | 180 | 36 | | |
| Sqrt | 1520 | 16 | | |
| Log | 3620 | 40 | | |
| Exp | 2240 | 34 | | |

In addition to its normal mode of operation, each arithmetic operation has a "permutation map" version. This version allows one to access elements of a vector by using indirection through a table of indices, making possible arbitrary selection and re-ordering of vector elements. Some common signal processing functions, such as matrix multiplication and the fast Fourier transform, can be performed quickly with permutation maps.

To support manipulation of virtual data, there are also primitives for allocation and deallocation, and for getting data into and out of virtual data objects. Since virtual data live outside of the Smalltalk environment, their storage space is not automatically reclaimed—as it is for normal Smalltalk objects—and so it must be explicitly allocated and freed by the user. The virtual data objects containing the handles *are* inside the environment, but the data that the handles point to is outside it. Furthermore, virtual data typically do not live through a save/quit/restart cycle in Smalltalk and must be regenerated by the user at the start of each login session.

Finally, there are primitives for storing data to, and reading data from, external files. These are fairly low-level primitives, oriented toward handling various formats of the streams of (audio) samples we are currently working with. There are other primitives for transferring data to and from the user's environment (e.g., turning virtual vectors into Smalltalk Array objects), and for data type conversion.

## How Well Does It Work?

The most important goal of the VDSP project is to make a simple, standard interface for signal processing operations so that writing high-level portable code is easy. Though we have not yet had a chance to implement VDSP on more than one hardware platform, we believe that it will be quite easy to carry an application written using VDSP from one implementation to another. Having the abstractions of virtual processor and virtual data has made it easier to write code for vectorized computations in the simple filter and transform applications we have finished to date. The abstractions allow one to separate the operation desired, such as a vectorized multiplication, from the implementation details; such separation greatly helps simplify thinking about the operations.

A second goal is to speed up numerical computation. Smalltalk is not really designed for optimized arithmetic operations the way, say, Fortran is, but VDSP helps get around this problem by allowing for reasonably fast vectorized operations. Table 2 summarizes timings for some common operations in the current implementation. The VDSP timings are shown for the version that uses the Macintosh II's (TM of Apple, Inc.) internal MC68881 math coprocessor for VDSP operations.

*Mellinger et al.*

The simple VDSP benchmarks measure roughly a factor of 10 improvement for floating-point arithmetic, a factor of 20 or more for integer arithmetic, and varying improvements from 5 to 70 for more complex operations. Note that these improvements are obtained without special hardware. Further speedups will be achieved with the use of dedicated signal processing devices.

A third goal of the VDSP project was to explore the use of object-oriented programming for signal processing. Though our experience is yet slight, it seems as though the object-oriented model can significantly help ease the task of programming. The concepts of virtual processor and virtual data map directly to classes in Smalltalk, so it was easy to write the Smalltalk end of the VDSP implementation. The few applications we have built on top of the system were also simple to implement using the object model and the classes defined by VDSP.

## Current Status

The current VDSP implementation runs on an Apple Macintosh II computer using a Smalltalk-80 system from ParcPlace Systems, Inc. for the high-level operations and APDA's MPW C compiler and loader for the low-level primitives. This implementation uses the 68881 coprocessor to do floating-point and integer operations, and the Macintosh II's native operating system for file input/output and memory management. We are also working on another interface for a hardware card from Spectral Innovations, Inc., which contains a special-purpose signal-processing chip, the AT&T DSP-32.

## Future Work

The computational model described so far does not include any graphics operations, but applications that require real-time graphics will depend on integrating a graphics kernel with the signal processing kernel, and we have begun work in that direction.

Regarding DSP chips, we are interested in the use of the Motorola 56001. In particular, when CCRMA

receives NeXT machines, and Smalltalk becomes available on them, we will be able to put the portability of the VDSP system to another test. This implementation should test the notions of virtual processor and virtual data better than any other, since the 56001 works with different data sizes than either of the implementations finished or under way.

Since the low levels of the VDSP system—the user primitives written in C—operate on objects, it is possible to use object-oriented systems other than Smalltalk for the high level, such as object-oriented extensions of Lisp and C.

We also contemplate building an operation compiler that would speed up the interface slightly and let the user mostly forget about storage allocation and temporary variables. Currently, the user must explicitly allocate space for all temporary vectors used in a computation, which is annoying at best. The operation compiler would let the user specify an *operation block*, a block of Smalltalk code for a complicated vectorized computation. The compiler would preprocess the block, determine what storage needs to be allocated for the block's functions and what VDSP calls need to made to execute it, and store this information. When the user evaluates the block later, the stored information would be used to execute the block operations quickly and with no need for explicit allocation and deallocation of temporaries.

Last, but not least, we plan to bridge the gaps between block-oriented and stream-oriented computation, by developing a "stream of blocks" model, and to extend our model for the use of multiple interconnected signal processors.

## References

Goldberg, A., and D. Robson. 1983. *Smalltalk-80: The Language and Its Implementation*. Reading, Massachusetts: Addison-Wesley.

Kopec, G. E. 1985. "The Signal Representation Language SRL." *IEEE Transactions on Acoustics, Speech, and Signal Processing* 33.

# Addresses of Authors

**Glendon Diener**
CCRMA, Department of Music
Stanford University
Stanford, CA 94305
grd@CCRMA.Stanford.edu

**Henry Flurry**
CPAT, School of Music
University of Michigan
1100 Baits Dr.
Ann Arbor, MI 48109
HenryF@Magnificat.CPAT.UMich.edu

**C. Fry**
150 Walnut St.
Somerville, MA 02145

**Kurt J. Hebel**
Symbolic Sound Corp.
P. O. Box 2530, Station A
Champaign, IL 61825
Hebel@CERL.UIUC.edu

**David Jaffe**
NeXT, Inc.
900 Chesapeake Dr.
Redwood City, CA 94063
David_Jaffe@NeXT.com

**Glenn Krasner**
ParcPlace Systems, Inc.
1550 Plymouth St.
Mountain View, CA 94043
glenn@ParcPlace.com

**Henry Lieberman**
Visual Language Workshop
MIT Media Laboratory
20 Ames St., Room 446
Cambridge, MA 02139
lieber@media-lab.media.mit.edu

**David Mellinger**
CCRMA, Department of Music
Stanford University
Stanford, CA 94305
davem@CCRMA.Stanford.edu

**Stephen Travis Pope**
Nomad OD/CMR
P. O. Box 60632
Palo Alto, CA 94306
stp@CCRMA.Stanford.edu

**Xavier Rodet**
IRCAM
31, rue St. Merri
F-75004 Paris
rod@ircam.ircam.fr

**Carla Scaletti**
Symbolic Sound Corp.
P. O. Box 2530, Station A
Champaign, IL 61825
Scaletti@CERL.UIUC.edu

# DATE DUE

| | | | |
|---|---|---|---|
| | | | |
| | | | |
| | | | |
| | | | |
| | | | |
| | | | |
| | | | |
| | | | |
| | | | |
| | | | |
| | | | |
| | | | |
| | | | |
| | | | |
| | | | |
| | | | |
| | | | |
| | | | |

Demco, Inc. 38-293